Charles E. Freedeman is associate professor
of history at the State University of New York,
Binghamton.

Joint-Stock Enterprise in France, 1807–1867

Joint-Stock Enterprise in France

From Privileged Company to Modern Corporation

1807–1867

by Charles E. Freedeman

THE UNIVERSITY OF NORTH CAROLINA PRESS · CHAPEL HILL

Library of Congress Cataloging in Publication Data

Freedeman, Charles Eldon, 1926–
    Joint-stock enterprise in France, 1807–1867.

    Bibliography: p.
    Includes index.
    1. Corporations—France—History.   2. Stock companies—
France—History.   I. Title.
HD2855.F73   338.7'4   78-26674
ISBN 0-8078-1359-1

For Joyce

Contents

Tables

Acknowledgments

This work owes much to the services of librarians and archivists, both in this country and in France. Special thanks are due to Monsieur Suriano, Archivist at the Chamber of Commerce of Paris; Monsieur F. Martin, Bibliothécaire at the Chamber of Commerce of Lyon; Monsieur Lacour, Director of the Departmental Archives of the Rhône; Madame Felker, Director of the Departmental Archives of the Seine; and the staff of the National Archives in Paris.

I gratefully acknowledge financial assistance from the Dean's Fund at Northern Illinois University for summer grants in 1964 and 1967, from the Harvard Graduate School of Business Administration and the Baker Library for a fellowship during the summer of 1965, from the Foundation of the State University of New York for grants in 1969 and 1970, and from the American Philosophical Society for a grant from the Penrose Fund in 1971.

I owe a great debt to my early mentors in French history, Mrs. George Eynon and Ralph H. Bowen, and to Shepard B. Clough, who introduced me to the discipline of economic history. I benefited from Rondo Cameron's encouragement, good advice, and editorial expertise over the years. I am indebted to the readers of The University of North Carolina Press and to Charles K. Warner. Their critical reading of the manuscript saved me from many factual and stylistic errors. A special note of thanks is due to Don Kelley for his counsel and friendship.

Introduction

> *I weigh my words when I say that in my judgment the limited liability corporation is the greatest single discovery of modern times, whether you judge it by its social, by its ethical, by its industrial, or, in the long run,—after we understand it and how to use it,—by its political effects. Even steam and electricity are far less important that the limited liability corporation, and they would be reduced to comparative impotence without it.*
>
> Nicholas Murray Butler

By the mid-twentieth century the modern business corporation had passed through three distinct stages of development. The privileged trading and manufacturing companies of the seventeenth and eighteenth centuries constituted the first stage. The government itself often acted as promoter for these companies, and their role was conceived in terms of the prevalent mercantilist philosophy. Coming under heavy attack in the second half of the eighteenth century, most joint-stock companies were shorn of their exclusive privileges; but fearful of the monster they had helped to rear, governments retained control over their formation.

The second stage, encompassing the first two-thirds of the nineteenth century in most Western countries, subjected the creation of joint-stock companies to government consent, particularly if shareholders were to enjoy limited liability. The hopes of government officials that the use of the joint-stock company might be limited, or even wither away, foundered with accelerated industrialization and transportation improvements. Enterprises that demanded large amounts of capital required a new and flexible institutional structure. An increasing portion of the business community chafed under governmental restrictions and, while employing all sorts of sophisticated subterfuges and substitutes, and occasionally resorting to illegality, gradually gained the strength for an all-out assault on the system, culminating with the third stage of free incorporation and limited liability.

It is with the second, or transitional stage, that this study is concerned. Although this study is limited to a single country, the rise of the corporation was a general Western phenomenon, an integral part of the development of capitalism. In view of its importance, it is surprising that the history of the corporation has attracted relatively little attention from scholars. One reason is perhaps that it involves consideration of law, politics, and economics, to which the compartmentalized division of academic disciplines in France and elsewhere has imposed an artificial barrier.

I have attempted to guard against the error of the historian who knows the outcome of his story and is tempted to see a linear development. The nature of the corporation was not foreordained and its development simply a tale of how the ideal was realized. The differences exhibited in corporate law and structure in Western countries should be sufficient to dispel that view (although international capitalism exerted pressures for a degree of uniformity, even in the nineteenth century). Contemporaries were divided about what form the corporation should take. Different options were available. Some enjoyed a temporary run, but it is not inconceivable that they might have ended in the mainstream. The corporation was a man-made instrument that bore the marks of the political and economic milieu from which it emerged. Legislators, jurists, bureaucrats, economic theorists, and businessmen all contributed to its shaping.

I have attempted to trace the origin, development, and role of the two types of French joint-stock company, the *société anonyme*, which required the consent of the government, and the *société en commandite par actions*, which could be freely formed. The first, and until now the lone, historian of French joint-stock enterprise for this period was Charles Lescoeur, whose still useful work is now a century old.[1] As a lawyer, Lescoeur took a predominantly legal approach. Without neglecting the legal aspects, I have tried to integrate the political and economic sides into the story.

Some claim that the restrictions on the use of the corporation (*société anonyme*) retarded French economic development. I would not argue against this proposition, but its truth is largely irrelevant. Certainly a more liberal attitude toward the authorizing of *sociétés anony-*

mes would have had a beneficial effect on development,[2] but why should France's institutions be expected to have been more perfect than those of her neighbors? In fact, until 1856, because of the existence of the *société en commandite par actions*, a viable corporate substitute, French law on joint-stock companies was as liberal as any and more liberal than most.

Commercial law in general, and corporate law in particular, has lagged behind rather than anticipated the needs of business, owing to the conservative attitudes of legislators and jurists. The greater the lag, the more serious the barrier to development. If the lag is not too great, however (and its degree may be ascertained by comparison with other developing countries), it can be considered an advantage rather than a disadvantage. The point of view adopted here is that, at least until 1856, France was well served by its law governing joint-stock enterprise, even though this state of affairs was a matter more of accident than of design. The drafters of the *Code de Commerce* could not foresee the use to which the *société en commandite par actions* would be put. French law on joint-stock enterprise, rather than constituting a barrier to development, facilitated it.

Joint-Stock Enterprise in France, 1807–1867

1 The Beginnings of Joint-Stock Enterprise in France

L'ordre public est intéressé dans toute société qui se forme par action, parce que trop souvent ces enterprises ne sont qu'un piège tendu à la credulité des citoyens.
Archichancelier Cambacérès, 1807

Colbert's Ordinance of 1673, France's first commercial code, attempted to define and establish the basic structure of the most prevalent types of business organization. Jacques Savary (1622–90), an ex-businessman turned government official, took the leading role in the drafting of this ordinance. Because the provisions of the ordinance were brief and imprecise,[1] Savary undertook the task of further clarification by publishing, two years later, a businessman's manual, *Le Parfait Négociant*, which presented, interpreted, and elaborated upon the provisions of the ordinance. This manual was popular and went through many editions, the last appearing in 1800.[2] The authority of Savary's manual was enhanced by his having been the chief drafter of the ordinance, and the courts normally accepted his manual as the authoritative commentary.

The ordinance distinguished two types of business organizations: (1) the partnership (*société générale*), established by formal agreement, whose major characteristic was the unlimited liability of the partners, and (2) the *société en commandite*, a limited (or silent or sleeping) partnership, which had one or more active partners who were subject to unlimited liability, and one or a number of individuals (*commanditaires*) who supplied capital but did not participate in the management of the enterprise,[3] and whose liability was limited to the amount of capital they contributed. Public registration was required for these two forms of business organization.[4] A summary of their provisions was to be registered at the local consular court or, lacking such a court, at some other designated place. They were also to be

[3]

posted in a public place. Savary's manual provided models for the drafting of partnership and *commandite* agreements.

In the Ordinance of 1673 the emphasis was on persons, rather than enterprise. The registration requirements did not include information on the amount of capital of the enterprise; it was the names of the principals that were considered important. The regulations governing both types of business organization were defined by the liability of the principals to the public: all partners in a *société générale* and the active partner(s) of a *commandite*.[5]

The foregoing description gives to these forms a precision and clarity that, in fact, they did not possess. The provisions of the ordinance were often ignored in practice. Business custom was at least as important as the statutory provisions.[6] Sometimes a partner escaped unlimited liability by inserting a clause in the agreement limiting his liability.[7] The identity of the silent partners (*commanditaires*) who supplied the capital in a *commandite* was often made public, and many *commanditaires* apparently participated openly in the administration of the enterprise.[8] The Ordinance of 1673 contained specific provisions concerning the registration of the terms of partnership and *commandite* agreements. These registration requirements were largely ignored. Before the Parlement of Bordeaux in 1787, the *procureur général* charged: "It is difficult to conceive how a law so explicit in its provisions, whose object is so important and of such interest for public security and valuable for business confidence, has been allowed to fall into complete disuse."[9] In the eighteenth century, registrations for Paris averaged only between five and ten a year; in Rouen, only sixty-three were registered over a period of seventy-one years.[10]

The ordinance did not recognize any form of joint-stock company. Joint-stock companies were considered exceptions to the common law and a matter of royal prerogative, to be organized by charters granted by the crown. Typical were the overseas trading companies enjoying exclusive trading privileges with certain areas, such as the East India Company, organized in 1664. In effect, they were quasi-public institutions. The shareholders in these companies were generally subject to unlimited liability, and their shares were, with certain restrictions and formalities, transferable. Two other types of joint-stock companies made their appearance, without benefit of statute, particularly in the last third of the eighteenth century. One developed by dividing the capital of a *société en commandite* into shares.[11] The other type of joint-stock company was simply an unregistered society of shareholders, distinguishable from a partnership in that the shares could be sold. According to Henri Lévy-Bruhl, these were more numerous than the *commandite par actions*.[12]

In 1778 the minister of justice, Hué de Miromesnil, instituted a commission to draft a new commercial code to modernize, clarify, and expand the provisions of the Ordinance of 1673.[13] The commission finished its draft of the code in 1782, and the following year it was submitted to the Parlement of Paris, which took no action in spite of repeated requests by Miromesnil and his successor, Chrétien François de Lamoignon, during the 1780s. The main reason the Parlement buried the project undoubtedly was its hostility to the consular courts, which deprived it of jurisdiction over profitable commercial cases.[14] In the realm of business organization the draft code did not go beyond the provisions of the Ordinance of 1673 except in providing clearer definition of the forms of business organization and strengthening the provisions regarding registration. The draft did not recognize the existence of joint-stock companies, although unincorporated societies of shareholders and the *commandites par actions* were already numerous.

The joint-stock enterprises of the *ancien régime*, although they instituted many innovations in the joint-stock company, generally failed to satisfy two of the basic criteria of the nineteenth-century corporation: limited liability for shareholders and negotiability of shares. In the East India Company the liability of the shareholders was unlimited, although the directors appear to have possessed limited liability.[15] Only in the 1780s did limited liability for shareholders make its appearance by means of clauses in the charters limiting the liability of shareholders to the amount represented by their shares.[16]

Numerous impediments interfered with the negotiability of shares. Some charters required the consent of the board of directors for any transfer of shares; others gave the board the right of preemptive purchase on behalf of the company. In some instances the seller remained officially a member of the company, the sale of shares being regarded as a private arrangement with the purchaser and remaining unknown to the company. Also, there were prohibitions against the alienation of shares to foreigners and non-Catholics.[17] Not only were there institutional deficiencies—the Paris Bourse dealt in the shares of a few large companies—but considerable public hostility existed against stockjobbing in the eighteenth century.

The entry under "stock-jobbing" in Malachy Postlethwayt's *Universal Dictionary of Trade and Commerce* (1757) is as illustrative of this prejudice in France as in England. Twelve reasons were advanced why stockjobbing was detrimental to the commerce of the nation; four dealt with government securities and eight with stockjobbing in the shares of trading companies. Among the reasons advanced against trading in the shares of trading companies was the objection that "the domestic traffic in the stocks of companies, so engrosses the thoughts of proprietors, that the national commerce often suffers, for want of that money being employed in a free trade which might prove much more to the advantage of the Kingdom, as well as to that of the stockholders themselves, if they employed the same property in the general trade. These considerations may, perhaps, furnish the weightiest objections that can be urged against all joint-stock companies."[18] Also, the exclusive privileges enjoyed by companies chartered by the crown came under increasing criticism in the eighteenth century; the attacks by Montesquieu and Adam Smith are the best known.

Confusion existed over the nature of shares. Some did not represent equal portions of capital; others did not represent any capital at all. In some companies the shares took the name of currency units, the capital (*livre*) being divided into *sols* or *onces* and subdivided into *deniers*. There could be any number of *sols*, rather than the twenty of the *livre tournois*, but there were usually only sixteen *onces* and twelve *derniers* per *sol* or *once*. Because the nominal value of the *sol* was generally high, the subdivision permitted shares of considerably smaller value. The *sols* of the mining companies of Anzin and Aniche had nominal values of 2,500 and 11,000 *livres* respectively, and those of the famous crystal manufacture of Saint Gobain were valued at 127,000 *livres*.[19]

Some of the privileged companies chartered by the crown issued different kinds of shares. Savary des Bruslons, in his *Dictionnaire universel de commerce*, distinguished three types of shares: (1) the regular share (*action simple*), representing a portion of ownership in the company; (2) bonds (*actions rentières*) returning only a fixed rate guaranteed by the crown and analogous to *rentes* on the Hotel de Ville; and (3) preferred shares (*actions interessées*) having a fixed return, guaranteed by the crown, and also the right to share in dividends after a fixed amount had been distributed to the regular shareholders. This last type of share was created especially for ecclesiastical orders.[20]

Bearer shares (*actions au porteur*), which were not registered in the name of the owner and could be transmitted without formality, had been issued early in the century by companies organized by the Scottish financial genius John Law. They appeared in the decade preceding the Revolution and were well known to the speculating public in the 1780s.[21] Shares with coupons were also introduced to facilitate the payment of dividends.[22]

Many joint-stock companies made provision in their charters for stockholders' meetings, but most restricted the vote to those holding a certain number of shares. Large companies often set up boards of directors to administer the enterprise. Other companies made no provision for stockholders' meetings. Where they did exist they were usually without real power. Most large companies (those with capital of over 1 million *livres*) were formed in Paris, the only important capital market in France, and their directors and shareholders also met there. The number of shareholders was generally small: Anzin had only nineteen shareholders in 1757.[23]

Joint-stock enterprises tended to be concentrated in a few sectors of the economy. Ordinary partnerships and *en commandite* partnerships were adequate for the needs of domestic commerce, as long as the amount of capital needed remained relatively small. But in sectors where large amounts of capital were required, the traditional forms of organization and the regulations governing them were clearly inadequate. The first joint-stock companies in France were overseas trading companies chartered by the crown and enjoying exclusive privileges. Appearing slightly later were large manufacturing concerns enjoying the patronage of, and often subsidized by, the crown. The crown also chartered a few banks and public utilities. Those joint-stock companies chartered by the crown were by far the largest of the *ancien régime*. Unregistered companies of shareholders were employed primarily for mining and metallurgical enterprises. In port cities the *commandite* with shares was developed for outfitting merchant ships, usually for a single voyage.

The nobility invested heavily in joint-stock enterprise. The *commandite par actions* and the unregistered company of shareholders afforded nobles an opportunity for investment that did not involve them directly in commerce, which they regarded as incompatible with their dignity, or subject them to any publicity. Those who invested were the influential court nobility, and nobles of recent origin whose fortunes had been made in business.[24] Investment by the nobility was particularly heavy in *commandites par actions* organized to outfit ships for trading voyages.[25] In time of war, nobles also invested in privateering ventures, organized as *commandites par actions*, operating out of Nantes, Saint Malo, and Marseille.[26] The nobles' closeness to the land led to heavy investment in mining and metallurgical enterprises organized as unregistered companies of shareholders.[27] This type of organization was typical of coal mines at the end of the *ancien régime*, though the number of stockholders was usually small.[28]

The reappearance of bearer shares in the 1780s, after a long hiatus following the collapse of John Law's system, enabled nobles and other investors to conceal their identities more effectively. These shares were exempt from any formalities of transfer, though their holders ran the risk of loss and theft. In spite of their disadvantages—companies disliked them because they would not permit further calls on shareholders for capital—they were popular with the investing public. At the time of the reorganization of Le Creusot in 1787, Ignace de Wendel, after failing to get funds from the crown, noted that "only the public could provide the capital for a large scale enterprise and the only way to get public participation was to create bearer shares."[29] De Wendel recognized the great advantage to shareholders of being able to recover their capital by selling their shares at any time.[30] Even Calonne, the minister of finance, found it expedient to float government loans by means of bearer securities.[31]

Two great speculative booms in the shares of joint-stock companies occurred in the eighteenth century. Both involved the shares of privileged companies chartered by the crown. The first, part of a general speculative mania that was European in character and saw the South Sea bubble in England and the tulip mania in Holland, involved shares in the bank and trading companies founded by John Law. The collapse of this boom in 1720 left in its wake a revulsion against banks of issue and joint-stock companies, which retarded the development of both of these institutions in France.

After unsuccessful attempts to suppress speculation following the collapse of Law's system, the Paris Bourse was founded in 1724, in part to enable the government to police transactions in government securities and other shares. Before 1724 these functions had been performed by unlicensed intermediaries meeting on certain streets or in cafes, such as the famed rue Quincampoix during the Law boom. Sixty licensed brokers were to handle all transactions in government securities and other shares, although the negotiation of bills of exchange did not require the use of intermediaries. Until its suppression during the Revolution, the Bourse was housed in the Hotel de Nevers, the present location of the Bibliothèque nationale.

The second great speculative boom occurred in the 1780s. This boom involved not only government securities but the shares of such quasi-public companies as the Caisse d'Escompte (founded in 1776), the Paris Waterworks Company (1784), the New Company of the Indies (1785), and a life insurance and two fire insurance companies (1786–88). The total issue of these companies amounted to over 76 million *livres*.[32] Another company whose shares were heavily traded on the Paris Bourse was the Bank of Saint Charles in Madrid, founded in 1782 and headed by a French merchant, François Cabarrus. Some of these companies were involved in government finance; some, in fact, were schemes to enable the hard-pressed government to borrow money. The small number of speculators consisted of nobles, wealthy bourgeois, and foreigners.[33] The techniques of speculation were sophisticated, including buying on margin and dealing in futures. Well-orchestrated campaigns to depress or raise the value of shares of certain companies were a characteristic feature.

These excesses contributed to the closing of the Bourse and the suppression of all joint-stock companies during the Revolution. On 27 June 1793, the Convention, under pressure from the Paris sections that blamed speculators for the depreciation of *assignats*, decreed the closing of the Bourse.[34] On 24 August a law suppressed the Caisse d'Escompte, the life insurance company, and all enterprises "whose capital funds were in the form of bearer shares, or negotiable shares, or by inscriptions on a book transferable at will."[35] In the future only the legislature would be permitted to authorize the formation of joint-stock companies. A variety of reasons contributed to this action: hostility of the Paris *sans-culottes*, corruption in the large companies, the depreciation of the *assignats*, for which the companies were partly blamed, and the belief that speculation in shares decreased the funds available for government borrowing.[36]

Except for the large joint-stock companies chartered by the crown, whose shares had been traded on the Bourse, it seems unlikely that the Convention's prohibition had much effect. Although the Directory authorized the return of joint-stock companies (law of 1 November 1795 —30 Brumaire year IV), it did not provide any framework or impose any restrictions. Promoters were allowed free rein, but questions concerning the legal status of their creations remained unresolved. The early preoccupation of the Bank of France, created in 1800, with the liability of its administrators and shareholders illustrates the uncertainty over these matters.[37] The Consulate quickly took steps to remedy this uncertainty by providing a common framework for all joint-stock companies.

In 1800, Vital-Roux, a merchant of Lyon, published *De l'influence du gouvernement sur la prospérité du commerce*, in which he called for the drafting of a commercial code. The new code, he said, should be drafted by merchants because of their experience. "The worker who runs the machine knows its faults better than the intellectual who describes it."[38] Vital-Roux's wish was granted the following year, when he was appointed to the commission charged with preparing the draft of a new code.

This commission, appointed by the First Consul on 3 April 1801 (13 Germinal, year IX), numbered seven persons, most of whom possessed either legal or business backgrounds.[39] Within eight months the commission completed its draft.[40] In his report to the consuls, the minister of the interior, Jean Antoine Chaptal, claimed that, in the main, the new draft code merely reproduced the provisions of the ordinances of 1673 and 1681. Chaptal added that what new provisions there were stemmed from experience and suggestions emanating from large commercial centers.[41]

The commission possessed some knowledge of the Miromesnil reform project, but it is uncertain if its members had access to the final

text of this draft code. The commission report admitted that some fragments of the work of the Miromesnil Commission had been communicated to them by a former member of that commission.[42] However, a
comparison of the two drafts—in which there are many similarities—
and the relatively short time in which the commission completed its
work, strongly suggest that the commission may have had access to
the final draft of Miromesnil's code.[43]

The draft of the commission recognized only one type of joint stock
company, the *société anonyme*, and required that this form of business
organization be authorized only by the government. The text of the
draft code was then submitted to all the courts of appeal, tribunals
of commerce, and chambers of commerce throughout the country
for their advice.[44] The members of these institutions, primarily businessmen and jurists familiar with business practices and needs, gave
careful consideration to the draft; their observations fill three large
volumes.[45] The provision requiring that all joint stock companies be
authorized by the government raised numerous objections. Although
only the appeals courts of Brussels, Dijon, Caen, Abbeville, and Paris
objected to the requirement of authorization of all share-issuing enterprises, the objections of commercial tribunals and chambers of
commerce, both more representative of business opinion, were more
numerous. The commercial courts of Abbeville, Bayonne, Brussels,
Dijon, Eu and Tréport, Geneva, Havre, Rochefort, Lyon, Marseille,
Nantes, Saint-Brieuc, Saint-Malo, and Strasbourg raised objections,
as well as the chambers of commerce of Lyon, Marseille, Nancy,
Nantes, Rouen, Saint-Brieuc, Saint-Malo, and Strasbourg. Urged to
do so by the government, many commercial courts and chambers
deliberated together and issued joint opinions.[46] All contended that the
requirement would be gravely injurious to commerce. Some noted that
the requirement was justified for banks, for companies possessing an
exclusive privilege, such as the overseas trading companies of the
ancien régime, or for large enterprise, but not for ordinary business
ventures, such as the outfitting of ships and manufacturing enterprises.
Typical of the responses on this point were the observations of the
commercial tribunal of Havre:

The authorization of the Government, which this article requires, is undoubtedly necessary for large enterprises which might have some connection with
the public interest, such as the Bank of France or other establishments of this

type, and privileged companies, if they are to be formed. But this requirement
. . . must not be applied to individual enterprises which are ordinarily formed
with shareholders such as the outfitting vessels for commerce, privateers,
manufacturing establishments, etc., because these enterprises are ordinary
commercial operations which are regulated and must be regulated by contracts
between the interested parties.[47]

   After taking into account the objections and suggestions of the
courts and chambers of commerce, the commission revised its initial
draft. The commission report, which accompanied the revised draft,
denied any intention of subjecting share-issuing *sociétés en commandite* to governmental authorization, but it recognized that the objections were not without substance, as the original text contained no
provision expressly permitting the division of the part of the *commanditaires* into shares.[48] The commission added a provision allowing the
capital of a *société en commandite* to be divided into shares.

   The draft was then transmitted to the Conseil d'Etat, where it was
allowed to languish for several years until Napoleon ordered that its
consideration be expedited. The economic crisis of 1805–6, bringing
in its train a large number of business failures, appears to have convinced the emperor of the utility of uniform and precise regulations to
govern commerce.[49] The draft was first revised by the section of the
interior of the Conseil d'Etat, after which it was submitted to the
Conseil's General Assembly. Altogether the General Assembly devoted more than sixty sessions to the *Code de Commerce*, four of
which were presided over by the emperor himself. The General Assembly dealt with title 3 of the code, concerning business organization, during five sessions in January and February 1807.[50]

   During these sessions some key provisions of the draft code were
challenged. Some members of the Conseil wished to eliminate the
société en commandite as a separate form of business organization.
Merlin de Douai claimed that it resembled the *société anonyme*, an
opinion that was ably refuted by Regnaud de Saint-Jean d'Angély,
who argued that the *société en commandite* constituted a distinctly
different form of business organization. A more liberal provision regarding the formation of *sociétés anonymes* was suggested by Jean
Baptiste Treilhard, one of the ablest members of the Conseil. He
proposed that government authorization be required only for those corporations having some connection with public order or the state. He

even suggested the possibility of leaving the decision on whether the corporation required authorization to the shareholders themselves.[51] This proposal was attacked by both Regnaud de Saint-Jean d'Angély and the archchancellor, Jean Jacques Cambacérès. "The public order," according to Cambacérès, "is involved in every company that issues shares, because far too often these enterprises are only a trap set up for credulous citizens."[52] Regnaud de Saint-Jean d'Angély reminded the members of the excesses of former companies and noted that, without careful surveillance by the government, frauds would be numerous.[53] It was also pointed out that the emperor had already demonstrated his opposition to allowing *sociétés anonymes* to be formed without government permission by ordering the minister of the interior to require all such existing enterprises to submit their charters for approval. Cambacérès also expressed some reservations over the wording of the article allowing the capital of a *société en commandite* to be divided into shares. He feared it might "allow a veritable *société anonyme* to conceal itself behind the facade of a *société en commandite* to avoid obtaining government authorization."[54]

The code, once approved by the Conseil d'Etat, was passed by the docile Tribunat and Corps Législatif without serious difficulty. The final vote on it took place on 15 September 1807, and its provisions became effective 1 January 1808.

The new *Code de Commerce* recognized three forms of business organization: (1) the *société en nom collectif*, (2) the *société en commandite*, and (3) the *société anonyme*. The *société en nom collectif* was a regular partnership in which any partner could act for the others[55] and all partners were subject to unlimited liability. Whereas the ordinary partnership implied a number of individuals all actively engaged in the enterprise, the *société en commandite* was a "limited" (or "sleeping" or "silent") partnership in which one or a number of active partners (*gérants*) managed the enterprise, and one or a number of passive or "limited" partners (*commanditaires*) contributed capital or other assets to the enterprise but were denied participation in management, under pain of loss of limited liability. The *gérants* of a *commandite*, like the partners of a *société en nom collectif*, were subject to unlimited liability. The *commanditaires*, described in the code simply as lenders of capital (*bailleurs des fonds*), possessed limited liability and were to receive an agreed-upon share of the profits. Article 38 of the code provided that the capital of the *commandite* might be divided into shares, which in effect created two types of *société en commandite*: the *société en commandite simple* and the *société en commandite par actions*. The right to issue shares made the latter a type of joint-stock company.

The *société en commandite*, as conceived by the drafters of the code, was for a small or medium-sized enterprise, such as a partnership might engage in, but with added flexibility that the partnership did not possess. As we have already seen, this form of enterprise was widely used in coastal cities for trading ventures. It had permitted the nobility of the *ancien régime* to invest in business enterprises without fear of losing their titles. Early nineteenth-century glossators habitually described the *commandite* as a form admirably suited to the needs of inventors in search of capital. The drafters of the code did not foresee that allowing the capital of a *commandite* to be divided into shares would enable it later to serve for large enterprises.

The form of business organization intended for large enterprises, then quite rare in France, was the *société anonyme*. A corporation in the modern sense, its organization was modeled after the privileged companies of the *ancien régime*. The capital of the *société anonyme* was divided into shares that were easily transferable. All stockholders possessed limited liability. The *société anonyme* was administered by agents, who were not necessarily stockholders themselves and who could be removed by the stockholders. Unlike the partnership and the *société en commandite*, where the name of the enterprise was the name of one or more persons subject to unlimited liability, the *anonyme* was designated by the object of the enterprise. A *société anonyme* could be formed only with the express permission of the government by means of a decree approved by the Conseil d'Etat and signed by the emperor. Regnaud de Saint-Jean d'Angély, in his *exposé des motifs* before the Corps Législatif on 1 September 1807, explained the purpose of *anonymes* and the reason for government authorization:

Sociétés anonymes or associations of shareholders have, of necessity, also attracted the attention of the drafters of the code. These associations are an effective means of encouraging large enterprises, of bringing foreign capital to France, of associating small fortunes and almost the poor with the advantages of large *spéculations*, of adding to the public credit and the circulating funds of commerce. But too often these associations, poorly organized from the beginning or poorly administered in their operations, have jeopardized the fortunes of stockholders and administrators, altered momentarily the general credit, and imperiled public tranquility.

It has been recognized that a company of this type can exist only after a legal act, and that the intervention of the government is necessary to verify from the beginning on what basis the operations of the company would rest, and what consequences it would have.[56]

A regulation of seven articles issued by the minister of the interior on 21 December 1807 set forth the procedure for obtaining the authorization of a *société anonyme*.[57] Requests for authorization were to be submitted to the prefect of the department. Each request was to include a description of the object of the enterprise, the period of its duration, the names and addresses of the stockholders, the capital of the enterprise, the dates by which the capital was to be paid up, the seat of the enterprise, the mode of its administration, and its draft charter. If all the capital was not subscribed, and the subscription was to be completed after governmental authorization, then at least one-fourth of the capital had to be paid in. The prefects were required to report on the status and character of the promoters and stockholders and to give their opinions on the utility and chances for success of the enterprise.

The request for authorization, with related documents, and the report of the prefect would then be forwarded to the minister of the interior. After being examined by the ministry, the request would be transmitted to the Conseil d'Etat, which, after an examination of its own, decided to authorize or reject. Authorization became final after the signature of the head of the state. Once the enterprise was authorized, changes in its charter had to be secured by the procedure required for initial authorization. This long and tortuous process offered no guarantee for final success. Existing *sociétés anonymes* were to request authorization following the prescribed procedure within six months after 1 January 1808.

The judgments of modern French historians on the code tend to be negative. The backward-looking, restrictive, and repressive provisions of the code are held responsible for retarding economic development and inhibiting the growth of enterprise. In short, the code owed too much to the ordinances of Colbert's time and did not sufficiently take into account eighteenth-century developments and future needs. Items in point are its harsh provisions regarding bankruptcy—hardly surprising in an era that regarded harsh punishments as a deterrent to crime—imprisonment for debt, and restrictions on credit instruments. On the positive side, the code provided a useful legal codification, improved the commercial courts, provided for swift and relatively inexpensive commercial justice, and established the framework of modern business organization. Although founding a *société anonyme* by these provisions may have been difficult, it was easier than obtaining legislative approval. In fact, the provisions governing business organization were more liberal than those found elsewhere.

Less than twenty *sociétés anonymes* were authorized during the First Empire.[58] Although the provisions of the code and the regulation of 1807 laid down the basic framework of the enterprise and the procedure for the granting of authorization, much concerning the structure of these companies was left to the discretion of the agencies who played a role in their authorization. Thus, the early precedents in handling requests for authorization are important.

The first company to receive authorization was the Entreprise Générale de Messageries, a Paris-based company organized during the Directory to transport goods and passengers. In his report to the emperor, the minister of the interior noted that the Chamber of Commerce of Paris, which had examined the charter, and the prefect of police of Paris were in agreement that, ''from the viewpoint of the morality of the entrepreneurs and the utility of the enterprise, combining prudence, wisdom and good faith, authorization presents no inconvenience for morals, public order, and the probity of commerce.''[59] The minister did require modification of the provision in the charter that paid a rate of interest to the shareholders higher than the legal rate.[60] In the opinion of the Chamber of Commerce of Paris, the administrators and shareholders were subject to unlimited liability under previous laws, and granting them limited liability as a *société anonyme* might give rise to future litigation based on retroactivity. The ministry did not share these apprehensions. The Conseil d'Etat, section of the interior, offered no objections, requesting only that the ministry furnish a balance sheet for the enterprise prior to definitive approval. The Entreprise de Messageries was authorized by decree on 2 July 1808.

The Entreprise de Messageries was also the first *société anonyme* to request changes in its charter. In 1809 the company was permitted to double its capital, raising it to 2 million francs, divided into shares of 10,000 francs and half shares of 5,000 francs. The duration of the enterprise was extended to 1840.[61]

Provisions for stockholders to receive interest in addition to dividends on their shares were common in early corporations, even if the interest had to be taken from capital. The ministry and the Conseil d'Etat did not object to interest, only to the rate of interest. A provision in the proposed charter of the company for the Dessèchement des Marais de Bourgoin et Braugnes, stipulating that shareholders receive 9 percent interest, was judged to be illegal, imprudent, and onerous.[62] This company was refused authorization in 1808 on the grounds that its charter provided for the unlimited liability of shareholders and for future calls on shareholders for additional capital, which the ministry of interior characterized as contrary to the nature of a *société anonyme*.[63] The minister of the interior informed the prefect of the Aude in 1809 that the proposed Compagnie des Salines d'Estarac did not fulfill the requirements for authorization as an *société anonyme* because neither the capital of the company nor the value of each share was fixed.[64]

The directors of the century-old Saint-Gobain company, considering the company to be a *société anonyme*, applied for authorization. The prefect of police of Paris consulted the Chamber of Commerce, which argued that because the shareholders were subject to unlimited liability, the company was actually a partnership. The chamber recognized that partnerships are designated by the names of one or more of the partners but thought that the Saint-Gobain company which had always been known as the Manufacture (Royale) des Glaces, could legally retain its old name.[65] The company was denied authorization, although it is not clear if the Conseil d'Etat accepted the arguments of the Chamber of Commerce of Paris.

Those companies that received authorization were engaged in a wide variety of enterprises. There were four forges or foundries, a coal mine, a canal, three theaters, a coach company, a bridge company, a sawmill, a company to produce vegetable dyes, a company to manufacture sugar from beets, and a secondary school. Some of these enterprises were already in existence in 1808 and, like the Saint-Gobain Company, applied for authorization as required by law. Their size also varied. The capital of the Fonderies de Romilly, originally founded during the *ancien régime*, was 1,760,000 francs divided into 55 shares of 32,000 francs, each share being subdivided into *coupons* of 8,000 francs.[66] The capital of a company for the construction and maintenance of a theater at Le Mans was 18,000 francs, divided into 120 shares of 150 francs.[67] The capital of the company Culture de Pastel et la Fabrication de l'Indigo at Mulhouse consisted of 400 bearer shares at 100 francs.[68] During the empire, the Conseil d'Etat permitted shares of widely varying nominal value, the subdivision of shares into *coupons*, the payment of interest on shares, and the issue of bearer shares.

From the beginning, the Conseil d'Etat assumed great discretionary power in granting authorization. In its advisory opinion rejecting the authorization of the Manufacture de Draps des Hautes-Alpes à Embrun in 1809, which the minister of the interior had recommended authorizing, the Conseil noted that, "because *sociétés anonymes* have no agent who is personally liable, in the best interest of commerce they cannot be authorized without the greatest caution."[69] Though the personnel and organization of the Conseil would change over the next sixty years, this remained a guiding principle.

2 The Rise of the *Société Anonyme*, 1815–1833

Les sociétés par actions conviennent aux entreprises qui exigent de gros capitaux, et qui doivent durer plus longtemps que la vie d'un homme.

Mais en même temps on ne peut espérer de succés dans une société par actions, qu'autant qu'elle a pour objet une affaire dont l'administration peut être simple et facilement contrôlée.

Jean-Baptiste Say, 1829

Early Years, 1815–1820

The early years of the restoration witnessed an increase in the number of companies requesting authorization. There was some confusion among promoters about the procedure to be followed in obtaining authorization, as well as some uncertainty about the nature and structure of a *société anonyme*. In order to lessen the confusion and uncertainty, the ministry of the interior issued two *instructions*, the first on 22 October 1817 and the second on 11 July 1818, codifying the procedures and requirements that had been established by the ministry and the Conseil d'Etat.[1] These *instructions* made it clear that authorization was not a mere formality but would be granted only after careful consideration and with adequate safeguards to prevent these companies from being "a snare for public credulity."[2] The government would verify "that the object of the enterprise was real and legal; that the enterprise actually existed, not as a mere prospectus without substance, but based on a contract, a subscription of funds to assure its existence, and actual shareholders and not simply fictitious associates who lent their names to promote public subscription of shares."[3]

The government would take care that the announced capital figure for the enterprise was realistic for the object of the enterprise and that

[19]

its payment by the shareholders was assured. The requirements for authorization were designed to protect both the shareholders and the public, but at the same time the government disclaimed any responsibility for the future success of the enterprise. These safeguards were all the more important because *sociétés anonymes* "existed especially for large and risky operations that would not be undertaken without this type of company. It is proper for public banks, the operation of mines, canals, marine insurance, etc.—all large enterprises that it is important to encourage."[4] Respecting the principles of freedom of commerce, the government would not grant exclusive privileges to any commercial or industrial enterprise, as had been the practice during the *ancien régime*.

The charters of all *sociétés anonymes* had to contain, according to the *instruction*: "the operation or operations that the company proposes to undertake, one or more of which must be incorporated into the company's name; its official seat; the length of time for its duration; the amount of its capitalization; the manner in which it shall be formed, either by permanent or transferable personal subscriptions, or by shares either in the name of the owner or bearer shares; the dates by which the capital is to be paid in; and the method of administration."[5] If the subscription of shares was to be completed after authorization, then at least a quarter of the capital had to be subscribed. On the administration of the enterprise: "The first administrators can be temporarily designated by the charter; but, in conformity with Article 31 of the code, the directors of *sociétés anonymes* are only agents necessarily serving a term and revocable; all shareholders must have equal rights in proportion to their contribution; charters cannot reserve for any individual, as initiator of the company, founder, or any other reason, special rights to the enterprise, neither to perpetual and irrevocable administration nor to any levy on the profits, other than a salary attributed to the duties of management."[6]

Finally, the first *instruction* clearly spelled out the duties of the prefects. They were to forward each application and related documents to the ministry, adding their advice on whether the enterprise was legal and likely to be successful. Also, the prefects were to report "on the status and morality of the subscribers of shares, particularly in the case . . . where the subscribers of only a quarter of the capital are known and the rest is to be subscribed, and especially on the directors of the enterprise; [and] on the substance of the subscribers, to assure that they are capable of paying, either when the enterprise is formed or when prescribed, for the shares they have subscribed."[7]

The second instruction was issued in 1818. Addressed by the ministry to the prefects and chambers of commerce, it laid down further requirements for authorization emanating from the Conseil d'Etat. The duration of the company, subject to government approval, was to be stated in its charter. The Conseil justified this provision on the grounds that "the confidence merited by the initial founders of a *société anonyme* is one of the matters taken into consideration by the government at the time when authorization is accorded. After a certain time, death or the voluntary transfer of shares substitutes new shareholders for the original ones. It is in the public interest that, to continue, the enterprise be expressly reauthorized at the end of its term, and submitted again to the approval of the government, in order that the government can refuse authorization if the new shareholders do not appear to be worthy of confidence."[8]

The draft charter also had to specify that if a certain portion of the capital of the enterprise were lost, the enterprise was obliged to dissolve itself. The establishment of a reserve fund, to be raised by taking a portion of the annual profits, was required. No dividends were to be paid if the capital of the enterprise fell below its nominal figure. For these requirements to be enforced, all companies would have to submit balance sheets every six months to the local commercial tribunal, to the local chamber of commerce, if any, and to the prefect. For further publicity, the charters of all *sociétés anonymes* were to be published in the local press as well as in the official *Moniteur*.[9]

Insurance companies, upon which promotional activity in the early years of the restoration was concentrated, were the primary concern of the second *instruction*. In 1815 there were no insurance companies in France, the two fire insurance companies and the life insurance company founded in 1786–87 having disappeared during the Revolution. By 1820 eight insurance companies existed in Paris. The first to be organized was the Compagnie Royale d'Assurances Maritimes, authorized 11 September 1816 and reorganized in 1820 at the time of the creation of two additional companies, with the same shareholders and directors, for life and fire insurance. Another important group was the Compagnie d'Assurances Générale, composed of three companies for marine insurance (22 April 1818), fire (14 February 1819), and life (22 December 1819). The Conseil also authorized the Phénix (1 September 1819) and the Compagnie Commerciale d'Assurances Maritime (22 April 1818). These were all large companies mainly organized and controlled by private Parisian bankers of the *haute banque*. The founders of the Compagnie Royale group included the firms of Jacques Laffitte, James Rothschild, the Périer brothers, Jean Hottinguer, and Dominique André and Cottier. The Compagnie Royale group was also the largest: the capitalization was 30 million francs for the life insurance company,[10] and 10 million each for the fire and marine insurance companies. Outside Paris, there were by 1820 a marine and a fire insurance company in Bordeaux and marine insurance companies in the port cities of Rouen and Nantes. In the 1818 *instruction*, the Conseil d'Etat had decided that no insurance company that insured more than one type of risk would be authorized.[11] The Conseil considered marine insurance particularly risky—a well-founded opinion, as both the Compagnie Royal d'Assurances Maritimes and the Compagnie Commerciale d'Assurances Maritimes disappeared within a few years.

Mutual insurance companies for the purpose of indemnifying losses among their members also appeared. In 1809, the Conseil d'Etat ruled that such companies had to be authorized by the government.[12] Although, strictly speaking, they were not commercial companies within the meaning of the *Code de Commerce*, because they sought no profits, they were assimilated to the *anonyme* form. The first mutual company, for protection against fire, appeared in Paris in 1816. An additional 2 mutual fire insurance companies were founded in 1818, 8 in 1819, and 8 in 1820. The first mutual life insurance company, founded in 1820, was apparently stillborn, and its authorization was revoked in 1827. In the sixty years after 1817, over 170 mutual companies were formed, including some for protection against hailstone damage to crops, animal mortality and epizooty, and conscription.

The government authorized three regional banks of issue, one at Rouen in 1817 and the others at Nantes and Bordeaux in 1818. The motive of the founding of the Bank of Rouen was the suppression of the branch of the Bank of France there at the end of the empire. The primary function of all three was the discounting of commercial paper. Local private bankers, who did not welcome the competition, opposed the founding of the banks of Bordeaux and Nantes.[13] The Bordeaux bank was the largest, capitalized at 3 million francs, followed by Rouen at 1 million and Nantes at 600,000. The bank at Nantes experienced difficulty raising its capital and was not able to begin operation until 1822.[14] The next wave in the creation of departmental banks did not begin until the mid-1830s.

The first large mortgage bank, the Caisse Hypothécaire, was authorized in 1820 with a capital of 50 million francs. Not particularly successful, the Caisse expired in 1847 after the government refused to reauthorize it.[15] At about the same time the government refused to authorize a somewhat analogous Banque Foncière, projected by a certain Harel and backed by a group of nobles and large landed proprietors. Its draft charter of 1820 stipulated a capital of 135 million francs. The prefect of police of Paris reported favorably on the affair, but the Conseil d'Etat denied authorization in April 1821.[16] The organizers attempted to meet, in part, the objections of the Conseil d'Etat and submitted a new draft charter, which at the same time extended the operations of the projected company to include commercial credit and changed its name to Banque Foncière et Commerciale. In July the ministry submitted the project to the Conseil Générale du Commerce,[17] composed of luminaries of the *haute banque* and commerce, which raised numerous objections to the enterprise and recommended that it be refused authorization. The organizers introduced further revisions in its draft charter in October 1821 and reduced the capital of the enterprise to 45 million francs. Further changes were made in January 1822, all in vain, for the Conseil d'Etat rejected the proposal in April 1822.[18]

The organizers then founded the company as a *société en commandite par actions* to escape the necessity for authorization. Alarmed, the minister of the interior queried the minister of finance, Count de Villèle, on possible legal grounds for stopping the promoters. Villèle concluded, "Although it appears to me unlikely that the results will correspond to the hopes of the founder, I think, provided that the head of the enterprise and his associates conform to the provisions of the *Code de Commerce*, which regulates this type of business organization, the government does not have the right to interfere in their operation any more than for other enterprise founded on a basis either better or worse."[19] The minister's worries were needless, for the bank was stillborn. Although the objections of many of the members of the Conseil Général de Commerce could be attributed to the dislike of a possible rival, it is difficult to escape the conclusion that the project was poorly conceived.

Another innovation of the restoration period was the establishment of savings banks (*caisses d'épargnes et de prévoyance*), aimed at inculcating the virtue of thrift among the poor. These banks invested their deposits in government *rentes*, the interest of which was credited to the accounts of depositors. Benjamin Delessert and other members of the Parisian *haute banque* founded the first of these banks, the Caisse d'Epargne of Paris, in 1818. The organizers requested the *anonyme* form because they "wished their association to be subjected to the formalities of commercial *sociétés anonymes* to insure confidence, although they ruled out any idea of profit."[20] The patrons contributed government *rentes* with an annual income of 1,000 francs to endow the Caisse of Paris. This initiative spread to other departments, where the lead in founding *caisses* was taken by prefects, chambers of commerce, and municipal councils.[21] By the end of 1833, 27 *caisses* had been founded. But the most active period of foundation occurred between 1834 and 1837, when 244 new *caisses* were organized.[22] By the end of 1847 there were 354 *caisses* in operation, with 175 branch offices.[23]

Among *sociétés anonymes* authorized during the period 1815–20 were four in the mining and metallurgical sector: two coal mines (Decize and Montrelais) and two metallurgical companies, the Mines de Fer de Saint Etienne, which proposed to install coke-operated smelting furnaces, and the Forge du Bas Rhin. The report of the engineer who investigated the Montrelais coal mine argued against the authorization of any coal mine as a *société anonyme* on the grounds that this form of organization lacked the spirit of conservation and foresight in its mining methods, was incapable of prompt and concerted action, and was not responsive to official regulation to the degree obtained when the concession was in the hands of the proprietors of the topsoil.[24] The operation of a mine by a *société anonyme* would be "slow, incoherent, and without any guarantees."[25] He concluded that these disadvantages outweighed the advantage of the larger capital that could be raised by an *anonyme*.[26]

Another *anonyme* authorized during the period 1815–20 was the important Manufactures de Glaces et de Verres de Saint-Quirin, an enterprise dating back to the *ancien régime*. This enterprise, the first authorized under the restoration, was wholly owned by four individuals who listed as their motives for requesting authorization the "desire to assure the continued existence and success of their enterprise, to facilitate its transmission to their heirs and to maintain insofar as possible the ownership and administration within their families, to retain unity of management and simplicity of administration, while avoiding the dangers of a large number of stockholders. . . ."[27] Another motive given was the desire of one of the owners, Baron Pierre Louis Roederer, a member of the Napoleonic Senate—the request for authorization was instituted before the fall of the empire—not to see his name involved in litigation before the commercial tribunal.[28] The owners took the charter of the Fonderies de Romilly, authorized in 1808, as their model.[29] The division of the capital of this enterprise was indicative of the desire to retain family control. The capital of over 2 million francs was divided into four shares, each share being subdivided into twelve *coupons*. Each *coupon* had a nominal value of 42,000 francs.

Altogether, thirty-two regular *sociétés anonymes*, twenty mutual insurance companies, and three savings banks were authorized during the period 1815–20 (table 2.1).

TABLE 2.1 Companies Authorized, 1815–1820

Year	Regular SAs	Mutual Insurance Companies	Savings Banks
1815	1	0	0
1816	3	1	0
1817	5	0	0
1818	10	2	1
1819	5	8	1
1820	8	9	1
Total	32	20	3

All but a few of the thirty-two *sociétés anonymes* were large companies, with nominal capital of a million francs or more. The largest was the Caisse Hypothécaire, with a capital of 50 million francs (never entirely realized). The shares of most of these companies were not widely held because of their limited number and high denomination. Most shares had denominations of between 1,000 and 5,000 francs. The Compagnie d'Assurances de Bordeaux, authorized in 1818, divided its capital (4,800,000 francs) into 192 shares of 25,000 francs each. Two-thirds of this company's shares were registered in the owner's name (*actions nominatives*) and one-third were bearer shares. Forty-four shareholders subscribed for the registered shares, each holding from 2 to 4 shares.[30] The same group of Bordeaux businessmen and capitalists, led by Pierre Balguerie, also helped found the Bank of Bordeaux and two bridge companies, all in the same year.[31] The shares of the bank and the two bridge companies were 1,000 francs, and the combined capital of these four companies totaled 11,600,000 francs.

Paris, of course, offered greater promotional opportunities. Nineteen of the thirty-two companies had their seats in Paris, even though the firms might carry on their activities elsewhere. The developing capital market in Paris permitted the raising of larger amounts of capital from a more numerous investing public. In addition to the Caisse Hypothécaire, which issued 50,000 shares of 1,000 francs, the three Compagnies Royale d'Assurances had a combined capital of 50 million francs: 30 for the life company, and 10 each of the fire and marine insurance companies. The nominal value of their shares was 5,000 francs. The shares of six of the thirty-two companies, all Paris-based insurance companies, were quoted on the Paris Bourse in 1820. Apart from government securities, the shares of only two other companies were quoted: the Bank of France and Trois Vieux Ponts sur la Seine, both authorized by statute prior to the promulgation of the *Code de Commerce*.

An increasing number of companies issued bearer shares. Some companies satisfied the desire for bearer shares by issuing both shares registered in the name of the owner and bearer shares. The Compagnie d'Assurances Maritime Contre les Risques de la Guerre divided its capital of 3 million francs into 300 registered shares of 8,000 francs each and 600 bearer shares of 1,000 francs each.[32]

In spite of the existence of a few large companies that tried to attract capital from a large number of investors, most companies possessed, initially, between 15 and 150 stockholders, numbers that would rule out the partnership form of organization. Promoters and investors were becoming increasingly aware of the superiority of the *anonyme* form over the partnership because of the former's limited liability, negotiable shares, and longevity.

The Société Anonyme, *1821–1833*

In the period 1821 through 1833, the annual average formation of *sociétés anonymes* reached nine per year, as compared with five for the period 1815–20. Probably as many more projected companies did not receive authorization, for one reason or another.[33] Consideration of requests for authorization was beginning to constitute an important

TABLE 2.2 Formation of *Sociétés Anonymes*, 1821–1833

Year	Number	Initial Nominal Capitalization (Francs)
1821	6	13,297,000
1822	14	40,355,000
1823	8	91,627,000
1824	9	9,960,000
1825	6	11,700,000
1826	13	38,480,000
1827	8	14,596,000
1828	11	30,785,000
1829	13	43,695,000
1830	8	19,524,044
1831	11	12,945,000
1832	9	7,126,000
1833	3	2,330,000
Total	119	336,420,044

Source: Compiled from the company charters in the *Bulletin des lois*.

part of the workload of the bureau of commerce of the ministry and of the committee of the interior and commerce of the Conseil d'Etat. Almost half the enterprises formed during this period (fifty-eight) were capitalized at one million francs or more.

After 1825, the period was one of depressed economic conditions, marked by many failures in the traditional banking structure.[34] This depression is only imperfectly reflected in the yearly capitalization figures in table 2.2. In some cases, the credit squeeze offered an added inducement to "go public" either for the creation of a new enterprise or for the reorganization of an old one. This was particularly true of some mining and metallurgical firms.

Many different types of firms employed the *anonyme* form. Table 2.3 shows the distribution of firms and their initial nominal capitalization by sector of the economy.

Companies involved in the transportation revolution were the most numerous, with twenty-nine, and accounted for little more than half the total nominal capitalization. Of these, ten canal companies accounted for 138 million francs. The most important canals (table 2.4)

TABLE 2.3 *Sociétés Anonymes*, 1821–1833, by Sector

Sector	Number	Initial Nominal Capitalization (Francs)
Transportation	29	181,000,044
Mining and metallurgy	22	48,617,000
Banking and insurance	13	33,786,000
Glass and crystal	8	17,364,000
Bridges	13	9,887,000
Textiles	5	8,580,000
Gas and water	4	7,660,000
Paper	3	5,175,000
Other	22	24,351,000
Total	119	336,420,044

Source: Compiled from company charters in the *Bulletin des lois*.

were constructed by the state, with private companies providing the capital. Syndicates of bankers gained concessions to supply the capital on the basis of competitive bidding, the key feature being the rate of interest the company would accept, for example, 6 percent for the Canal de Monsieur and 5.1 percent for the Burgundy Canal.[35] The companies then floated bonds that entitled the holders to fixed annual returns and amortization in forty-five years. In addition to the bonds, the initial subscribers received for each share a participation share (*action de jouissance*) that entitled the holders to half the net returns from the canals for a number of years (ninety-nine for the Canal de Monsieur and forty for the others), to begin after the bonds had been amortized. The bonds and the participation shares were negotiated separately on the Bourse.[36] Work on the canals progressed slowly, being finished only in the early 1840s. The method of government construction and private financing was criticized then and later, on the one hand by those who advocated private construction and financing, and on the other by those who wanted state construction and financing. Had the credit of the government been better, the latter alternative almost certainly would have been adopted.

France's first three railroad companies adopted the *anonyme* form. The first, in 1824, was for the twelve-mile line from Saint-Etienne to

TABLE 2.4 Large Canal Companies, 1821–1833

Company	Year	Initial Nominal Capitalization (Francs)
Canal de Monsieur (Rhône to Rhine)	1821	10,000,000
Canal from Arlès to Bouc	1822	5,500,000
Burgundy Canal	1822	25,000,000
Ardennes Canal	1823	8,000,000
Duc d'Angoulème Canal (Somme)	1823	6,600,000
Company of Four Canals (Loire Lateral, Brittany, Berry, and Nivernais canals)	1823	68,000,000

Andrézieux on the Loire, capitalized at 1 million francs. The line from Saint-Etienne to Lyon, authorized in 1827, and two years later the Loire railroad connecting Andrézieux to Roanne were intially capitalized at 10 million francs each. All three of these lines were industrial lines, primarily for hauling coal, and locally raised capital provided most of the financing.

Also organized as *anonymes* were thirteen steamship companies to provide for the transport of passengers and merchandise on the rivers and coast of France. The government authorized the first, Transports Accéléres par Eau, designed to provide service between Paris and Le Havre, in 1822. The mortality rate among these companies was high. For one thing, the steamboat was still in an experimental stage. The ill-fated Compagnie de la Navigation du Rhône par la Vapeur, organized by a merchant of Lyon, Gaillard-Malézieux, was authorized

TABLE 2.5 Large Metallurgical Enterprises, 1821–1833

Company	Date of Authorization	Initial Nominal Capitalization (Francs)
Fonderies et Forges de la Loire et l'Isère	1822	1,200,000
Forges d'Audincourt	1824	4,500,000
Hauts Fourneaux et Forges de Pont Kallecq et Mines de Quimper	1826	1,700,000
Houillères et Fonderie de l'Aveyron	1826	1,800,000
Mines, Forges et Fonderie du Creusot et de Charenton	1828	10,400,000
Forges et Fonderies de Imphy	1829	4,000,000
Fonderies et Forges d'Alais	1830	6,000,000

in June 1826. In March 1827 a boiler explosion destroyed its first steamship, *Le Rhône*, on her maiden voyage. Gaillard-Malézieux, along with the ship's designer and the principal stockholders, perished in the disaster.[37]

Among mining and metallurgical enterprises, most of the largest iron-producing firms smelting with coke adopted the *anonyme* form (table 2.5). The capital requirement was large, especially because the latest English technology was being adopted; the smallest firms soon found it necessary to raise additional capital. The Loire et l'Isère company raised its capital to 4 million francs in 1823.[38] The Aveyron company doubled its capital in 1829 and again (to 7.2 million francs) in 1832.[39] An ordinance of 14 January 1830 authorized the Pont Kallecq company to raise its capital to 2.8 million francs, but the company disappeared the same year.[40] Two Englishmen, Aaron Manby and Daniel Wilson, took over the ailing Creusot works, where the first French coke-smelted iron in the 1780s had been produced. The decision to form an *anonyme* was motivated by the need for additional capital to finance an ambitious expansion plan. The Creusot company failed in 1833 with liabilities of 11 million francs.[41] The necessity of raising additional capital was an important motive in the choice of the *anonyme* form for the Imphy company, which was originally a four-man partnership. Three of the partners were old and wanted to withdraw most of their capital from the business; the fourth was unable to continue the firm with his own limited resources.[42]

If the *anonyme* form was attractive to some, the older generation of ironmasters—including Nicolas Rambourg, for example—considered transformation of their enterprises into *anonymes* virtually unthinkable; they preferred to do without needed capital rather than risk losing control or having to share control with others.[43] Most *anonymes* were founded on the basis of old enterprises. The Audincourt company succeeded the partnership Saglio, Humann et Compagnie, and the Loire et l'Isère company succeeded the *société en commandite* Louis Frèrejean père et fils et Compagnie.[44] The Alais company, however, was basically a new company, founded under the leadership of Marshal Nicolas Soult.[45]

Besides the metallurgical companies already mentioned, most of which possessed their own coal mines, the government authorized three coal companies, seven other metallurgical enterprises, two marble quarries, two slate quarries, and the large Salines et Sels de l'Est (1826), capitalized at 10 million francs.

The most important activity in the financial sector was the authorization of nine insurance companies, four of which were based in Paris: the two Union companies, one for fire insurance and the other for life insurance, each capitalized at 10 million francs; the Soleil fire insurance company, capitalized at 6 million francs; and a small company (capital 100,000 francs) to insure the life of horses. The five outside Paris were all for marine insurance, two in Le Havre, two in Nantes, and one in Bordeaux. Two stillborn mortgage banks were authorized in Paris in 1821,[46] and the depression resulted in the creation of two semipublic discount banks in Limoges and Reims in 1831 to replace discount institutions that had disappeared. Of the nine other such banks created, none employed the *anonyme* form.[47]

The Conseil d'Etat refused to authorize the Société Commanditaire de l'Industrie, the only important bank to be projected during this period. An investment bank, the Société Commanditaire was to promote industrialization by providing long-term capital for new enterprise. The founders, led by Jacques Laffitte, included prominent French and foreign bankers, industrialists, merchants, and influential politicians and nobles.[48] Its proposed capital of 100 million francs would have made it the largest enterprise in France. The first 50 million of its capital, divided into 5,000 registered shares of 5,000 francs and 25,000 bearer shares of 1,000 francs, had already been subscribed by the founders, and transactions in promises for future delivery of shares (*promesses d'actions*) at a premium were already taking place.[49]

Although Villèle, the chief minister, reputedly favored this enterprise, it evoked considerable apprehension among other government officials. According to a contemporary, M. A. Jullien, the Conseil denied authorization because of (1) the presence of foreign bankers among the promoters, including Baring of London, Hentsch of Geneva, and Bethmann of Frankfurt; (2) the large size of the capital; and (3) the potential degradation of the nobility involved (e.g., Talleyrand and the Duc de la Rochefoucauld) through association with bankers and industrialists.[50] Had the founders been willing to exclude the foreigners, reduce the capital to 25 million francs, and accept two commissioners appointed by the government, with the power to veto any operation, it appears likely that authorization would have been granted in 1826. But by then, as Bertrand Gille suggests, the depression that had begun at the end of 1825 had undoubtedly cooled the ardor of the promoters.[51] The refusal to authorize this bold innovation, a generation before the creation of the Crédit Mobilier, strongly supports those who have argued that the Conseil d'Etat helped retard French economic development. But the question of authorization went beyond the confines of the Conseil. The issue was political as well as economic, a part of the struggle for power during the restoration between the bourgeoisie, spearheaded by bankers, and the old landed aristocracy.

The most important firms in the glassmaking and crystal industry were *sociétés anonymes*. Saint-Quirin had already been incorporated in 1815, and four more large firms followed during this period (table 2.6). In addition, there were four smaller firms, capitalized at between 300,000 and 800,000 francs. The shares of all these firms were fairly closely held. Baccarat had only eight shareholders, which caused the Conseil d'Etat to object that it resembled a partnership.[52] The eight shareholders each held a single share having a par value of 125,000 francs. None of the glassmaking companies issued shares whose par value fell below 5,000 francs. The Baccarat and Saint-Louis compa-

TABLE 2.6 Large Glassmaking Companies, 1821–1833

Company	Date of Authorization	Initial Nominal Capitalization (Francs)
Compagnie des Verreries et Cristalleries de Vonèche-Baccarat	1824	1,000,000
Manufacture de Glace et Verreries de Commentry	1828	5,000,000
Compagnie des Verreries de Saint-Louis	1829	1,200,000
Manufacture Royale des Glaces de Saint-Gobain	1830	8,064,000

nies, which specialized in crystal, cooperated in marketing their products to avoid directly competing with one another, as did the two glassmaking giants, Saint-Quirin and Saint-Gobain.[53] The Commentry firm was in liquidation the year following its authorization, with Saint-Quirin and Saint Gobain eventually acquiring its factory and stocks.[54]

Bridge companies were organized as *anonymes* to supply the necessary construction costs in return for the right to collect the tolls for a certain number of years. Because they were organized on the basis of concessions from the government, which regulated their responsibilities and rights, their authorization as *anonymes* did not generally give rise to difficulties.

Only a few of France's numerous textile enterprises assumed the *anonyme* form, one in 1825 and four in 1826. Four were large enterprises, capitalized at 1 million francs or more. Their rarity might seem surprising in an industry where many large firms existed. One reason was that old and well-established textile enterprises did not need to bring in outsiders. Another was the predominance of the family firm, in which internally generated capital usually sufficed for the needs of the enterprise. As Claude Fohlen has pointed out, "Auto-financing is particularly well adapted to an industry such as textiles, in which expansion of the means of production is accomplished by the addition of small units of capital."[55] Even the capital requirement for entry by new enterpreneurs was relatively low, so that outside capital, even if available, could be dispensed with. .

Besides three early gas companies, a water works, and three paper companies, the other *anonymes* were of highly varied sizes and characters, including theaters, model farms, bathing houses, a real estate development, and a newspaper.

Running the Bureaucratic Gauntlet

During the 1820s, as new problems developed and new conditions arose, the committee of the interior and commerce of the Conseil d'Etat continued to refine, add to, and occasionally change the requirements for obtaining authorization as a *société anonyme*. These requirements were embodied in the advisory opinions of the Conseil, which constituted a sort of administrative "jurisprudence," whose precedents formed the common law for corporate charters. Although the Conseil did not publish these advisory opinions, their contents were made known to the founders of each *société anonyme*.

Because notaries drafted the charters, and subsequently revised them, these notaries became generally familiar with what was, and what was not, acceptable to the Conseil d'Etat. The published charters themselves afforded convenient models. The less familiarity a notary had with this uncodified administrative "jurisprudence," the more unacceptable the draft charter was likely to be. Some notaries, particularly those outside the important industrial and commercial centers, had little occasion to draft company charters.

Undoubtedly, the depression that began in 1825 contributed to the increasingly cautious and restrictive attitude of the Conseil d'Etat on authorization. Between 1825 and 1830 many *sociétés anonymes* were dissolved after considerable losses for their shareholders; some ended in bankruptcy, with total losses to their shareholders and unsatisfied claims by creditors of the enterprise as well. The reaction of the Conseil d'Etat to these disasters, which were regarded as adverse reflections upon its own judgment, led to a more careful scrutiny of requests and a tightening of the requirements for authorization.

Although the Conseil d'Etat made the final decision to authorize, except for the signature of the head of the state, the role of the ministries was also important. The officials of the ministries of commerce and public works, in their examinations of requests for authorization, applied the requirements laid down by the Conseil d'Etat. In some instances the ministry simply rejected a request without further processing, on the grounds that the proposal did not meet the major requirements for a *société anonyme*. Or the draft charter might be returned to the promoters with specific suggestions on revision to meet the requirements for authorization. Another course was submission to the Conseil d'Etat of the request, along with the report of the *chef de bureau* (*rapport au ministre*) suggesting what changes ought to be required in the charter. The ministry's suggestions could be either ignored or adopted by the Conseil and enforced upon the promoters. The ministry did not always passively confine itself to applying the criteria laid down by the Conseil. It could and did suggest new departures, which, if accepted by the Conseil, became part of the administrative "jurisprudence." On one important occasion it successfully opposed the attempt of the Conseil to limit the use of the *anonyme* form to large enterprises of "public utility." Had the ministry not been successful, there might have been far fewer *anonymes*.

On the application for authorization of the Compagnie de la Verreries de Thuison, whose capital of 210,000 francs was represented by twenty-one shares of 10,000 francs, divided among six shareholders, the Conseil d'Etat attempted to limit further the use of the *société anonyme*. In its advisory opinion of 5 August 1825, the Conseil concluded:

> It would greatly extend the privilege of the *société anonyme* to apply it to associations whose objects were commercial operations on a limited scale or whose capital requirements were small; the authorization of the crown is required to establish them; public officials see that they observe the terms of their charters; the stockholders of these companies are assured that the capital represented by their shares is the only guarantee afforded to third parties in commercial operations, whereas all other types of business organization offer more extensive guarantees and the possibility of suits by a creditor against the debtor. All these considerations have led to the conclusion that the government must reserve the privilege of *sociétés anonymes* for companies that have as their objects the creation of establishments of public utility and that require the amassing of large sums of money; thus, the exploitation of mines, the opening of canals, and the founding of other companies whose public utility is demonstrated, which require the raising of large sums, attracting funds from persons unconnected with business and attracting erstwhile unproductive funds to industry, appear to attain the object of the law for the founding of *sociétés anonymes* better than the operation of a factory or a glassworks.[56]

Then, taking note of the small number of shareholders, the modest capital and limited operations of the enterprise, the Conseil concluded that these appeared to be sufficient reasons "to require the enterprise to assume one of the ordinary forms of business organization which confer a greater liability on the associates for their acts."

The ministry objected that the Conseil's proposal "contained divergent principles from those that have been followed until now"; and on the orders of the minister, Count de Corbière, the ministry submitted the matter to the Conseil Général du Commerce for its opinion.[57] The Conseil Général du Commerce came to the aid of the ministry, unanimously rejecting the contentions of the Conseil d'Etat:

> The proposed limitations are not precise. To explain the concept of *establishments of public utility*, the author of the proposal limits himself to citing

the *exploitation of mines and the opening of canals*. These types of enterprise have a special character in that they cannot be created without the approval of the government, but it does not follow that they possess exclusively the character of establishments of public utility. That character inheres in the same degree in a multitude of industrial operations that have no need for government approval. . . . In general no enterprise succeeds, no industry prospers, unless it is *useful to the public*. As for the size of the capital, the author of the proposal has not indicated the minimum he intends to fix for the capital of a *société anonyme*. This minimum, if it were possible to fix one, must vary according to the locality; a sum that would appear small for Paris would be large in the departments where industry was less well developed.

But, even in Paris, it would be convenient often to authorize a *société anonyme* founded with a small capital. If, for example, it involves attempting a new process, . . . would the promoters be forced to form a *société en commandite*? This would change their status; to force them to confine themselves to a *commandite* would restrict them from all participation in the direction of the enterprise and as a result could cause them to renounce it.

The proposal designates as a *privilege* the authorization given to a *société anonyme*. There would be a *privilege* only in the event of an exclusive concession of a branch of industry. This the government of the King will assuredly not grant. If the sharcholders of a *société anonyme* are liable only for the value of their shares, it is the same for the *commanditaires* of a *société en commandite*. It is true that the *commandite* has unlimited liability, but the *société anonyme* offers to third parties a guarantee lacking in all other forms of business organization, that of the publicity of its accounts and of its operations.

In deciding on requests for authorization of *sociétés anonymes*, the government functions as a jury. It decides according to the particular circumstances of each request and no general rule can be established to serve as a base for those decisions.[58]

In this conflict, the ministry was partly victorious. The Compagnie de la Verreries de Thuison was authorized, but its capital was raised to 400,000 francs.[59] Although the Conseil d'Etat gave way, it did not renounce the views it had set forth. It continued to regard incorporation as a *privilege*; it continued to apply, at least implicitly, the concept of *public utility*; and it generally viewed with a jaundiced eye any enterprise whose capital was small. Furthermore, the Conseil regarded with suspicion all promoters who were not well-known or well-established members of the business community.

In 1828, the Conseil d'Etat expressed similar sentiments in its opinion on a request to authorize the Moulin des Tuileries of Toulouse, capitalized at 240,000 francs. This was a partnership whose proprietors wanted the *anonyme* form to facilitate the transmission of their enterprise to their heirs. The Conseil d'Etat, noting that it was not a new or large enterprise and needed no additional capital, that other organizational alternatives existed, and that "the legislator, in permitting the creation of enterprises enjoying such great advantages, aimed to encourage, in the public interest, large industrial enterprise requiring the amassing of large amounts of capital and requiring to some extent the gathering of funds from the public," rejected the request.[60] According to the Conseil, it was for the government "to judge in each particular case the necessity, or at least the utility, of employing this form of business organization."[61]

Although the Conseil d'Etat and the ministry subjected each request to a careful and detailed consideration, the role of the prefect in the authorization process tended to be pro forma. Required by the *instruction* of 1817 to render an opinion on the utility of the enterprise and the character and substance of the promoters and shareholders, the prefect usually discharged his duty in a perfunctory manner.[62] Rarely was the prefect's report unfavorable. More often, the prefect strongly advocated the authorization of the enterprise and frequently, particularly outside Paris, inquired on behalf of the promoters about the status of the project during the long process leading to authorization. It can be assumed that the prefect was often on friendly terms with the promoters. His duties as the government's electoral agent required him to be interested in how they voted, and it was only logical that he should become an advocate of their interests. However, the prefect was forbidden from holding shares or participating in any way in enterprises organized within his jurisdiction.

Because they tended to be pro forma, the prefect's recommendations were not given much weight either within the ministry or by the Conseil d'Etat. The prefect served primarily as an intermediary, channeling documents and information between the founders on the one hand and the ministry and the Conseil d'Etat on the other.

Until the 1820s, it appears that chambers of commerce were consulted frequently on requests for authorization. The minister of the interior wrote the Chamber of Commerce of Paris in 1818 that the ministry valued its opinion on projected enterprises and that the advice of the chamber would continue to be solicited, as in the past. Therefore, he regarded as superfluous any provision requiring the administration to consult the chamber.[63] In spite of this assurance, consultation of chambers of commerce on requests for authorization occurred less frequently. When they were consulted, the initiative usually came, it appears, from the prefect.[64]

It also remained to be seen how the general requirements laid down in the ministerial *instruction* of 1818 concerning the duration of an enterprise, mandatory dissolution, reserves, and public accounting would be applied. The requirement that companies were to have a definite duration was justified on the grounds that reauthorization upon the expiration of the term of the enterprise gave the government an opportunity to reappraise it. As a means of control over the enterprise, this requirement was illusory. Because the period of duration seldom was less than twenty years (though never more than ninety-nine years), the government had little occasion before 1833 to deal with requests for reauthorization. Enterprises that managed to survive their terms were generally successful ones, and that success in itself constituted a strong argument for reauthorization. Within broad limits, it appears that promoters were permitted to set the length of their terms without interference. The duration of some companies was determined by external factors; the duration of bridge companies, for example, was fixed by the period during which they enjoyed the right to collect tolls.

All charters had to contain provisions requiring the dissolution of the enterprise if a certain portion of the capital were lost, usually between one-half and three-quarters.[65] Many charters, in addition to the required clause on mandatory dissolution, contained a clause regarding optional dissolution, giving the board of directors or stockholders the right to dissolve the enterprise if a certain portion of the capital had been lost, usually between a quarter and one-half. Within these limits the choice was apparently left to the founders, but outside this range the government raised objections. The Conseil d'Etat and the ministry both objected to a provision in the draft charter of the Boulangerie Mécanique de Lille, which permitted a single shareholder to force the dissolution of the enterprise after a third of the capital had been lost, as too restrictive.[66]

Charters also had to provide for a reserve fund to be raised by a levy against net profits, usually 5 percent or 10 percent, until the reserve fund had reached a certain amount, usually a figure between 10 percent and 20 percent of the enterprise's total capital. The Conseil d'Etat

objected to a reserve fund of 150,000 francs for the projected Boulangerie Mécanique de Lille as being disproportionate to the enterprise's
capital of 400,000 francs.[67]

Another provision of the *instruction* was the requirement, incorporated into the authorizing ordinance, that the enterprise submit a balance sheet (*état de situation*) every six months to the local tribunal of
commerce and chamber of commerce and to the prefect, who forwarded it to the ministry. The intent of this provision was to provide
third parties with information about the enterprise[68] and presumably
allow the government to ascertain if the corporation was observing the
provisions of its charter. The authorizing ordinance also contained the
provision that the government could dissolve the enterprise for non-
observance of its charter. Until 1838, when a government crackdown
occurred, companies seldom bothered to submit these balance sheets,
and when they did, the ministry made no attempt to use them as an
instrument of surveillance.

Although the Conseil d'Etat early had ruled that dividends could be
paid only from profits, and that no dividends could be paid if the
enterprise's capital fell below its stated capital, its policy regarding the
payment of interest to shareholders was shaped later. The Conseil
permitted early charters to stipulate the payment of interest to shareholders. This was a provision favored by promoters, becaused it made
shares appear analogous to government *rentes* and attractive to *ren-
tiers* because of the higher rate. At first the Conseil d'Etat generally
limited itself to stipulating that such interest could be paid only out of
profits,[69] so as not to reduce the capital of the enterprise. Toward the
end of the 1820s, the Conseil began to object to interest payments
altogether, and they were systematically barred from all corporate
charters as misleading to shareholders.[70]

In its examination of corporate charters, the government decided
whether sufficient working capital (*fonds de roulement*) had been provided for the operation of the enterprise and often forced promoters to
raise the capital.[71] Once an enterprise was authorized, it was difficult
for it to increase its capital by issuing additional shares, for changes in
the charter had to be approved by the procedure followed in original
authorization—a lengthy process. Nor could calls be made on shareholders above the par value of their shares. Borrowing was a possibility, but the Conseil d'Etat regarded it as an unwise course.[72]

Surprisingly, the Conseil d'Etat did not attempt to establish a policy on depreciation. Of course, depreciation affects various enterprises unequally. It is of little concern to banks and insurance companies, as they have few, if any, assets subject to depreciation. The Conseil could hardly avoid some awareness of the problem, because it was always interested in maintaining the integrity of an enterprise's capital. Possibly, the Conseil regarded the mandatory reserve fund as a way of covering depreciation. Some companies chose, out of either design or ignorance, to neglect it completely. It was a way of overstating profits or understating losses. For example, the Compagnie des Transports des Marchandises sur la Saône, authorized in 1829, was still carrying its boats at their original cost on the balance sheets of 1835 and 1836.[73] The draft charter of the Verreries de Lamotte provided for an annual depreciation of buildings and equipment of 2 percent. Brochant de Villiers, in his report to the Conseil Général des Mines, claimed that this figure was too low and proposed that it be raised to 5 percent for buildings and 6⅔ percent for equipment;[74] the Conseil d'Etat did not adopt this view. For reasons that are not clear, the final draft of the company's charter provided for annual depreciation of buildings and equipment of only 1 percent.[75]

The government permitted amortization of the capital shares of some early *anonymes*, such as bridge and canal companies. These, however, came to be regarded as special cases, resembling repayment of loans, as the Conseil d'Etat began to see provisions for the amortization of capital as detrimental to the integrity of the enterprise's capital; and this integrity, as the Conseil never tired of pointing out, was the only guarantee afforded to third parties. The idea of amortizing the shares of the enterprise, coupled with the issue of "industrial" or "participation" shares, attracted promoters. Bordeaux capitalists projected a number of these companies.[76] One such, the Paquebots à Vapeur de Bordeaux au Havre, requested authorization in 1832. The company, capitalized at 900,000 francs divided into 900 shares of 1,000 francs, proposed to buy and operate two steamships of 400 tons. The draft charter provided for amortization of its shares over a period of twenty-three years. Amortized shares would receive a premium. The order of amortization was to be determined by lot, and premiums ranged from 150 to 10,000 francs. During the period of amortization, the company would pay no dividends, only interest on the shares. All shareholders received a participation share for each capital share; once the capital shares had been amortized, the holders of participation shares would enter into ownership of the company. Shareholders found attractive the prospect of an annual return of 6 percent (only 5 percent until construction of the ships was completed); a minimum premium of 15 percent when one of the shares was amortized, with the possibility of a 1,000 percent premium, depending on the luck of the draw; and, after twenty-three years, if all went according to plan, possession of a valuable participation share. Both the ministry and the Conseil d'Etat rejected this arrangement.[77]

The government became more careful about authorizing new enterprises on the basis of the capital assets of an old enterprise, especially after the failure of many *anonymes* during the 1820s, alleged to have been caused, in part, by the exaggerated value placed on such assets. Some promoters organized *anonymes* as a means of realizing immediate profits for themselves or of dumping unprofitable enterprises upon the public. In order to make sure that assets were not overvalued, government officials appointed independent appraisers to make careful appraisals. This procedure often resulted in wide divergencies between the appraised value of assets and the value assigned the same assets by promoters. In some cases, promoters renounced a request for authorization rather than accept the government's appraisal.

A few *sociétés anonymes* had been permitted to use the designation "Compagnie Royale," but in the 1820s the Conseil d'Etat began to object to such designations, on the grounds that the failure of a company so named would reflect adversely upon the crown. Some exceptions were made. In spite of the objections of the Conseil d'Etat, the Société Royale pour l'Emploi des Laines Longues et Lustrées, authorized in 1826, retained the designation "Royale," owing to the insistence of the Duc de Doudeauville, one of the founders of the company and the minister of the household of the crown.[78] Another exception was the Institution Royale Agronomique de Grignon, authorized in 1827, which was sponsored by the aristocracy and for which Charles X provided the land.[79] The old Saint-Gobain company, authorized in 1830, already had the designation "Manufacture Royale," and the Conseil left to the crown the decision on whether the company would be allowed to retain it. The crown approved.[80] But, unless support could be gained from the crown, the designation was systematically denied, although requests for it were numerous.[81]

Every charter contained provisions on the administration of the enterprise. Administrative responsibility rested with a board of directors, chosen by the stockholders and subject to dismissal by them, although in some enterprises there was only a single director. In the latter case a number of *censeurs* might be provided to report on the administration of the enterprise to the stockholders. Although the draft charter could name a temporary board of directors, stockholders were empowered to choose new boards after authorization. Because directors were only agents of the company and subject to dismissal by the stockholders, the government systematically rejected any provisions in draft charters that would make their terms perpetual or grant them any special privileges, such as the right to a fixed percentage of the profits.[82]

Charters often required that directors possess a certain number of shares. In like manner, attendance and voting at stockholders' meetings generally was restricted to those owning a certain number of shares. In an age of high property qualifications for voting, it did not seem incongruous to deny small shareholders the right to attend and vote. On the other hand, charters often limited the number of votes a single shareholder could cast. Stockholders of the Compagnie des Bateaux à Vapeur pour la Navigation du Rhône, authorized in 1830, were limited to a maximum of three votes, regardless of the number of shares owned. Stockholders had to have three shares for one vote, six for two votes, and nine for three votes.[83] Such provisions were designed to prevent a single individual or a small group from controlling the enterprise.

Although restricting the vote to holders of a certain number of shares was general, there are examples of a more democratic procedure. Shareholders of the Compagnie des Transports des Marchandises sur la Saône, authorized in 1829, were permitted one vote for each share up to six votes, after which three shares were required for each additional vote; no shareholder was permitted more than ten votes.[84] The charter of the Hotel de Saint Jean à Toulouse stipulated only one vote per shareholder, regardless of the number of shares owned.[85] The Conseil d'Etat permitted the founders considerable discretion in these matters.

But the Conseil did intervene in the charter of the Compagnie du

Pont, Gare, et Port de Grenelle, authorized in 1826, to reduce the number of shares required for membership on the board of directors from fifty to twenty, and the number of shares to attend and vote at stockholders meetings from twenty to five. The Conseil was concerned less with giving representation to smaller shareholders than with making the clauses of the charter workable. The Conseil feared that with the passage of time and the greater diffusion of shares, it might be impossible to find enough owners of fifty shares to fill the board of directors and enough shareholders with twenty shares to provide a quorum for a stockholders' meetings.[86]

The authorization procedure for mining and metallurgical companies differed from that for other companies. The ministry of public works, rather than the ministry of commerce, was responsible for processing the request before it was submitted to the Conseil d'Etat. In addition to the report of the prefect, reports from the government's mining engineer for the district and his superior were required. After these reports had been evaluated by the Conseil Général des Mines, the ministry's division of mines advised the minister whether to submit the request to the Conseil d'Etat. The Conseil Général des Mines, a small body composed of the eight or nine highest-ranking government mining engineers and presided over by either the minister or, as usually was the case, the director-general of the division of roads, bridges, and mines, played the key role in enforcing upon promoters the administrative "jurisprudence" laid down by the Conseil d'Etat. Many projected *anonymes* were either rejected at this stage or renounced by the promoters when they found the requirements of the Conseil Général des Mines too onerous.

One such case involved a request for authorization in 1829 of the Usine Métallurgique de Gouille, capitalized at 1,250,000 francs. The report submitted to the Conseil Général des Mines in 1831 charged that the evaluation of the property of the Comte d'Archiac at 600,000 francs appeared to be much too high; ten and one-half shares of the capital had not yet been subscribed, which reduced the capital by 105,000 francs; and given the annual operating expenses calculated by the district engineer at 627,776 francs (the *gérant* of the enterprise, Joshua Glover, had estimated 600,000 francs), the capital for the enterprise was insufficient. The report also rejected as inadmissible a clause in the charter providing for the payment of 6 percent interest on the shares; this was "only a snare to attract subscribers." The charter had no clauses providing for optional or obligatory dissolution of the enterprise when a certain portion of the capital had been lost, as required by the ministry *instruction* of 11 July 1818.[87] The Conseil Général des Mines, in addition to specifying other changes in the provisions of the charter, decided that the capital must be raised by 350,000 francs and that the property of the Comte d'Archiac had to be formally appraised.[88] Some of the same objections were raised in 1842–43, when the enterprise again unsuccessfully attempted to obtain authorization. A third attempt by the enterprise succeeded in 1854.

Companies organized to prospect for coal were not authorized as *anonymes*. In the case of the Compagnie Départmentale du Haut-Rhin pour la Recherche de Mines de Houille, promoted by Florent Saglio and Georges Humann, both interested in the Audincourt company located in the same department, Brochant de Villiers concluded in favor of authorization in his report to the Conseil Général des Mines in 1822.[89] However, the Conseil advised against authorizing a company of this type,[90] and the ministry upheld the Conseil's position. In July 1826 the same report writer was able to convince the Conseil Général des Mines to authorize such a company (Société Havas), but the minister overruled the Conseil.[91] At the end of 1826, the Haut-Rhin Company again applied for authorization. In his report to the Conseil Général des Mines in April 1827, Brochant de Villiers recognized that "the jurisprudence adopted by the minister and the Conseil d'État holds that enterprises to prospect for coal may not be constituted as *sociétés anonymes*, because they actually have no commercial basis."[92]

In considering the request for authorization of the Mines de Houille de Norroy in 1831, the Conseil Général des Mines refused to allow the funds already expended on exploration for coal, estimated by the company at 124,000 francs, to be included in its capitalization, because inclusion of these funds would be misleading to the public. Needless to say, this was an inconvenient restriction for promoters. The working capital of the Norroy Coal Mines was judged to be insufficient, and the Conseil required that it be raised by 100,000 francs.[93] The company failed to comply with this last requirement, and authorization was refused a year later. The report to the Conseil Général des Mines noted that "if these mines of Norroy promise such a good return, it was extraordinary that in more than a year none of the new shares had been subscribed and none of the original shareholders, among whom there were rich persons, had seen fit to take additional shares."[94] The writer of the report added, "If *sociétés anonymes* in industry have for some years been in a state of public discredit, except perhaps those for the construction of bridges or roads and canals, it is principally because of the laxness with which they have been authorized, in allowing an exaggerated or illusory capital value, which has resulted in miscalculations and losses, and in their train the ruin of the majority of these *sociétés anonymes* to the great detriment of industry."[95]

Abuses did exist. Many promoters used the joint-stock company as a device to unload part or all of the ownership of an unprofitable or marginal enterprise on the public. But blaming administrative laxness for the failures of this period gives too little credit to the business cycle. In effect, government officials recognized that they had an implicit responsibility for the future success of those enterprises they authorized. Accordingly, on the eve of rapid industrial expansion, they attempted to apply the tightest possible controls, thereby limiting the use of the *anonyme* form as a vehicle of economic growth.

Another high government official, the mining engineer Beaunier, testified before the ministry of commerce investigation into the state of the iron industry in 1828, "The *anonyme*, marvelously applied to the construction of roads, bridges, and canals, is less suited for enterprises in which buying, manufacturing, selling, and making deals are involved."[96] This view echoes the opinion expressed over fifty years earlier by Adam Smith that the joint-stock company was suitable only for enterprises whose operations could be reduced to routines, such as (commercial) banking, insurance, canals, and water supply companies. Implicit in this view were the assumptions that the owners, through their boards of directors, had to administer the enterprises and that such boards could not make competent day-to-day decisions. This difficulty could be overcome only with the creation of a professional managerial class to whom authority could be delegated. In any case, whether suitable or not, there was no satisfactory alternative, when large amounts of capital were required, to the joint-stock company.

3 The Rise of the
Société en Commandite par Actions

Les affaires, c'est l'argent des autres.

Variously attributed

If promoters could obtain authorization for their enterprise as a *société anonyme*, they enjoyed, in addition to the legal advantages that the *anonyme* status conferred—such as limited liability and the freedom to sell their shares and withdraw their services from the enterprise at will—the government-created presumption that the enterprise was serious and solid, which facilitated the placing of shares and obtaining of credit. The public ignored the constant insistence of government officials that authorization did not constitute a guarantee; in fact, the cautiousness of government officials in according authorization belied their own disclaimers. The advantages of authorization had to be weighed against the difficulty of satisfying the stringent requirements and the length of time the procedure took, usually twelve to eighteen months, and with no guarantee of final success. The Conseil d'Etat also discouraged entrepreneurs by refusing to allow "promotional profits": entrepreneurs could not receive any special compensation for organizing the company, for previous efforts, or for cash outlay not represented by a tangible asset, which, in effect, reduced them to the same level as "the most recent" subscribers of shares. The big operators often remedied this situation by retaining large numbers of shares and then mounting huge publicity campaigns after which, if successful, the shares could be sold at a handsome premium. For those promoters who could not succeed in securing authorization, or to whom the disadvantages seemed too formidable, an alternative existed: *the société en commandite par actions.*

The first draft of the *Code de Commerce* contained no provision permitting the capital of a *société en commandite* to be divided into shares. Only after complaints from the commercial tribunals and cham-

[47]

bers of commerce, particularly those of coastal towns, requesting that the draft be revised to accommodate current business usage, was the provision allowing *commandites* to issue shares added. Although this provision occasioned serious opposition within the Conseil d'Etat, it was allowed to stand. In spite of these apprehensions, certainly no one, even in the wildest flight of imagination, could have foreseen the use to which the *commandite* would be put.

Under the provisions of the code, the *commandite par actions* possessed one or more administrators (*gérants*) who were subject to unlimited liability, as in a partnership, and whose names were the legal name (*raison social*) of the enterprise.[1] The ordinary shareholders (*commanditaires*) furnished capital and, provided they did not participate in the management of the enterprise, possessed limited liability. Because the mass of shareholders legally could not interfere in the management of the enterprise, the *gérant* was virtually omnipotent.

The *commandite par actions* was in many respects a promoter's dream. The legal formalities for the formation of the enterprise were minimal. Even the services of the omnipresent notary were optional. A summary of the main provisions of the enterprise's charter had to be registered at the local commercial tribunal, a formality requiring only the small fee of five and a half francs. The promoter could determine the terms of the charter. He possessed wide latitude concerning the provisions, subject only to the basic framework provided by the code and subsequent court decisions. He could place his own evaluation upon the assets, tangible and intangible, that he contributed to the enterprise, which could include compensation for his past efforts and ideas. He could even set his own future salary. The only limitation upon the appetite of the *gérant* was the necessity of convincing potential shareholders to part with their cash. The promotion had to look appealing.

By the 1830s, the charters of most *commandites* exhibited certain common characteristics. Most serious enterprises used the services of notaries; standard models of charters existed, which could be varied to fit the needs of the enterprise or the whims of the *gérants*.[2] Besides the provisions concerning duration, capitalization, denomination and type of shares, division of profits, dissolution, and liquidation, most charters came to provide for shareholders' meetings and councils of surveillance. One legal obligation of the *gérant* toward the shareholders was the rendering of financial accounts. The easiest way to present accounts was through annual stockholder meetings, at which a report from the *gérant* was read. Because shareholders had the right to verify the accuracy of these accounts, it was convenient to provide in the charter for a committee chosen by the shareholders from among themselves to perform this function. These committees became general and were formalized under the name of councils of surveillance (*conseils de surveillance*). To avoid expensive litigation in the courts, charters normally provided that internal conflicts between the *gérant* and shareholders be settled by compulsory arbitration. As in a partnership, the death of the *gérant* brought the dissolution of the enterprise. Because this provision was inconvenient and could be disastrous, many charters made provision for continuing the enterprise in the event of the death or withdrawal of the *gérant*.

Although the position of the *gérant* was legally dominant, it should not be assumed that the shareholders always adhered to the passive role assigned to them by the code. The use of straw men as *gérants*, to front for and do the bidding of powerful shareholders, was frequent, if the numerous denunciations of this practice are to be believed. The use of bearer shares enabled these shareholders to conceal their identities and thus escape losing limited liability for participation in management. This practice afforded one of the major reasons for questioning the legality of bearer shares and for the attack on bearer shares during the boom that began in 1836.

The question of whether *sociétés en commandite* would be permitted to issue bearer shares (*actions au porteur*), as an increasing number of them did, especially in Paris, came before the courts in 1830. In 1828 a *société en commandite*—Armand, Lecomte et Compagnie—was founded for the purpose of transporting merchandise; its nominal capital of 10 million francs was divided into 10,000 bearer shares of 1,000 francs each. Some disgruntled shareholders brought suit in 1830 to have the company's charter declared null and void on the grounds that bearer shares were illegal for *sociétés en commandite*. Their position was supported by briefs from two distinguished members of the Paris bar, Charles Persil and A. M. J. J. Dupin (Dupin ainé), whose major argument was that the issue of bearer shares effectively nullified Article 28 of the *Code de Commerce*, which prohibited shareholders (*commanditaires*) of a *commandite* from participating in the management of the enterprise on penalty of losing limited liability; if the shareholders could not be identified, they could violate the prohibition of Article 28 with impunity. Briefs supporting the legality of bearer shares were presented by Odilon Barrot, Philippe Dupin (Dupin jeune), and Devaux. The commercial tribunal of Paris, on 14 August 1830, decided in favor of the legality of bearer shares, principally on the grounds that the code, in permitting *commandites* to issue shares, did not expressly prohibit bearer shares.[3] This decision was upheld in appeal by a decision of the Royal Court of Paris on 7 February 1832.[4]

Even before the definitive resolution of the question whether a *commandite* could issue bearer shares, this form of business organization was beginning to acquire some importance in Paris and in other commercial centers. Although information regarding the numbers and the capitalization of *commandites par actions* is far from satisfactory, it is nevertheless possible to arrive at some conclusions. Between the promulgation of the code in 1807 and the mid-1820s, the *commandite par actions* appears to have been little used. For most enterprises the partnership still sufficed. The availability of the *commandite par actions* was not well known, and, probably most important, the willingness to hold negotiable shares was only gradually taking hold. What paved the way for the triumph of the *commandite* was the difficulty of obtaining authorization for the *société anonyme*.

The advantages of the *commandite par actions* over the *société anonyme* have already been discussed. In relation to the partnership,

TABLE 3.1 Registration of *Sociétés en Commandite par Actions*, 1826–1837

Locale	Number	Initial Nominal Capitalization (Francs)
Paris[a]	1,106	1,117,098,740
Rest of France[b]	673	430,282,000
Total	1,779	1,547,380,740

[a]MU, 1838, Rapport de la Commission, p. 1010.
[b]Compiled from reports of the Cours Royaux in AN, BB[30] 278.

the *commandite* possessed the advantage of being able to raise large sums and issue negotiable securities, and the omnipotence of the *gérant* was undoubtedly attractive to ambitious entrepreneurs. In the 1830s, contemporaries were convinced, rightly or wrongly, that the popularity of the *commandite* rested upon its ability to issue bearer shares. Bearer shares were particularly prevalent among companies registered in Paris.

The *commandite par actions* enjoyed a greater popularity in Paris than in other parts of France, even allowing for the great economic and commercial importance of the capital. The commercial tribunal in Paris, from 1826 until the end of 1837, registered 62 percent of all *commandites par actions*, representing 72 percent of the total nominal capital (table 3.1). The annual figures for Lyon, an important commercial and industrial center, show that the *commandite par actions* was little used, at least until 1838 (table 3.2). In Lyon, the traditional forms of organization—the partnership and the simple *commandite*— remained dominant. In the important silk industry, the *commandite par actions* was almost completely ignored.[5]

Figures for France, excluding Paris (table 3.3), show that the number of *commandites* for the period 1826–30 was small, although the

TABLE 3.2 *Sociétés en Commandite par Actions* Registered at the Commercial Tribunal of Lyon

Year	Number	Year	Number
1821	0	1831	3
		1832	1
1825	7	1833	3
1826	7	1834	5
1827	5	1835	1
1828	4	1836	3
1829	6	1837	9
1830	4	1838	19

Source: Compiled from AN, BB[30] 278, and AD, Rhône, 8U, Sociétés: Constitutions et Modifications.

Note: Years 1822–24 not included in sample.

nominal capitalization was significant. After an eclipse from 1831 through 1835, the number and nominal capitalization of *commandites* jumped dramatically in 1836. The distribution of the *commandites par actions* by economic sector shows that they were used for many kinds of enterprise, but bulking largest were those enterprises requiring large amounts of capital. Both in numbers and in nominal capitalization, mining and metallurgy, banking and insurance, and companies involved in transporting goods and passengers predominated (table 3.4).

In 1833, the commercial tribunal of Paris registered sixty-six *commandites par actions*, representing a nominal capital of 28,394,000 francs. Exactly one-half (thirty-three) of these *commandites* were enterprises involving the publication of newspapers, periodicals, and

TABLE 3.3 Registration of *Sociétés en Commandite par Actions*, France except Paris Area, 1826–1837

Year	Number	Initial Nominal Capitalization (Francs)
1826	40	42,047,000
1827	41	21,803,000
1828	29	19,238,000
1829	44	16,642,000
1830	29	24,528,000
1831	20	4,124,000
1832	31	5,227,000
1833	27	6,824,000
1834	35	17,264,000
1835	37	15,486,000
1836	85	76,151,000
1837	106	93,627,000
Exact date unknown	149	87,321,000
Total	673	430,282,000

Source: Compiled from AN, BB[30] 278. The year of registration is unknown for 22 percent of the companies, but it may be assumed that the relationships among the various magnitudes would not be significantly affected.

books.[6] A breakdown of the *commandites par actions* formed in the boom year of 1837 shows the continued favor this form of business organization enjoyed in the publishing industry. Two of these companies were themselves spawned by the joint-stock company boom: the

TABLE 3.4 *Sociétés en Commandite par Actions*, France except Paris Area, 1826–1837, by Sector

Sector	Number	Initial Nominal Capitalization (Francs)
Transportation (steamship companies, coach lines, etc.)	126	64,942,000
Banking and insurance	92	85,841,000
Mining and metallurgy	81	116,912,000
Textiles	57	28,513,000
Newspapers, periodicals, printing companies	51	4,293,000
Sugar refining	39	9,165,000
Light manufacturing (hardware, candles, soap, bricks, etc.)	30	7,333,000
Paper and chemicals	27	9,097,000
Commerce (retail and wholesale)	27	4,844,000
Real estate and farming	20	38,790,000
Flour mills and sawmills	18	7,594,000
Glass and earthenware	15	11,258,000
Gas and water	15	7,790,000
Bridges	11	14,750,000
Miscellaneous enterprises (baths, theaters, schools, fishing, restaurants, race tracks, etc.)	64	19,160,000
Total	673	430,282,000

Source: Compiled from AN, BB[30] 278.

stock market newspapers *L'Actionnaire* and *La Bourse*. The first, guided by Agénor Adolphe François, formerly a partnership capitalized at 40,000 francs, transformed itself into a *commandite par actions* in December, capitalized at 175,000 francs divided into shares of 500 francs. *La Bourse*, capitalized at 150,000 francs, issued 500 shares of 200 francs and 500 shares of 100 francs, bearer or registered at the choice of the holder. The founder of *La Bourse*, Gustave Sicard, attributed 100 shares of each denomination to himself as compensa-

TABLE 3.5 *Sociétés en Commandite par Actions* Registered at the Commercial Tribunal of Paris in 1837, by Sector

Sector	Number	Initial Nominal Capitalization (Francs)
Publication (newspapers, books, periodicals)	94	21,753,000
Transportation	39	47,230,000
Mining and metallurgy	26	58,390,000
Manufacturing (paper, glass, bricks, leather goods, hardware, sugar refining)	26	20,740,000
Banking and insurance	22	116,100,000
Commerce (retail and wholesale)	17	7,729,000
Real estate and agricultural enterprise	11	34,550,000
Textile	10	9,300,000
Cultural enterprises (theaters, schools, art galleries)	10	5,188,000
Bridges	9	5,000,000
Gas	2	5,000,000
Miscellaneous	21	11,458,000
Total	287	342,438,000

Source: Compiled from AD, Seine, D31, U³, cartons 70–74.

tion for his effort.[7] Neither of these papers survived the collapse of the boom that had given them life.

Although publishing enterprises were the most numerous, approximately one-third of the total nominal capital went into banking and insurance, and almost half of that amount went into a single firm, Jacques Laffitte's Caisse Générale du Commerce et de l'Industrie (nominal capital 55 million francs, of which only 15 million was (realized).[8] The combined transportation and mining and metallurgical sectors accounted for another third, with the remaining sectors accounting for the last third (table 3.5).

Laffitte's *caisse*, the largest of the enterprises registered in Paris in 1837, issued shares of 5,000 francs. The eighty shares of the metallurgical concern run by the Schneiders at Le Creusot each had a par value of 50,000 francs.[9] These were the exceptions. The shares of most enterprises ran from 100 to 1,000 francs. Few fell below 100 francs, though 50-franc shares were issued by Fortuné Jüestz et Compagnie, organized to transport goods and passengers between Paris and Fontenay; its 5,000-franc capitalization made it the smallest company registered at Paris in 1837.[10] Most shares issued by Paris companies were bearer shares, which were more popular in Paris than elsewhere. The same range of par values for shares prevailed in the rest of France.

These figures concerning *commandites par actions* are for registrations; it should not be assumed that all of them became operating enterprises. Many were stillborn because of failures to raise sufficient capital to begin operation. Some double counting is involved, for some companies were registered at more than one commercial tribunal. The procelain-manufacturing enterprise of Decaën frères, capitalized at 1,600,000 francs, was registered at the commercial tribunals of both Paris and Lyon.[11] Among operating companies there was often a considerable discrepancy between the nominal capital and the realized capital. Louis Wolowski, highly knowledgeable in these matters, estimated the sums involved in *commandites par actions* in early 1838 at more than a billion francs—"a calculation exempt from exaggeration"[12]—yet this figure appears to be too high. Jacques Bresson, in relating nominal capital to actual capital for companies that failed in 1839, estimated that only one-third of the capital of these companies was realized.[13] If, in order to account for stillborn enterprise, double counting, and unrealized capital, we employ the conservative estimate that one-fifth of the over 1,500,000,000 francs of nominal capital for *commandites par actions* registered during the period 1826–37 was realized, the resulting figure is more than 300 million francs. It is still an impressive figure and more than the approximately 295 million invested in *sociétés anonymes* for the same period. It cannot be doubted that *commandites par actions* played an important role in French industrialization.

This spectacular rise of the *commandites par actions* was not without effect on traditional institutions, which viewed the *commandite* as a threat. The Bourse, which with few exceptions quoted only government *rentes* and the shares of *sociétés anonymes*, saw a dangerous competitor operating outside its purview; the Bank of France and the *haute banque* viewed with alarm the creation of discount banks; the ministry of finance saw an avalanche of *commandite* shares as weakening the market for government *rentes*; those with vested interest in existing *sociétés anonymes* felt the challenge. Seizing upon certain abuses in some share-issuing *commandites*, many businessmen found it easy to convince themselves, in the unlikely instance that any such doubts existed, of the identity of their own interests and those of the country. It proved to be an effective device for waging war upon a dangerous competitor.

Public officials watched with apprehension as the boom in *commandites par actions* gathered steam throughout 1837. There was a growing conviction that some government action would have to be taken to stop this speculative frenzy. In July, the Bank of France complained to the minister of finance about "the invasion of the *société en commandite*, which has been diverted from its true purpose," and asked for government action.[14] The following month, A. G. Aubé, the outgoing president of the commercial tribunal of Paris, called for legislation to prevent fraud in the *commandite par actions*.[15] In the fall of 1837, Emile Vincens, a member of the Conseil d'Etat, produced a short book on joint-stock companies, which attacked the abuses in *commandites par actions*.[16] The *commandite*, he charged, was being used even for large enterprises for which it was not suited.[17] Increasingly, *commanditaires* were interfering in the administration of the enterprise, the sole preserve of the responsible *gérant*. Some *gérants* were simply straw men, fronting for the large shareholders.[18] In many cases, the *commandite par actions*, instead of employing the names of responsible *gérants* to designate the enterprise, were appropriating names stating the object of the enterprise, which were reserved for *sociétés anonymes*.[19] These *commandites* wished to appear in public in the guise of *sociétés anonymes*. Vincens proposed the complete elimination of the *commandite par actions* through the abrogation of Article 38 of the *Code de Commerce*. Only the *société anonyme*, which in Vincens's view was also in need of some reform, should be permitted to issue shares.[20]

Reform sentiment led to the appointment of a commission in late 1837 to draft a bill on the *commandite par actions*. Its fifteen members included the minister of justice, who presided; the ministers of finance and commerce; the undersecretary of state for justice; and the Directeur du Mouvement des Fonds from the ministry of finance. Three others, including Vincens, were members of the Conseil d'Etat. Of the others, five had legal backgrounds, one was an official of the Paris Bourse, and the Comte d'Argout was governor of the Bank of France. In more than a dozen meetings held between 19 November 1837 and 25 January 1838, the commission hammered out a bill whose main provision was the complete elimination of the *société en commandite par actions*. From the minutes of the commission it is clear that this solution to the problem of abuses in the *commandite par actions* was more stringent than even the government desired.[21]

From the outset the commission divided into three groups of about equal size. First were those, such as M. Vandermarcq, a *syndic des agents de change* of the Paris Bourse, who desired purely and simply the suppression of the *commandite par actions*, the course of action already suggested by Vincens. Few *commandite* shares were listed on the Paris Bourse. The suppression of the shares of all *commandites* would eliminate a tough competitor and presumably enhance those *anonyme* shares and government *rentes* in which the Bourse specialized. A second group, in which were to be found the ministers of justice and finance, wanted severe restrictions on the *commandite par actions*, including government authorization analogous to that required for *sociétés anonymes*. A third group wanted only moderate restrictions designed to curb the worst abuses. Among these was A. G. Aubé, the commission's only businessman and a former president of the commercial tribunal of Paris, who proposed simply to forbid bearer shares, provide guarantees against fictitious *apports* by *gérants*, and not permit shares below a certain denomination.[22]

At a second meeting of the commission on 25 November, a proposal to rescind Article 38 of the *Code de Commerce*, which would eliminate the *commandite par actions*, gained only five affirmative votes. However, on 9 December the commission reversed itself, and those supporting total abolition were joined by some of those who had wanted only moderate reform. The latter apparently concluded that if the *commandite par actions* had to be authorized, it would be distinguished from a *société anonyme* only in that it had a *gérant* subject to unlimited liability and stockholders who could not participate in management. It seemed simpler to eliminate the *Commandite par actions* and rely on the Chamber of Deputies to draft a more acceptable bill. Even Minister of Justice Félix Barthe expressed the fear that the proposed bill would face a hostile reception in the Chamber.[23] His apprehensions were justified.

The bill also contained restrictions applicable to *sociétés anonymes*. There were to be no bearer shares, unless completely paid up; dividends could be paid only from profits; and directors were liable in case fictitious dividends were paid. Provision for optional or compulsory arbitration was also to be eliminated from company charters as a means of settling internal disputes, and such disputes would be decided by commercial tribunals.

To help circumvent criticism of the slowness of the Conseil d'Etat in considering requests for authorization of *sociétés anonymes*, the government issued an ordinance on 5 February 1838 creating a new committee of public works, agriculture, and commerce within the Conseil. The government hoped that this reform, which involved dividing the workload of the old committee of the interior, would speed up the process of granting authorization.

On 15 February 1838, Barthe introduced the reform bill and justified its provisions to the Chamber. He cited statistics showing the tremendous increase in the number and nominal capitalization of joint-stock companies registered at the commercial tribunal of Paris: from 55 companies with a nominal capital of 15 million francs, represented by 28,000 shares, in 1833, to 288 companies with a nominal capital of 361 million francs, represented by 586,000 shares, in 1837.[24] Some *commandites par actions* had even issued shares of 50 and 20 francs to tap small savings, and mounting publicity had accompanied the issue of new shares. According to Barthe, abuses in this form of enterprise were rampant; some were created simply to swindle the unsuspecting investor: "We have witnessed speculators organizing an enterprise on the basis of greatly overvalued property or inventions whose ineffectiveness was soon demonstrated, soliciting capital subscriptions on the basis of chimerical assets, placing in charge of the enterprise an insolvent director, detaching themselves from the risks of inevitable catastrophe, and realizing enormous profits by the sale of shares that they attributed to themselves in exchange for their contribution of overvalued assets. In the end, gullible shareholders are left with value-less paper in return for the money they have paid in."[25] These abuses afforded ample justification for the elimination of the *commandite par actions*, which, according to Barthe, served no useful purpose.[26] For large enterprise, the *anonyme* form was available; for small enterprise, there was the *société en commandite* without shares. To those who would complain about the slowness of authorization of a *société anonyme*, Barthe contended that creation of large enterprise should not be rushed and that the recent creation within the Conseil d'Etat of a new committee would speed the process of authorization.[27]

Two days after the introduction of the bill, the minister of justice, desiring to have fuller knowledge of the extent of the *commandite par actions* outside Paris, requested the Cours Royaux to forward to the ministry a complete list of all *commandites par actions* organized within their jurisdictions since 1826, including information on the nature of each enterprise, the number and nominal value of shares, and the nature—registered or bearer—of the shares.[28]

As was to be expected, the commission's solution seemed draconian to many. Even while the government's bill was being drafted, Charles Persil, a deputy and former minister of justice, advocated in the December issue of the *Revue française* the more moderate course of prohibiting bearer shares and modifying Article 38 so as not to allow the nonmonetary contribution of the *gérant* to be represented by negotiable shares.[29]

Paillard de Villeneuve, well informed of the discussions taking place within the commission, sounded the alarm against their decisions in the 27 November and 1 December issues of the *Gazette des tribunaux*.[30] For France, he wrote, legislation to stimulate the mobilization of capital was essential: "That is the purpose of the *commandite*, undoubtedly not as it was conceived in the *Code de Commerce* at a time when commerce and industry were still little developed, but as it must exist today in the present state of ideas and institutions."[31] Eliminating the *commandite* was no solution for the problem of abuses. "Sooner or later, abuses will decline in the face of public good sense, but bad laws last a long time."[32]

A more detailed analysis, proposing remedies similar to those advanced by Paillard de Villeneuve, was provided by Louis Wolowski's *Des Sociétés par actions*, which strongly influenced the counterproposal drafted by the Chamber's committee.[33] Wolowski subjected the government's bill to a detailed criticism. The *commandite par actions* was too important to eliminate, especially because the *société anonyme* could not fill the void. Government authorization, according to Wolowski, was neither a defense against abuses nor a guarantee of the future success of the enterprise, as the failure of numerous *anonymes* illustrated. Moreover, the authorization of a *société anonyme* "gave rise to more or less well-founded suspicions of favoritism."[34]

For Wolowski, the chief victims of abuses in the *commandite* were not third parties but the shareholders who were "fooled by fictitious assets and fraudulent promises, excited by the allurement of imaginary dividends, and barred from any right of participation in the management of the enterprise."[35] While the stockholders were ruined, the *gérant* got rich. Wolowski proposed a series of reforms that would correct the abuses in the *commandite*. The reforms included (1) expanding the role of the shareholders in the formation and dissolution of the enterprise, (2) providing safeguards against both the overvaluation of assets provided by the *gérant* and the stipulation in the charter of excessive privileges for the *gérant*, (3) preventing the *gérant* from escaping financial loss if the enterprise proved to be unprofitable, and (4) prohibiting the payment of dividends not covered by profits. The Chamber's committee adopted all these reforms in its counterproposal to the government bill.[36]

The Chamber's committee to examine the bill was particularly distinguished, consisting of nine members under the presidency of J. M. F. Nicod, with Charles Legentil acting as secretary and *rapporteur*. Four members of the committee were businessmen: Legentil, Hippolyte Ganneron, A. N. Lafond, and Louis Lebeuf;[37] both Lafond and Lebeuf were also regents of the Bank of France. Juridical arguments that the *commandite par actions* had been deformed from its intended role had less appeal for this committee than for the lawyer-dominated government commission.

The committee began by deciding that the *commandite par actions* was not only useful but necessary for the development of French industry and that, without grave inconveniences, its place could not be taken by the *société anonyme*. According to the committee, the strength of the *commandite par actions* lay in its freedom of foundation, the exclusive power of the *gérant* to administer the enterprise, and the personal liability of the *gérant*. These qualities were not to be found in a *société anonyme*:

> The *société anonyme* does not have unity of direction, personal liability, and direct and personal interest in its administration. It has been said, with reason, that the business of everyone is the business of no one; consequently, it has not been unusual for some enterprises, which combined all the necessary requirements for success, to have failed because of the vices inherent in the *société anonyme*.
>
> If an enterprise is subject to unforeseen accidents, to the appearance of frequent difficulties that require prompt decisions, and if this enterprise is hindered in every instance by the necessity for and slowness of discussion, it is doubtful if such an enterprise can prosper.[38]

Then, knowingly or unwittingly, the committee report echoed the famous passage in Adam Smith on the limitation of joint-stock companies:

> The *société anonyme* is suited only for simple operations, involving a single business that, once established, can operate easily and without difficulty. It is above all suited to large enterprises of public utility, such as bridges, canals, railroads, etc., which call for millions for their execution, long years to be completed, and ask, as the price for their enormous outlay, concessions lasting 50 or 100 years. For these colossal enterprises, it would be difficult to find a man rich enough to offer a serious pecuniary liability and bold enough to undertake it.
>
> On the other hand, for a factory, a manufacturing concern, a commercial or industrial establishment, which faces incessant competition, fruitful and rapid decisions are required. For all operations requiring spontaneity of action and freedom of movement, it is to the *commandite* that one will turn by preference.[39]

It was necessary, the committee argued, for commercial law to take
account of social attitudes and institutional arrangements peculiar to
France. The joint-stock company was more important for France than
for England, where large fortunes were concentrated in the hands of a
landed aristocracy, and where fortunes accumulated in industry remained invested there. In contrast, French landholdings were small
and fortunes accumulated in business were diverted to acquisition of
land. In England one or a small number of individuals would put up
the capital for an enterprise; in France, recourse to a large number of
persons was necessary.[40]

The committee agreed with the government that grave abuses existed in the *commandite*:

> What is taking place before our eyes? The promoter of a company alone, or
> with a small number of associates, drafts the charter. He evaluates his contri-
> bution at an exaggerated figure. He stipulates in the charter excessive privi-
> leges for his own profit. All the shares are subscribed by his creatures. He
> carefully picks a well-known banker for the enterprise, placing it, to all
> appearances, under the bank's patronage. He publishes the prospectus and
> numerous advertisements. Talk and publicity at any price are essential, for
> they produce a handsome return. The seduced shareholder comes running to
> subscribe, only to find all the shares taken, but he is allowed to acquire some
> at a 25 percent premium. Ask him what he has bought, the name of the *gérant*,
> the type and nature of the enterprise, and he doesn't know. He knows only the
> market quotation and dreams only of what that quotation will be tomorrow. In
> this manner a contract, which is collective in nature, comes into being without
> examination, discussion, or challenge.[41]

The committee proposed to remedy these and other abuses by restrictive legislation.[42] In order to prevent the fraudulent promotion of
commandites by *gérants* without substance, the *gérant* would have to
furnish at least 10 percent of the capital to be represented by inalienable shares. The shareholders were also to be given a role in determining the provisions of the charter. Before the company could be formed,
the shareholders were to meet and deliberate on the definitive draft of
the company's charter. The services of a notary were to be required. A
council of surveillance was to be mandatory for every *commandite par
actions*. This council, chosen by the stockholders, would verify the
accounts of the enterprise (though it was enjoined from participating
in management of the enterprise); the council also possessed the power

to convoke a stockholders' meeting for the purpose of dissolving the enterprise. Bearer shares and shares of small denominations were to be prohibited. Shares had to be in denominations of at least 500 francs for companies with capital of 100,000 francs or more, and 100 francs for companies whose capital was under 100,000 francs. No dividends could be paid except from verified profits, a provision that the bill also extended to *sociétés anonymes*. Finally, penal sanctions were provided for violation of the bill's provisions. As could be expected, both the government and the committee bills provoked considerable public reaction.

Further to confirm official fears, the trial of the promoters of the Compagnie des Mines de Saint-Bérain et de Saint-Léger in the summer of 1838 dramatically exposed to public attention some of the typical abuses in the *commandite par actions*.[43] The company was organized in July and August 1837 by Auguste Cleemann, a Parisian banker who was interested in a number of other *sociétés en commandite par actions*, mostly Paris publishing companies, and by David Samuel Blum, an ironmaster from Dijon. The names of neither Cleemann nor Blum appeared in the by-laws of the company, although Cleemann's younger brother Louis was designated the sole *gérant* of the enterprise.[44]

Blum acquired the mines in 1835 for 800,000 francs and claimed to have invested 347,000 francs in improvements, undoubtedly an exaggerated figure. (The property had changed hands in 1828 for 110,000 francs, though it was claimed again that several hundred thousand francs of capital improvements had been made between 1828 and 1835.) The mines were turned over to the *commandite* in exchange for 3,500 shares having a nominal value of 3,500,000 francs, a value that the plaintiffs claimed to be exaggerated. These shares were divided equally between Auguste Cleemann and Blum. The company was capitalized at 4,500,000 francs, represented by 4,500 shares with a nominal value of 1,000 francs.[45] Because the *gérant*, Louis Cleemann, had subscribed 100 shares, the prospectus and advertisements claimed that only 900 shares were offered for public subscription; in fact, however, Auguste Cleemann sold 1,150 of his 1,750 shares and Blum all or most of his.

Publicity for the promotion was placed in the hands of a M. Justin, a pioneering advertising man whose services eventually cost the company about 40,000 francs. Justin located for Cleemann a mining engineer, Theodore Virlet, who journeyed to the site of the mines in Saône-et-Loire and wrote a highly favorable report on the prospects of the mine, for which he received 500 francs; he received one share in the enterprise in addition, for the right to publish his report, which enjoyed a wide circulation. He also became the chief engineer of the mine at an annual salary of 6,000 francs.

Justin's publicity campaign was well organized; advertisements appeared in the major Paris newspapers and throughout France, excepting only the area in which the mines were located. These ads often carried Virlet's entire report and the ubiquitous rosy view of the present state and future prospects of the enterprise. To Justin we owe the slogan "La houille est la pain de l'industrie." The prospective shareholders were told that the coal was of superior quality (it was not) and that a production of 3,000 to 4,000 hectolitres a day was assured within a short time. Production costs were estimated as assuring a profit of forty centimes per hectolitre; further, the mine was placed advantageously close to the Canal du Centre. The prospectus, of which 2,400 copies were printed, contained an illustration of smoking chimneys and a railroad, which actually depicted the nearby mines of Blanzy.

The campaign netted about 2,000 shareholders, mostly small investors holding one or two shares, at whom the subscription campaign was obviously aimed. As an added inducement, the shares were to bear interest of 5 percent.[46] Auguste Cleemann, representing himself as personally disinterested, wrote to potential shareholders claiming that extraction was 2,000 hecolitres a day (it was actually around 400). To a Nîmes banker, he estimated that the shares would yield 8 to 10 percent a year. In fact, the main pits of the company, those of Saint Charles, either were threatened with cave-in or had begun to cave in while the shares were being sold.

Whatever might be said about these practices, were they illegal? The Tribunal Correctionnel of Paris decided that though the lies and exaggerations of the prospectus were immoral, they were not illegal. The court applied this same judgment to the other actions of the promoters, who were acquitted. Only some of the original plaintiffs appealed to the Cour Royale of Paris (the plaintiffs had had to bear the costs of the first trial, plus expensive lawyer fees), which, after a lengthy trial, decided on 22 August 1838 that Blum and Auguste Cleemann were guilty of swindling, sentenced each to three years imprisonment and fines of 3,000 francs, and ordered restitution to the plaintiffs of 324,000 francs plus 32,450 francs interest. The two men fled before they could be taken into custody. They were unfortunate in that they were tried in the supercharged atmosphere of 1838 when abuses in the *commandite* had aroused so much interest. In calmer times, they might well have been acquitted. In fact, they had done no more than many another promoter. Opponents of the *commandite*, however, failed to profit from this confirmation of their dire pronouncements.

The 1838 session of the legislature ended, while the Saint-Bérain case was still being tried, without the two bills being considered. Under the circumstances, this neglect might appear surprising. It has been asserted that the hostility of the business community inside and outside the Chamber to both bills caused them to be dropped.[47] Another explanation advanced is that the passage of either bill would have necessitated liberalizing the formation of *sociétés anonymes*.[48] Neither of these explanations is satisfactory. The business community was not united, and a version of the committee bill easily could have been passed. The real explanation was that the session of 1838 was marked by bitter political quarrels between Count Molé, head of the government, and the leaders of the opposition, Adolphe Thiers, François Guizot, and Odilon Barrot; and Barrot was a member of the Chamber's committee. The Molé government had suffered a series of embarrassing reverses at the hands of the Chamber in 1838,[49] and consideration of the bills on the *commandite par actions* would undoubtedly have subjected it to another defeat. Thus, personal political rivalries in the Chamber reprieved the *commandite par actions* for eighteen years.

4 The *Société Anonyme* in the Railroad Age, 1834–1859

L'esprit d'association, qui a enfanté des merveilles en Angleterre, en Amérique, et partout où il s'est developpé avec une certaine énergie, s'enracine chaque jour davantage dans les moeurs francaises, et promet de donner bientôt à notre industrie un essor prodigieux.

Malepeyre and Jourdain, 1833

The Coming of the Railroad, 1834–1846

Though their growth was numerically less spectacular than that of the *sociétés en commandites par actions*, *sociétés anonymes* continued to grow in number and size during the period 1834–46. Compared with 119 for the preceding thirteen-year period (1821–32), 221 *anonymes* were authorized. The total capitalization grew from 336 million francs for the period 1821–33, to approximately 1.5 billion francs for 1834–46. Of this sum, 80 percent was pledged in the three boom years of 1838, 1845, and 1846 (table 4.1).

The most significant change over the previous period was the growth of investment in railroads. Whereas only three short coal-carrying lines had been authorized before 1834, twenty-seven railroad companies were organized within the next thirteen years, initially capitalized at over 1.2 billion francs, and accounting for about 80 percent of the total capitalization for all *anonymes* (table 4.2). Another sector of rapid growth was insurance: from nine companies for the period 1821–33 to sixty-six for the period 1834–46, with a quadrupling in the capitalization. Canal shares, the leading sector of the previous period, declined to about one-fourth its former level, reflecting the shift from the canal to the railroad age.

Construction of France's railroad network was delayed as government and parliament groped toward a general policy on who would construct the lines and how they would be financed. In 1838, the Chamber of Deputies rejected a government bill for state construction of the major lines, a rejection owing as much to hostility in the Chamber toward the Molé government as to distaste for the principle of state construction. What finally emerged was a compromise, embodied in the railroad law of 1842, which provided for state acquisition of the right of way and preparation of the road bed (the infrastructure), with private companies laying the rails, providing the locomotives and rolling stock, and operating the lines (the superstructure).[1] Some companies also received aid from the state in the form of loans—the Paris-Rouen line received a loan of 14 million francs from the government in 1840—and guaranteed interest on their shares—in 1840 the

TABLE 4.1 Formation of *Sociétés Anonymes*, 1834–1846

Year	Number	Initial Nominal Capitalization (Francs)
1834	12	18,596,000
1835	13	35,854,500
1836	13	16,353,567 (for 12[a])
1837	28	49,477,000 (for 24)
1838	26	217,627,000 (for 24)
1839	8	7,900,000
1840	10	40,300,000 (for 5)
1841	16	26,157,000 (for 14)
1842	16	9,270,000 (for 9)
1843	12	52,670,000 (for 11)
1844	21	23,910,000 (for 16)
1845	28	569,108,000 (for 20)
1846	18	377,185,000 (for 15)
Total	221	1,444,408,067 (for 183)

Source: Compiled from company charters in the *Bulletin des lois*.

[a]Beginning in 1836, the capitalization for some *sociétés anonymes* is not recorded in the charter. Therefore, the annual totals for initial nominal capitalization include only those enterprises for which the capitalization is known.

government guaranteed 4 percent interest on the shares of the Paris-Orleans Company, which assured their ready acceptance. Legally, such a company was a lessee from the government for the length of the concession, usually between forty and ninety-nine years, after which ownership and operation of the line would revert to the state. When the concession expired, the company would be reimbursed for its property. Of course, the company hoped to make sizable profits from the operation of the line during the life of the concession.

Also contributing to official hesitations concerning the construction and operation of railroads by private companies was the speculative boom in 1837–38, characterized by stockjobbing on a large scale in the shares of *commandites par actions*, to which the unprecedented volume of railroad shares (it was thought) would certainly contribute. A fear, bordering upon the irrational, of unbridled speculation (*agoitage*) was a major preoccupation of bureaucrats, lawyers, and some deputies during the late 1830s. The stringent conditions laid down for

TABLE 4.2 *Sociétés Anonymes*, 1834–1846, by Sector

Sector	Number	Initial Nominal Capitalization (Francs)
Railroads	27	1,211,750,000
Insurance and banking	72	141,100,000
Transportation (except railroads)	26	46,137,000
Bridges	39	10,077,067 (for 19)
Mining and metallurgy	12	2,801,000 (for 3)
Gas	11	1,667,000 (for 4)
Sugar refining	7	7,600,000
Textiles	4	5,490,000
Paper	5	4,700,000
Other	18	13,086,000 (for 16)
Total	221	1,444,408,067 (for 183)

Source: Compiled from company charters in the *Bulletin des lois*.

concessions also discouraged promoters, whose expectations of profits were not as grandiose as those envisioned by government officials. The unprofitability of the two Paris-Versailles lines was not a good advertisement for railroads. The terms of the concession of the Paris-Le Havre Company, authorized in 1838, were quite unfavorable; the company surrendered its concession in 1839 after failing to raise its capital of 90 million francs.[2] The depression that began in 1839 greatly reduced the availability of capital. James de Rothschild apparently declined to accept the stringent conditions for the construction of the Nord Railroad in 1843, delaying the beginning of that line for two years.[3]

Only in 1845 did the requirements of the government and the expectations of promoters combine to produce the authorization of eleven companies capitalized at over 500 million francs (table 4.3). The gigantic sums involved transformed the nature and scope of the French securities market. Thousands of new investors, who had never before owned a share of stock, joined in the rush for railroad shares. The Nord Railroad Company, finally formed in 1845 under the aegis of James de Rothschild, was capitalized at 200 million francs, which made it the largest joint-stock company ever created in France. The

TABLE 4.3 Railroad Companies, 1834–1846

Year	Number	Initial Nominal Capitalization (Francs)
1835	1	6,000,000
1837	3	19,250,000
1838	5	180,000,000
1840	1	36,000,000
1841	1	6,000,000
1843	2	40,000,000
1845	11	554,500,000
1846	3	370,000,000
Total	27	1,211,750,000

Paris-Lyon Company, authorized the following year, was also capitalized at 200 million francs.

The advent of the railroad age produced some liberalization in authorization requirements, although the Conseil d'Etat initially attempted to force railroads to meet the stringent conditions required of other *anonymes*. In considering the charters of the Paris-Orleans and Paris-Le Havre companies in 1838, the committee of commerce of the Conseil d'Etat rejected the provision that the shares of the companies be negotiable after 25 percent of their value had been paid in. The committee voted to require that the shares could not be negotiated upon the Bourse until fully paid up. The companies apparently convinced the minister of commerce, Martin du Nord, that negotiability of shares after 25 percent had been called was essential to the successful promotion of the companies. When the charters of these companies came before the General Assembly of the Conseil d'Etat for final action, the minister personally presided. But in spite of the minister's hope for a reversal, the General Assembly voted to uphold the decision of the committee, which conformed to the established jurisprudence of the Conseil. Much to the Conseil's surprise, its decision was overruled by the Council of Ministers, and the authorizing ordinance signed by the king gave the companies what they wanted.[4] Reversing a decision of the Conseil was a rare occurrence, and the action had the effect of establishing a precedent to be followed by the Conseil for the shares of future railroad companies.

The government also overruled the Conseil by allowing interest of 3 percent to be paid upon shares of the Paris-Rouen Company, authorized in 1840, during the period of construction.[5] Because this interest would have to be paid from the company's capital, it was contrary to one of the Conseil's most cherished precedents. According to A. G. Aubé, òne of the rare businessmen ever to serve on the Conseil, it was difficult to convince the Conseil that the companies could not be successfully promoted without these provisions.[6] The normally omnipotent Conseil discovered that, in face of the railroad interests, its jurisprudence had to give way to the realities of the marketplace.

The insurance sector also grew rapidly during the period 1834–46. Sixty-six companies were authorized, most of them during the boom years 1836–38 and 1843–45 (table 4.4).

Thirty-eight companies, capitalized at 47.2 million francs, specialized in marine insurance. Half were founded in Paris, with Le Havre (nine) and Bordeaux (seven) accounting for most of the others. Many were capitalized for as little as 500,000 francs; only three companies, all based in Paris, were capitalized at more than 2 million francs: Union des Ports (1836) at 5 million, Lloyd Français (1837) at 6 million, and the Chambre d'Assurances Maritimes (1837) at 3 million.

Unlike marine insurance, which gained acceptance in France before the nineteenth century, fire insurance became established only between 1820 and the middle of the century. Five important fire insurance companies, located in Paris, already existed by 1834: Phénix (1819), Assurances Générales (1819), Royale (1820), l'Union (1828), and Soleil (1829). The growing public acceptance of fire insurance and the handsome returns enjoyed by some of the earlier companies stimulated the formation of new ones. In the ten-year period between 1836 and 1845, seventeen fire insurance companies were authorized with a nominal capitalization of 60 million francs. Thirteen of these were

TABLE 4.4 Insurance Companies, 1834–1846

Year	Number	Initial Nominal Capitalization (Francs)
1834	4	3,300,000
1835	1	1,000,000
1836	6	11,700,000
1837	4	20,000,000
1838	8	23,200,000
1839	2	4,500,000
1840	1	500,000
1841	4	7,200,000
1842	4	8,400,000
1843	7	11,600,000
1844	12	16,200,000
1845	7	14,100,000
1846	6	5,200,000
Total	66	126,900,000

Parisian companies. Except for Le Nord, a company in Lille capitalized at 500,000 francs, all were capitalized at 2 million francs or more. La France, the largest, was authorized in 1837 with a nominal capital of 10 million francs. Competing with these fire companies, whose insurance against loss was based upon the payment of premiums, were a large number of mutual companies; these were not joint-stock companies, as there were no shareholders, but authorization by the Conseil d'Etat was required.

Insurance companies exhibited peculiarities not found in other *sociétés anonymes*. The nominal value of most fire insurance shares was 5,000 francs, but only a small fraction of the amount was called. For example, only 100 francs of the 5,000-franc shares of the La France company was paid in. But shareholders were required to deposit for each share, as a guarantee, government securities worth 900 francs, which remained the property of the shareholder. With only a small amount paid in, the rate of return could be quite spectacular; dividends of 100 percent or more of the amount paid in were not uncommon. Of course, shareholders were liable for the full amount of their shares. Another difference was that often the board of directors had the right to prevent the sale of shares to an individual who in their eyes did not offer sufficient guarantees, unless the buyer deposited government securities equivalent to the total nominal value of his shares.

Although the amounts called upon the shares of most insurance companies were only 5 or 10 percent of their nominal values, insurance companies possessed large sums representing paid premiums that in due course would be disbursed to cover losses of the assured, to pay dividends, or to supplement the company's reserve. Life insurance companies, however, had sums for long-term placement. The funds of most insurance companies went into national and local government bonds and securities guaranteed by the state (e.g., canal shares). The life branch of the Assurances Générales company channeled large sums into real estate and shares of the Bank of France.[7] The board of directors of the life branch of l'Union decided in 1836 to employ 20 to 25 percent of the company's funds in the purchase of real estate.[8]

The shares of sixteen fire insurance companies and seven life insurance companies were listed on the Paris Bourse in 1846, but most companies were closely held, and shares only occasionally changed hands. Control of most fire and life companies rested in the hands of Paris bankers.

Life insurance progressed slowly. In addition to the three existing life insurance companies founded during the restoration (Assurances Générales in 1819, Royale in 1820, and l'Union in 1829), nine new companies, nominally capitalized at 20 million francs, were founded in Paris between 1842 and 1846. Four of them were founded solely for the purpose of administering tontines, which enjoyed a brief vogue in the 1840s.[9] Tontine companies, most of which were not *sociétés anonymes*, were more numerous and also attracted more clients than ordinary life insurance companies, a trend that was reversed only in the 1850s. For the first twenty years of its existence, the l'Union company seldom wrote more than a million francs' worth of policies a year, except during the cholera epidemic of 1832, when the figure exceeded 3.5 million despite a temporary raising of premiums.[10] The other life insurance companies were doing no better. The only one of the new companies to survive more than a few years was the Phénix, which was authorized in 1844.

The Conseil authorized two other insurance companies, one to insure against hailstone damage to crops in Lille and the other to insure the life of animals in Tarbes (Haute Pyrénées).

Banking, too, gained during this period. Six new departmental banks, founded between 1835 and 1838, joined the three previously authorized banks at Rouen (1817), Nantes (1818), and Bordeaux (1818) (table 4.5). Because these were banks of issue, the government exercised extreme caution in their authorization. Government officials

TABLE 4.5 Departmental Banks, 1834–1846

Bank	Year	Initial Nominal Capitalization (Francs)
Lyon	1835	2,000,000
Marseille	1835	4,000,000
Lille	1836	2,000,000
Havre	1837	4,000,000
Toulouse	1838	1,200,000
Orléans	1838	1,000,000
Total		14,200,000

tended to regard the issue of paper money as something like a modern version of alchemy. The Bank of France was consulted, and its restrictive advice was generally accepted.[11] The charters of these new banks followed the model of earlier departmental banks and also that of the Bank of France. Note issue and accounts payable on demand (*comptes courants*) were not to exceed specie holdings of the bank by more than three to one. Weekly reports on the amounts of each bank's issue, deposit liabilities, and specie holdings were to be submitted to the prefect. Discounting operations were carefully restricted in geographical area, term, and type of bills.

The initiative for founding and the ownership of these banks was, and remained, local. Although the capital of some banks was initially subscribed by as few as ten persons, the shares, uniformly of 1,000 francs, were eventually distributed among several hundred shareholders.[12] The charter of the Bank of Lyon, the first of the six created in this period, permitted shareholders to receive interest of 4 percent on the par value of their shares, but such interest could be paid only from current earnings or from past earnings in the bank's reserve fund. This provision was dropped from subsequent charters. As with the Bank of France, stockholders' meetings were limited to a certain number of the largest shareholders: fifty for Lyon, seventy-five for Marseille, and sixty for Lille.

These bank foundings and further pressures for improved banking facilities in provincial centers brought about a reversal of the attitude of the Bank of France toward the creation of branch offices, which the bank had opposed as unprofitable since the restoration. Faced with the possibility of becoming the "Bank of Paris," the bank reacted by creating thirteen branch offices between 1836 and 1848, some of them created specifically to head off the formation of departmental banks.[13] Next, the bank openly opposed the creation of additional departmental banks,[14] and its stand was probably decisive in the refusals to authorize several of them. Finally, in 1846, the Bank of France adopted a policy of restoring its monopoly of note issue by gradually absorbing departmental banks.[15] At that time it was a question of the renewal of the charter of the Bank of Bordeaux, which was to expire in 1848. The severe depression beginning at the end of 1846, exacerbated by the Revolution of February 1848, gave the Bank of France its chance; it absorbed all nine departmental banks, each shareholder in the departmental banks receiving an equal number of shares in the Bank of France.

Apart from the six departmental banks, no other banks were authorized, although at least a dozen projected banks of various kinds attempted to secure authorization as *sociétés anonymes*.[16] Some of these were not serious projects, but others had solid backing.[17] The number of projected agricultural banks, designed to lend to farmers, provides testimony to the need for this type of institution. The promoter of one of them wrote to the minister of commerce in 1845 that his bank proposed to lend to farmers at 5 or 6 percent, "instead of the 10 to 12 percent or more that notaries charge."[18] Other banks failing to receive authorization were discount banks, mortgage banks, and banks to retire debts.[19] The ministry and the Conseil d'Etat exhibited extraordinary caution in dealing with these projects: banks were indeed a sensitive matter.

In the transportation sector, apart from railroads, twenty-six *sociétés anonymes* were authorized. Of these, seventeen were steamship companies; some connected France's Atlantic and Channel ports and provided service between French ports and London, Holland, Hamburg, Portugal, and Russia. Steamship companies were also organized for internal transport on the Seine, Rhône, and Garonne rivers. As the risks were great, the joint-stock form was ideal for these companies. They were of medium size: the smallest, to connect the ports of Le Havre and Caen, was capitalized at 250,000 francs; and the largest, to provide service between Le Havre and Russia, was capitalized at 1,600,000 francs. Four small companies for land transport and a larger company to provide taxi service in Paris, the Compagnie des Voitures de Place, capitalized at 800,000 francs, secured authorization. The total capitalization of these twenty-two companies to carry passengers and freight on water and land amounted to less than 10 million francs. The rest of the transportation sector comprised four canal companies, with a capital of over 36 million francs.

Thirty-nine companies to finance the construction of bridges were organized as *sociétés anonymes*. This was three times the number organized between 1821 and 1833 and marked the high point in the private financing of bridge construction. The capital involved was approximately 20 million francs.

With the coming of the railroad age, the iron industry and coal mining steadily expanded and consolidated. Iron producers continued to acquire coal mines to assure sources of supply. The trend toward enlarging firms by expanding capacity or by mergers accelerated. Technological advances in the iron industry required the investment of ever larger amounts of capital. These developments strained the ability to survive of most family firms and of traditional partnership forms of business organization, adding to the irreversible trend toward adoption of the joint-stock form of business organization. By 1846, seven of the ten largest firms, based on capitalization, were joint-stock companies.[20]

This impulsion toward the joint-stock form is only imperfectly reflected in the number and capitalization of *sociétés anonymes* authorized during this period: the Conseil d'Etat authorized twelve firms with a total capital of approximately 18 million francs. Both the numbers and capitalization were less than half that for the previous period (1821 to 1833). In part, this was because many of the largest firms were already *anonymes* by 1834, although the large Creusot firm, an *anonyme* from 1828 until its bankruptcy in 1833, was reorganized as a *société en commandite par actions* under the Schneider brothers in 1836. Some firms became *commandites par actions* because of the difficulties in gaining authorization for *anonymes*. At least as many firms attempted and failed to receive authorization as were successful.

One such firm was the Chatillon-Commentry Company, organized in November 1845 by the merger of two large enterprises into a *commandite par actions*, with the intention of transforming itself into an *anonyme*. Its capitalization at 25 million francs made it the largest metallurgical enterprise in France. The fate of its request is indicative of the difficulties involved in obtaining authorization. The dossier in the National Archives contains the reports in January and February of 1846 of seven departmental prefects giving their opinions on the charter and the persons involved in the enterprise.[21] The prefect of Nièvre also communicated the charter to the Chambre Consultatif des Arts et Manufactures of Nevers for its opinion. To meet some of the preliminary objections, a new charter was drafted in June 1846. Because it was a mining and metallurgical concern, the ministry of public works, the Conseil Général des Mines, and a hierarchy of mining engineers were involved, in addition to the prefects, the ministry of commerce, and ultimately the Conseil d'Etat.

It was, indeed, a formidable array of hurdles.[22] All the assets of the company had to be inventoried and evaluated—the inventories to be supplied by the company and an evaluation made by the government mining engineers before the matter could be submitted to the Conseil Général des Mines. Throughout 1847, there were numerous complaints from government engineers that the inventories supplied by the company were insufficient to provide the basis for an evaluation: these men expected every shovel to be counted. The process was far from complete in December 1847, when the minister of public works informed the minister of commerce that, since the drafting of the new charter in June 1846, the company's assets had changed. The company had acquired one new coal mine and leased ten of those it owned; it had constructed eight new puddling furnaces at Commentry and two new blast furnaces at Montluçon; and it had two more under construction. Further, it had issued 1,000 additional shares. The draft charter would have to be revised to reflect these changes. Additional financial information would be needed, especially on the amount of working capital. Also required were more detailed inventories of the firm's real assets: "Instead of the detailed inventory and evaluation that have been requested, the company has furnished a general inventory with an overall evaluation of important objects."

The minister's suspicion was aroused by the failure of the company to produce its balance sheet for 1 July 1847. He recommended that the company be required to present a new charter and produce a complete and detailed inventory. Finally, he raised the question, "At what point is it inconvenient to allow the gathering of such a large number of metallurgical establishments in the hands of a single *société anonyme*?"[23] Ten months earlier, Minister of Commerce Cunin-Gridaine, in a letter of 23 February 1847 to the minister of public works, had posed the same question: "Do you see any inconvenience that these various establishments . . . are to be united into a single company?"[24] As it turned out, neither minister had to answer this question. The Revolution of February 1848 ended for a time action on the company's request for authorization, though it is probable that the company had renounced serious effort before the end of 1847. In 1857, the company unsuccessfully renewed its attempt; a third attempt in 1861–62 resulted in authorization.

A large concentration of coal mines, the Compagnie des Mines de la Loire, failed to obtain authorization despite repeated attempts extending over eight years. In this particular case, the question whether to authorize the company was not confined to the normal administrative channels but became a hotly debated public issue. The company united thirty-three of the sixty mining concessions in the Loire basin and accounted for about 80 percent of the basin's total production.[25] The initial impulse behind the formation of this gigantic combination was technical. The effort to prevent flooding of the mines forced various concessions to cooperate, under the urging of the government.[26] Falling profits in 1837 led to some cooperative marketing arrangements. Another period of falling profits resulted in a series of fusions in 1844–45, culminating with the merger of rival combinations in November 1845.[27]

Initially organized as a *société civile*, a form of quasi-joint-stock company permissible for coal mines, the company occupied an anomalous status as a business enterprise. To what extent a *société civile* could legally engage in commercial activities was open to question. The attractiveness of its shares was lessened because the shareholders of a *société civile* were subject to unlimited liability. The minister of finance vetoed the quotation of its shares on the Paris Bourse in 1846 and again in 1848.[28] The Bank of France (in 1845) and the Comptoir d'Escompte of Paris (in 1848) both refused to grant the company discount privileges because it was a *société civile*.[29] To escape from its questionable legal status, the company actively sought authorization as a *société anonyme*.

Its enemies, alleging that it was an illegal and dangerous monopoly, were numerous and vocal.[30] They included a large number of businessmen and the mayor, municipal council, newspaper, and Chamber of Commerce of Saint-Etienne. Liberal economists saw the company as a threat to free competition; radicals were critical of the company's labor policies, accusing it of responsibility for bloody strikes in 1846. Some lawyers claimed that the merger of mining concessions was illegal. The Chamber of Deputies debated the company's legal status and policies, presenting an occasion for Lamartine to exercise his great oratorical skills, to the company's detriment.

Though its enemies were numerous, the company had its supporters: numerous businessmen from Lyon and Paris; many important and influential politicians, including Odilon Barrot; its own bevy of lawyers and paid publicists; for a brief time its own newspaper in Saint-

Etienne; and even a liberal economist, J. A. Blanqui. The question of
authorization became a political matter to be decided at the highest
level. After receiving approval in the council of ministers, the company was on the verge of being authorized in 1848, when the July
Monarchy fell.[31]

To meet the changed conditions, the company in March 1848 modi-
fied its draft charter to guarantee coal prices below a certain maximum
and to provide for the participation of workers in company profits and
representation of the workers on the board of directors.[32] Before this
maneuver could bear fruit, the political climate changed again. Next
the company sought to obtain authorization by statute. A government
bill was introduced for this purpose at the end of 1848 but was withdrawn in January 1849.[33] The company continued its efforts, but a
long strike at Rive-de-Gier in the summer of 1852 tarnished its public
image. In October the government prohibited its projected merger
with the large Grande'Combe Mining Company. The company's failure to meet the growing demand for coal alienated important business
interests that had formerly favored it. Changes in administrative personnel with the coming of the Second Empire placed enemies of the
company in key positions.[34] Finally, the company was forced to accept division into four separate companies as the price for authorization of the successor companies in 1854.

Although there were some important enterprises organized as *sociétés anonymes* in the paper industry, in other sectors they played a
limited role. In the emergent gas industry, eleven *sociétés anonymes*
were organized, but *commandites par actions* were more numerous.
Anonymes were rare in the textile industry, where partnerships and
proprietorships continued to dominate. Such diverse enterprises as
municipal theaters, a school, public baths, a newspaper, docks, and
mills, many of them quite small, employed the *anonyme* form. The
capitalization of the lone newspaper *Courrier de Lyon*, authorized in
1842, was only 32,000 francs. Many newspapers employed the *commandite par actions* form. Joint-stock companies, organized before
1834, dominated glassmaking, and the important glass company of
Saint-Quirin, Cirey, et Monthermé, initially authorized as an *anonyme*
in 1815, was reauthorized in 1841 upon the expiration of its charter.
Its capital had grown from 2 to 10 million francs, though its shares
were still closely held by only a few families.[35]

Depression, Revolution, and Boom, 1847–1859

The depression that began in 1846 was particularly severe, because it stemmed from combined agricultural and industrial causes. Crop failures in 1845 and 1846 led to higher food prices, resulting in a drastic drop in the demand for textiles and other consumer goods.[36] This period also saw the end of the railroad boom that had begun in 1842. Railroad shares declined sharply on the Paris Bourse in the fall of 1846. Not only was the capital market unable to absorb new shares, but many shareholders failed to meet calls on old shares. Most railroad shares had been floated at 25 percent down with successive annual payments of 25 percent spread over three years, which, it was believed, made the shares more easily marketable. Because the construction costs were spread over a period of years, there was no need to call all the capital at once. Railroad shares floated in 1843, 1844, and 1845 were still draining the capital market in 1846. Simultaneously, British investors, whose holdings of French railroad shares were large, though almost certainly less than the one-half estimated by Jenks,[37] were attempting to repatriate their capital. With the addition of new flotations in 1846, the cumulative effect amounted to more than the capital market could absorb.

The failure of shareholders to meet calls and the inability of railroad companies to borrow meant an end to construction on lines that were far from being completed. Thousands of workers in railroad and railroad-linked enterprises lost their jobs. Railroad shares lost about a quarter of their value in 1846. The crisis worsened in 1847, but a normal grain harvest and the stabilization of share values on the Bourse at the end of 1847 led some to predict that the worst was over and that the new year would see the beginning of recovery. Whatever may have been the validity of these hopeful prognostications, the Revolution in February, to which the depression was a major contributor, exacerbated the depression by introducing political instability. Proposals to nationalize the railroads and force large enterprises to institute profit sharing with their workers further undermined business confidence.

The nominal capitalization of newly authorized *sociétés anonymes* reflects these developments (table 4.6), especially if account is taken of the failure of the Lyon-Avignon railroad line, authorized in 1847

for 150 million francs, to raise its capital, and its surrender of its
concession to the state the following year. Successful new capital
issues for the period 1847 to 1851 were virtually nonexistent. Omitted
from table 4.6 are the nominal capitalizations of eighteen companies
authorized between 1847 and 1851, the charters of which enumerated
no capitalization figures. The largest and most numerous of these
companies were in the mining and metallurgical sector. Although the
motive of most of them was to obtain additional capital, both by
borrowing and by issuing new shares, their authorizations represented
changes in the form of organization of existing enterprises and not
new creations. Although their nominal capital, and the nominal capital
of other companies in this category, would substantially increase the
figures for 1847–51, the totals would remain greatly inferior to those
of the preceding and following years.

The end of political uncertainty with the coup d'état in December

TABLE 4.6 Formation of *Sociétés Anonymes*, 1847–1859

Year	Number	Initial Nominal Capitalization (Francs)
1847	9	153,987,000 (for 6)
1848	9	7,800,000 (for 6)
1849	10	3,010,000 (for 5)
1850	8	7,400,000 (for 4)
1851	3	unknown
1852	18	475,928,850 (for 17)
1853	22	213,264,500 (for 16)
1854	25	102,750,000 (for 13)
1855	18	235,630,000 (for 9)
1856	12	8,600,000 (for 8)
1857	6	599,150,000
1858	11	10,560,000 (for 7)
1859	10	103,600,000
Total	161	1,921,680,350 (for 107)

Source: Compiled from company charters in the *Bulletin des lois*.

1851, a favorable international economic environment, and positive government encouragement inaugurated a boom beginning in 1852. The nominal capitalization of *sociétés anonymes* clearly reflects the boom (see table 4.6). Most of this capital represents new investment, particularly in railroads and banks, which dominated the boom of the 1850s (table 4.7). If we estimate the capitalization of the fifty-four companies not represented in the totals at 200 million francs, then the nominal capitalization of the railroad and the banking and insurance sectors amounts to over 80 percent of the total. The total nominal capital of *sociétés anonymes* for the period 1847–59 increased by about 500 million francs over the preceding period, 1834–46.

After a five-year hiatus, the railroad boom resumed its course in 1852, with the authorization of eight lines (table 4.8). Railroad policy in the 1850s aimed first at the completion of the lines interrupted by the depression, and second at the consolidation of the shorter lines into six large companies, to facilitate the building of feeder lines. Although inclusion of figures for the nominal capital of shorter lines later ab-

TABLE 4.7 *Sociétés Anonymes*, 1847–1859, by Sector

Sector	Number	Initial Nominal Capitalization (Francs)
Railroads	20	1,486,850,000
Banking and insurance	53	254,100,000
Mining and metallurgy	22	6,360,000 (for 3)
Transport (except railroads)	17	61,170,000 (for 9)
Real estate development	8	79,128,850 (for 6)
Gas	8	114,500 (for 1)
Textiles	6	2,100,000 (for 2)
Bridges	5	unknown
Other	22	31,857,000 (for 13)
Total	161	1,921,680,350 (for 107)

Source: Compiled from company charters in the *Bulletin des lois*.

sorbed or merged into one of the large companies involves double counting, the impact of railroads on the capital market of the 1850s was more extensive than even these inflated figures would indicate. Costs of construction continued to be underestimated, and companies found it more convenient to borrow by issuing bonds (*obligations*) than by issuing additional shares. Some companies preferred a policy of borrowing rather than increasing equity capital so as to maximize anticipated dividends on capital shares.[38]

Although some corporations issued bonds before the 1840s, bonds became significant only when railroad companies began to issue them in large numbers in the 1840s.[39] The railroads first resorted to bonds to avoid depressing the market for shares already issued and to tap the savings of cautious and modest investors. Though they were at first issued in denominations of 1,000 francs or more, the "democratic" bond of 300 francs was pioneered by Paulin Talabot and Emile Pereire in the late 1840s.[40] The Second Empire was the golden age of the low-priced bond that had a nominal (and redemption) value of 500 francs but was sold at whatever the market would bring, generally between 300 and 400 francs. By the end of 1856, the railroads had realized over 1.3 billion francs from bonds, and the six main lines issued almost 1.8 billion francs' worth of bonds between 1862 and 1867.[41] Almost all railroad bonds carried a government guarantee of the interest.

During the period 1847 to 1859, the fifty-three banking and insurance companies represented one-third of all companies and 12 percent of the total capital (see table 4.7). Forty-seven were insurance

TABLE 4.8 Railroads Authorized, 1847–1859

Year	Number	Initial Nominal Capitalization (Francs)
1852	8	347,200,000
1853	5	179,650,000
1854	1	25,000,000
1855	4	197,000,000
1857	1	588,000,000

companies with capital varying from 300,000 to 6 million francs. Of
the insurance companies, thirty-two were for marine insurance, nine
for life, three for fire, and three for crops and animals. There were six
banks (table 4.9), three of which were land mortgage banks founded
in 1852 to fill an important gap in French financial institutions by
providing long-term agricultural credit at a lower rate of interest. They
were empowered to raise funds for loans by issuing bonds. Although
they were originally intended to be the first of a series of relatively
independent regional banks, the authorities later decided that a single,
semiofficial, Paris-based, bond-issuing institution was preferable to a
dozen independent institutions, which might have difficulty placing
their bonds. Authorized in July 1852, the Banque Foncière de Paris
was within a year rebaptized the Crédit Foncier de France, with its
capital raised to 60 million francs and its area of operation extended
from the seven departments around Paris to all of France, except for
the six departments served by the Marseille and Nevers banks.[42] In
1856 these two banks were absorbed by the Crédit Foncier de France.

   Although the creation of land mortgage banks had been under serious study since 1850, the coup d'état of December 1851 paved the
way for their formation. Complaints about lack of long-term rural
credit and high interest rates were of long standing, but earlier projects
had failed to win the government's approval. It is surprising not only

TABLE 4.9 Banks Authorized, 1847–1859

Bank	Year	Initial Nominal Capitalization (Francs)
Banque Foncière de Paris	1852	25,000,000
Banque Foncière de Marseille	1852	3,000,000
Crédit Foncier de Nevers	1852	2,000,000
Société Générale de Crédit Mobilier	1852	60,000,000
Comptoir d'Escompte de Paris	1854	20,000,000
Crédit Industriel et Commercial (Paris)	1859	60,000,000

that such an institution was not created earlier, but also that, once it was organized, its operations in rural areas grew so slowly. During the Second Empire, the Crédit Foncier played a greater role in financing urban development, especially Haussmann's rebuilding of Paris, than in its intended purpose of providing agricultural credit.[43]

In November 1852, just a few days before the plebiscite on the creation of the Second Empire, the Conseil d'Etat authorized the Société Générale de Crédit Mobilier. An investment bank to finance the completion of France's railroad network in particular, and economic development in general, the Crédit Mobilier was an innovation of decisive importance.[44] The idea was not new, even in France. As early as 1822, the Société Générale had been founded in Brussels, though it played only a small role until after Belgium achieved independence in 1830. In France, Jacques Laffitte had tried and failed to secure authorization for the Société Commanditaire de l'Industrie in 1825. The promoters of the Crédit Mobilier, Isaac and Emile Pereire, both staunch Saint-Simonians, had elaborated upon the idea of a large investment bank in 1830.[45] Past efforts to found such a bank had foundered on the opposition of vested banking interests and fears of government officials in the ministries and the Conseil d'Etat. This opposition was still potent in 1852; creation of the bank required the support of the prince-president, to whom the idea appeared quite opportune, as he was, at that time, promising to promote economic development. Louis Napoleon ignored a last-minute plea from James de Rothschild to kill the project.[46]

The normal procedures for authorization were either bypassed or shortened. The Pereires negotiated directly with Victor Fialin Persigny, the minister of the interior. Subsequently they enjoyed a personal interview with Louis Napoleon, with whom they discussed details of the project. With agreement at the top, the views of ministry officials and the Conseil d'Etat, normally decisive, had little weight. The Bank of France was not even consulted. The potential resources of the Crédit Mobilier, which was capitalized at 60 million francs, were greatly expanded by a provision in its charter allowing it to issue long-term bonds up to 600 million francs. However, when the Pereires decided to take advantage of this provision in 1855, the government, bowing to hostile criticism, forced them to cancel their plans. Even without this resource, the Crédit Mobilier, during the fourteen years of its existence under the Pereires, enjoyed a meteoric career before succumbing to the blows of its political and banking enemies.[47]

The Comptoir d'Escompte de Paris, authorized in 1854, was the lineal descendant of the semiofficial Comptoir National d'Escompte created in Paris, in the wake of the depression and Revolution in 1848, to restore commercial credit gravely compromised by the disappearance of a number of discount banks and by the restrictive discount policies followed by those that survived. The comptoir was only one of many created under the terms of the provisional government's decree of 7 March 1848. This decree provided that a third of the capital of these banks was to be subscribed in specie by individuals, one-third by the city where the comptoir was located, and a third by the state, with the shares of the city and state in the form of municipal and state bonds. Only two signatures were required for discount (or one signature and a warehouse receipt, in the case of tangible goods), rather than the three required by the Bank of France. The Comptoir of Paris was founded the same day the decree was issued. Others quickly followed. By the end of May there were forty-four of them; eventually more than sixty were created.[48] These comptoirs played an important role during a difficult time, but most of them disappeared when the crisis was over. When the guarantee of the state and municipalities was withdrawn, the Comptoir of Paris reconstituted itself as an independent enterprise in 1854, dropping the appellation ''National'' from its name.[49] It soon ranged beyond discount activities, engaging in a wide variety of promotional ventures in France and abroad and also in the government loan business.[50]

The Crédit Industriel et Commercial—the victim both of bad timing connected with the downturn of the business cycle and of the hostility of the bureaucracy—was authorized only after several unsuccessful attempts. Originally projected in 1855 by a group of English bankers headed by William Gladstone, an Englishman who had been interested in French railroads since the 1840s, and Armand Donon, a French banker, the bank was to have been modeled on the English joint-stock banks. It was planned as a commercial bank specializing in interest-bearing deposits, checking accounts, the discounting of commercial paper, and short-term loans on the security of merchandise or negotiable securities.[51] The project was well advanced when it received its first setback with the government's decision in March 1856 to authorize no new joint-stock enterprise for the rest of 1856.[52]

By the end of 1856, a second project, under the title of Société Impériale de Crédit Commercial, was elaborated, but with the scope of its operations extended to include promotional activity. The Conseil d'Etat rejected this proposal on the grounds that the bank combined too many imprecise operations. The Conseil also refused to consider for authorization an investment bank projected by the *haute banque*, the Comptoir Impérial des Travaux Publics du Commerce et de l'Industrie, declaring its founding untimely.[53] When Gladstone and Donon protested the Conseil's action, it reaffirmed its position, adding that if the Société Impérial were authorized, there would be no ground on which the Comptoir Impérial could be refused.[54]

This might have been sufficient to discourage the promoters, but the powerful Count de Morny was involved in their project, and the promoters were assured of the benevolent attitude, if not yet the active support, of Napoleon III. A third project, for a Société Internationale de Crédit Commercial, was immediately elaborated, but its operations were to be limited to those envisioned by the first project, in order to satisfy the criticism of the Conseil d'Etat concerning the broad scope of operations. To Donon and the English bankers were added additional French interests, particularly the Saint-Simonian François Barthélemy Arlès-Dufour, and a group of German bankers. Half the capital of 120 million francs had been subscribed, one-third by each of the English, French, and German founders. For reasons that are not clear, this project rested in abeyance for about eighteen months, to be revived at the end of 1858 when the emperor ordered that authorization be expedited.[55] In vain did Minister of Commerce Rouher address a confidential letter to Napoleon III, attempting to persuade him to withdraw his support, on several grounds but particularly because of the prominent role of Morny in the affair. Because Rouher refused to submit the dossier to the Conseil d'Etat, the minister of finance, Pierre Magne, submitted it, asking for quick action as ordered by the emperor. Under this pressure the Conseil acted swiftly.

But before submitting the draft charter to the Conseil d'Etat, the ministries forced the Crédit Industriel et Commercial, as it was to be named, to accept many unwelcome restrictions as the price for authorization. Its capital was reduced, its president and vice-president were to be government appointees, and precautions were taken to prevent the founders from making exorbitant promotional profits. Shares for the founders were limited to about 5 percent of the total, and the rest were to be distributed on the basis of a public subscription at par under the control of the ministry of finance.[56]

Another unwelcome restriction limiting deposits to one and one-half times the paid-in capital quickly proved onerous. Within a year the bank requested that the limit be raised, pointing out that English deposit banks operated with deposits of ten times their capital. The commerce section of the Conseil d'Etat was unsympathetic: "Banks by their very nature run risks that no human prudence can avoid. The danger is particularly present in the case of demand deposits, which have become the almost exclusive speciality of the Société Générale de Crédit Industriel et Commercial."[57] To fears of its liquidity in times of crisis, the bank argued that shareholders had paid in only one-quarter of the par value of their shares, the remainder being subject to call; that its commercial notes were realizable from one to one hundred days and could be readily discounted; and that English deposit banks had weathered the crisis of 1857 without difficulty. The commerce section of the Conseil countered these arguments by observing that the stockholders in English deposit banks were subject to unlimited liability, unlike those of the Crédit Industriel et Commercial.[58] The Conseil was also appalled that the bank had violated its statutes as its deposits already amounted to three times its paid-in capital. The objections of the Conseil were overturned by higher authority, presumably the emperor; the bank received permission to raise its deposits from 15 to 60 million francs in February 1861.[59]

Clearly, for the Conseil d'Etat and the bureaucracy, banks were a fearsome thing. The Crédit Foncier, the Crédit Mobilier, the Comptoir d'Escompte, and the Crédit Industriel et Commercial, the only important banks authorized during this period, were all official or semi-official creations. The Conseil d'Etat was not consulted on the creation of the Comptoir of Paris in 1848; the initiative for the Crédit Foncier came from the government itself; and for the authorization of the Crédit Mobilier and the Crédit Industriel et Commercial, the resistance of the Conseil had to be overcome by the head of the state.

Other projected banks were less fortunate. At least sixty were either rejected or abandoned. Only a few got as far as the Conseil d'Etat. Many were not serious, dreamed up by would-be promoters without substance or support. For others there is insufficient documentation to judge whether they were potentially viable. But it is clear that many, with substantial interests behind them, could have played important roles.

About one-third of those projected were initiated between 1847 and 1851, with banks to provide agricultural credit predominating. From 1852 to 1859, the projects were fairly evenly distributed among (1) institutions designed to provide agriculture credit, (2) those primarily for discount, and (3) investment banks, modeled on or resembling the Crédit Mobilier. Some had multiple functions, and a few fit into none of these categories. These projections suggest that the availability of credit at reasonable rates for farmers and small businessmen remained a serious problem.

In 1853, the Pereires and Benoît Fould of the Crédit Mobilier proposed to create a Caisse Centrale des Sociétés de Crédit Mutuel, capitalized at 60 million francs.[60] This Caisse Centrale was to be the parent institution of smaller *caisses*, each specialized in providing credit for a certain branch of industry. In contrast to the Crédit Mobilier, which was designed to create and serve large enterprises, the Caisse Centrale was geared to providing the services of discount and deposit to small and medium-sized enterprises. The reports of the ministries of finance and commerce were not entirely unfavorable,[61] and it is not clear why the project was abandoned. Nothing in the dossier in the National Archives indicates that it was presented to the Conseil d'Etat.

Another institution designed to provide credit at low rates to small businesses, the Union de Crédit, attempted to obtain authorization beginning in 1852. It was modeled on a similar institution formed in Brussels in 1848 with the same name. With solid sponsorship (e.g., that of d'Eichthal and Bischoffsheim), the project was submitted to the Chamber of Commerce of Paris, which rendered an unfavorable opinion.[62] The ministry of finance suggested substantial changes in the bank's charter. Twice approved by the commerce section of the Conseil d'Etat, it was twice rejected by the General Assembly of the Conseil in 1855 and 1856. The Union de Crédit renewed its attempt in 1860, this time mustering outside support in its favor. Numerous Parisian merchants, small manufacturers, and artisans petitioned for its authorization. Count Siméon, a senator, wrote to Rouher on the bank's behalf: Arlès-Dufour had kind words for the project; and James de Rothschild was said to have promised his support if authorization were obtained.[63] All these efforts were in vain.

The ink was barely dry on the ordinance authorizing the Crédit Mobilier when the minister of commerce received the project for a similar institution, the Compagnie Financière et Industrielle, capitalized at 75 million francs. The seven founders, five of whom were deputies, claimed to have the backing of important bankers, industrialists, and merchants. They declared: "The Empire and public tranquility are inseparable, giving promise of immense undertakings. To facilitate their execution, we propose to found a company that will serve as an auxiliary and moderator to the one that exists. Without competition, the enterprise that has just been authorized would enjoy a dangerous privilege for a single company."[64] The founders quickly discovered that the government had no immediate intention of allowing the privilege to be shared.

Other serious requests for authorization of Mobilier-type banks were to follow. In 1853 came a request from the Omnium Lyonnais, which, though small (with assets of a little more than 3 million francs), had operated successfully since 1838.[65] Dominated by important bankers of Lyon, it had previously confined its operations to acquiring shares in local companies, an operation it now proposed to extend, giving it the appearance of a small Crédit Mobilier.[66] The Chamber of Commerce of Lyon advised against authorization on the grounds that the enterprise would constitute an "irresponsible power" and was "devoid of the character of *public utility*," which the chamber of commerce considered a requisite for authorization.[67] The prefect was favorable and the minister of finance raised no serious objection, but the project was interred by the ministry of commerce.[68]

Jules Mirès attempted in 1856 to gain authorization for his Caisse Générale des Chemins de Fer, a recently reorganized *société en commandite* capitalized at 50 million francs. A self-made man, Mirès got his opportunity in 1848, when he was able to purchase, with borrowed funds, the moribund *Journal des chemins de fer*. With this base, he organized in 1850 the Caisse des Actions Réunis, a *commandite* capitalized at 5 million francs, "the main function of which appears to have been speculation in the securities alternately vaunted and deprecated in the *Journal*."[69] Mirès transformed this enterprise into the Caisse et Journal des Chemins de Fer in 1853, with an increase in capitalization to 12 million francs. The transformation of the organization in 1856 and the request for authorization marked Mirès's attempt to move into elite circles.

The minister of commerce wrote to Mirès with the bad news on his request in July:

> I have submitted this matter to the Emperor in the council of ministers. His Majesty has decided that further consideration cannot be given to your request for authorization in view of the nature of the enterprise and the measures adopted with regard to other financial enterprises projected for the same object, notably the Compagnie l'Omnium at Lyon, and at Paris the Compagnie Financière et Industrielle projected by MM. de Espeleta, Calvet Rogniat, Dollfus, Koenigswarter and associates. If, in the past, it has appeared possible to stimulate business when it was depressed by political crises, to attract capital and channel it into industry by authorizing the creation of large banking and credit establishments in the *anonyme* form, these reasons do not exist today. By multiplying unnecessarily the number of these establishments, we shall arrive at the most unfortunate results of developing a type of governmental guardianship in large industrial centers, and of stimulating the taste for speculation and gambling on the Bourse to the detriment of legitimate commerce. Consequently, I cannot begin the processing of your project.[70]

The Caisse et Journal des Chemins de Fer remained a *société en commandite* and was even forced to postpone the raising of its capital from 12 to 50 million francs. The emperor's note of 9 March 1856 declared that no new enterprises giving rise to new capital issues would be authorized for the rest of the year. Although the business was a *commandite* and not subject to this prohibition, the minister of finance was able, through the Bourse, to block the new issue.[71]

On a more exalted level, the luminaries of the *haute banque*, including Rothschild, proposed to establish the Comptoir Impérial des Travaux Publics du Commerce et de l'Industrie in 1856, but the Conseil set aside the project as "untimely." Unlike Mirès's *caisse*, the Comptoir Impérial was not rejected out of hand; the project was processed through the Conseil d'Etat. The scruples expressed by the minister of commerce in his letter to Mirès apparently did not apply in this case. Although the financial status and political influence of the founders was of the highest order, the same was true of the opposition. This projected bank was the forerunner of the Société Générale pour Favoriser le Développement du Commerce et Industrie en France, authorized in 1864.

Another *commandite par actions*, the Union Financière et Industriel of A. C. Calley de Saint-Paul, requested authorization the following year. Its nominal capital was 120 million francs, but it issued only 100,000 of its shares, on which 250 francs had been called, reducing its realized capital to 25 million francs.[72] Its request suffered the same fate as did that of Mirès's *caisse*. The Union Financière continued as a *commandite* for three more years before disappearing.[73]

If the concept of investment banking as a necessary evil was gaining grudging acceptance in governmental circles, the authorizing of institutions with the novel idea of eliminating transactions in specie failed to win support. In 1853 the ministry considered the request for authorization of the Société de Crédit Industriel et Agricole projected in Paris by Louis Goupy. This institution, capitalized at 25 million francs divided into shares of 100 francs, planned to serve as an intermediary and to collect a commission on the exchange of goods and services. The exchange would take place either directly or by means of receipts for the deposit of merchandise or notes promising to provide a service (*bons d'échange*). The promoter claimed that operating without employing specie as a means of payment would help avert depressions such as those France had recently experienced.[74] The major argument for the viability and social utility of such an institution was the success of the Banque d'Echange, a *société en commmandite* established in Marseille in 1849 by C. Bonnard. Organized initially with a capital of 7,825 francs divided into shares of 25 francs, the Banque d'Echange was an undeniable success. In its first year of operation it handled almost 500,000 francs' worth of transactions, rising to over three and one-half million in 1852. The annual dividends on its 25-franc shares averaged almost 20 francs a share during the first four years of its operation. Encouraged by this success, Bonnard founded branches in Lyon and Strasbourg and finally, in 1853, founded in Paris the Comptoir Central, a *société en commandite* nominally capitalized at 100 million francs (its realized capital had reached 11 million francs by 1856). Bonnard requested authorization for the Comptoir Central in 1854, but the ministry of commerce had already reached a decision on the projected Société de Crédit Industriel et Agricole, which also doomed Bonnard's request.[75]

Consulted by the ministry on Goupy's bank, the Chamber of Commerce of Paris raised numerous objections, stressing the large capital and low value of 100 francs for the shares of the enterprise.[76] The minister of finance, Jean Martial Bineau, was worried more about the economic and social consequences should institutions of this type prove successful than about the possibility of their failure: "A considerable depreciation of precious metals would occur at a time when the discoveries of Australia and California threaten already to damage our monetary system. . . . Secondly, the success of the enterprise, and the founders have not concealed their thought in this regard, would lead to the ruin of retail business. . . . "[77] Bineau advised against authorization, and the minister of commerce concurred with his opinion.

Some requests coming to the ministry emanated from promoters without substance or from cranks. In this latter category was Alexandre Crétenier, who attempted to found the Société des Fils Peignés-Crétenier in 1842 as a *société en commandite* and erroneously solicited government authorization. In the troubled year 1848 he attempted to elicit government authorization for no less than three companies, two of which were banks: the Société Démocratique des Déchets de Fabrique et du Peignage, a "manufacture nationale démocratique" to be capitalized at 200,000 francs; Le Commanditaire de l'Industrie et du Commerce, capitalized at 6 million francs; and the Compagnie Française d'Exportation, capitalized at 100 million francs. In 1863, demonstrating an ability to move with the times, Créteneir wrote to the emperor from San Francisco requesting authorization for a Compagnie Franco-Mexicaine, with a capital of 5 million piastres, "to exploit the rich gold and silver mines of Sonora." The seat of the company was to be Napoleonville, a town yet to be built.[78]

Twenty-two mining and metallurgical companies were authorized between 1847 and 1859, eight of them during 1847–50 and fourteen in the three years from 1853 to 1855. Continued growth of demand for iron and coal necessitated huge new capital outlays, spurring enterprise to adopt the joint-stock form of organization. Even the depression prompted partnerships and *sociétés en commandite par actions* (or *sociétés civiles* for coal mines) to seek, often unsuccessfully, authorization as *anonymes*, motivated by the need for additional capital and easier credit. Growth in the average size of enterprises continued, horizontally through mergers and vertically through the acquisition of coal mines by metallurgical companies in order to insure adequate supplies of coal. The breakup of the Loire Mining Company in 1854 was an exception to this trend.

The charters of only three of the twenty-two enterprises contain figures for nominal capital, partly because of the reluctance of the government to make public its evaluations of a firm's nonliquid assets, lest the public regard the government's estimate as a guarantee, and also because of the difficulties inherent in making satisfactory evaluations. The total capitalization of these twenty-two companies can be estimated, however, as exceeding 100 million francs.[79] Of the four important metallurgical enterprises authorized between 1847 and 1850, three were former *sociétés en commandite par actions*, and one appears to have been a partnership (table 4.10).

The Fonderies et Forges de l'Horme began its quest for authorization in 1845. Jacques Ardaillon wrote to the minister of public works asking for speedy action on the company's request on the grounds that "the company is constituted provisionally as a *commandite par actions*. It is administered by a *gérant* who thus has the freedom to administer the enterprise without control. This is a state of affairs that does not afford as much security to the shareholders as a *société anonyme*, which has a director at its head who can act only under the authority of a board of directors. It is therefore urgent to change this temporary status."[80] His request that the normal administrative procedure be dispensed with was not granted.

Expansion was also a motive. The company wished to raise 1 million francs in additional capital, partly to undertake the construction of two additional blast furnaces. The government engineer reported that

TABLE 4.10 Large Metallurgical Companies Authorized, 1847–1850

Company	Year	Initial Nominal Capitalization (Francs)
Fonderies et Forges de l'Horme	1847	5,000,000
Hauts Fourneaux et Forges de Denain et d'Anzin	1849	10,000,000
Hauts Fourneaux de Montluçon	1849	3,000,000
Hauts Fourneaux de Maubeuge	1849	6,000,000

this addition would still leave insufficient working capital, a position adopted by the Conseil Général des Mines.[81] The company was thus forced to raise its capital an additional 1 million in order to achieve authorization in 1847.

The Hauts Fourneaux et Forges de Denain et d'Anzin, a *commandite par actions* that initiated its request for authorization in 1847, combined metallurgy with coal mining. Raising additional capital was an important motive in seeking authorization, and, as others had done, the promoters chafed over the slowness of the procedures. As often occurred, friction developed between the promoters and the government mining engineer. Answering a request for his report from the chief mining engineer of the district, mining engineer Comte replied:

Finally, if the petitioners want the affair to move more rapidly, they should have turned over to me long before now a detailed inventory and evaluation of all the objects that constitute the capital of the new enterprise. I am still waiting for this inventory, of which I have been given only certain information, and even this information is incomplete. . . . I have completely dropped the matter in order to stimulate a little good will from MM. Verret, Lelièvre et Cie., who have made me wait excessively for the information that I need on the operation of the forges of Denain and Anzin in 1846.[82]

Meanwhile the minister of commerce, Cunin-Gridaine, who had requested the minister of public works to expedite the affair in early November, became impatient. In a letter of 20 December 1847 to the minister of public works, he pointed out that, as no capital figure was being assigned in the charter of the enterprise, it seemed unnecessary to evaluate the nonliquid assets of the company.[83] In January he became more insistent:

I wrote to you last December asking for a speedy processing of the request and at that time I said that the necessary verifications could be effected rapidly because no evaluation needed to be made on the noncash assets. Today, the promoters have informed me that the engineer charged with verifying the existence and importance of the nonliquid assets has been under the impression that he must evaluate every object that composes these assets. This method of operation brings about long delays in the processing of the request and serves no useful purpose. The mission of the government is only to verify the material existence of all the assets belonging to the company, especially raw materials, merchandise, cash, and accounts receivable, which constitute the working capital. Therefore, there is no reason to make a detailed evaluation of every single object to be found in the factories.

. . . The processing of *sociétés anonymes* involves inevitable delays, which the government makes every effort to shorten. It is unnecessary that a simple verification, which should take a few days, can suspend action on an enterprise of great importance for many months. . . . [84]

A few weeks later, the July Monarchy was swept away by the Revolution of 1848, and the political situation, combined with the depression, made the company's position precarious. The promoters renewed, with the provisional government, their efforts to obtain authorization. The support of Lamartine was enlisted, and the promoters wrote to the new minister of commerce in a manner calculated to elicit action: "We employ 1,200 workers that we have retained until now at the cost of enormous sacrifices. With each day our means of obtaining credit diminish and the weight of our liabilities increases. To obtain the money to pay the numerous workers we employ, we are obliged to give lenders shares in the *société anonyme*, which will acquire legal existence only when it is authorized. If this resource fails, it will be necessary to suspend operations and dismiss 1,200 men for whom we have provided bread until now."[85] The ministers of both commerce and public works declared the matter to be "very urgent," but even a revolutionary government was unable to short-circuit the normal bureaucratic routine. More than two months elapsed before the Conseil Général des Mines considered the matter; final authorization was delayed until April 1849.

A major motive in seeking authorization for both the Hauts Fourneaux de Montluçon and the Hauts Fourneaux de Maubeuge was the raising of additional capital. Montluçon remained an *anonyme* for only four years, merging with its local rival, Fourchambault, and with other companies in December 1853. This new combination, a *commandite par actions* capitalized at 22 million francs, immediately tried to obtain authorization, but without success.[86]

Emile Martin, one of the masters of Fourchambault who did not enter the new combination, noted in his diary in February 1854, "Everywhere industrial enterprises are adopting the joint-stock form, . . . it is quite difficult not to conform to this trend."[87] By then, all the large metallurgical firms had already adopted the joint-stock form; some of the largest were *commandites par actions*. In addition to Fourchambault, Creusot and Chatillon-Commentry were *commandites*.[88] Another giant *commandite par actions*, the Compagnie des Hauts Fourneaux, Forges et Aciéries de la Marine et des Chemins de Fer, was created in 1854 with the merger of four *commandites*: (1) Forges et Aciéries d'Assilly (Jackson frères et Compagnie), (2) Forges de la Marine (Pétin, Gaudet et Compagnie), (3) Aciérie de Lorette (Neyrand, Thiollière, Bergeron et Compagnie), and (4) Forges et Hauts Fourneaux de Vierzon (Parent, Schaken, Goldschmidt et Compagnie). This combination lacked its own coal mines, a deficiency it attempted to remedy by acquiring in 1855 the new Compagnie des Mines de la Loire, one of the four successor companies formed when the old Loire Mining Company was broken up. Government opposition apparently prevented this merger.[89]

Although many coal mines were being absorbed by metallurgical firms, a number of large independents joined the ranks of *sociétés anonymes*. In addition to the four large successor companies to the gigantic Loire Mining Company, two large companies, the Grand' Combe Company (Gard) and the Mines de Charbon de la Mayenne et de Sarthe, were authorized in 1855. All of these were former *sociétés civiles* who found it convenient to escape from that anomalous status. Four small coal-mining companies were authorized during this period (1847 59), but many coal companies remained *sociétés civiles* or *commandites par actions*, in several instances because they were refused authorization.

In the transport sector, apart from railroads, twelve steamship companies, three land transport companies, and three canals were authorized between 1847 and 1859. The two largest were the Compagnie des Services Maritimes des Messageries Nationales, authorized in 1852 and capitalized at 24 million francs, and the Compagnie Générale Maritime, a project of the Crédit Mobilier, authorized in 1855 with a nominal capital of 30 million francs.[90] The Services Maritimes des Messageries Nationales was formed as a separate company, because the ministry of commerce was opposed to having the Messageries Nationales extend its operations outside France by taking over service, formerly provided by the state, to the eastern Mediterranean. The company was to purchase the state's equipment and receive an annual subsidy of 2,700,000 francs. The minister of commerce argued that this arrangement not only would violate the charter of the Messageries Nationales but would involve the company in two different operations, whereas, by principle, a *société anonyme* was to have only a single object. Given the operation of other *anonymes*, this distinction was rather arbitrary. The minister of finance argued that, because the assumption of the Mediterranean service by the Messageries Nationales had been approved by a law, statute took precedence over the provisions of the company's charter.[91]

The other steamship companies were smaller, their nominal capital ranging from 200,000 to 5 million francs. Three engaged in French coastal service and seven in river transport on the Seine, Rhône, and Saône. The only other large company in the transport sector was the Entreprise Générale des Omnibus, authorized in 1855 and capitalized at 12 million francs. This company, created by the merger of a number of smaller companies under the patronage of the Crédit Mobilier, possessed an exclusive concession for the city of Paris.

Seven of the eight real estate companies were large enterprises for the construction and operation of docks and markets, large urban projects related to Napoleon III's plans for the beautification of Paris, and similar schemes for Lyon and Marseille. One company, for the construction and operation of the Palais de l'Industrie in Paris, was a quasi-official enterprise. It was authorized in 1852 with a capital of 13 million francs, and the state guaranteed a minimum return of 4 percent on the 100-franc shares. After five years of heavy deficits, with prospects for the future dim, the state bailed out the stockholders by purchasing all the shares.[92]

The government authorized two companies in 1854, one for the construction of the rue Impériale in Lyon, capitalized at 7 million francs, and the other for the rue de Rivoli in Paris, capitalized at 24 million francs. The Compagnie de l'Hotel et des Immeubles de la Rue de Rivoli[93] was a Pereire enterprise, founded under the auspices of the Crédit Mobilier. The Conseil d'Etat strenuously objected to allowing the company to issue its shares at 100 francs: "The general rule followed for companies, even including those whose object has a character of undoubted public utility such as railroads, is not to permit shares of less than 500 francs."[94] The Conseil d'Etat was overruled.

The Pereires were not so successful when they attempted to triple the capital of the rue de Rivoli company. Their first request in 1856 was ruled out because of the note of 9 March banning new capital issues.[95] When the Pereires returned to the charge a year later, both the minister of finance and the Conseil d'Etat were hostile. Minister of

Finance Achille Fould informed the minister of commerce: "I think that the present state of the market, above all because of the numerous calls for funds this year for the construction of railroads, makes the raising of the capital untimely. It is likely to produce a new and troublesome disturbance of the market."[96] At the end of 1857 the Pereires lowered their sights and asked only that the capital be doubled, but they were turned down.[97]

Two other large enterprises in Paris were for docks and warehouses on the Seine at Saint Ouen (1856) and for the Villette stockyards (1858). In 1859, the government authorized both the Docks et Entrepôts de Marseille, capitalized at 20 million francs, and Jules Mirès's Société des Ports de Marseille, the first of Mirès's projects to be so favored. This latter company, organized temporarily in 1856 as a *commandite par actions*, pending authorization as an *anonyme*, was to finance construction on lands acquired from the city of Marseille. The par value of the company's 100,000 shares was fixed at 150 francs, short of the usual minimum of 500 required by the Conseil d'Etat. To secure authorization a conversion of shares was required at the rate of ten old shares for three new ones.[98]

Also authorized were eight gas companies, the largest of which was the Compagnie Parisienne, formed by the amalgamation of six *commandites par actions* in 1855, and capitalized at 55 million francs. Textiles remained virtually unrepresented, and there were only five bridge companies. Other authorized companies included enterprises in glassmaking, (among them that formed by the fusion in 1858 of the previously authorized Saint-Gobain [1830] and Saint Quirin, Cirey, et Monthermé [1841]), water supply, warehousing, light manufacturing, and food processing.

The size and diversity of *anonymes* grew during the 1850s. This very success and the growing dependence upon the joint-stock form made the existence of a two-tiered system separating *anonymes* and *commandites*, privileged and underprivileged, all the more intolerable. Even the favored complained about the inflexible molds, created by the Conseil d'Etat, to which they had to conform. Demands for reform burgeoned, and none were louder than those from the growing number who had been denied the fruits of governmental favor.

5 The Fall of the *Société en Commandite par Actions*

Il n'est pas dans les instincts des jurisconsultes de calculer les profits de la liberté.

André Cochut, 1861

The failure to pass legislation restricting the *société en commandite par actions* in 1838 did not end sentiment favoring reform, although the collapse of the boom made it seem less urgent. In 1839, only 121 *commandites par actions* were registered for all of France,[1] compared with more than 400 for 1837, and 301 for the first seven months of 1838 in Paris alone.[2] France's premier stock-market publicist, Jacques Bresson, although he condemned both the government and the committee bills of 1838 as too restrictive, was not unwilling to see some reform. He defended the use of bearer shares as long as they were fully paid up. He also suggested adding the requirement that all capital be subscribed and at least one-half paid in before the *commandite* could be definitively constituted.[3] The abuses of 1836–38 could not be repeated, according to Bresson, because shareholders had profited from their experience: "Wisdom and reason have replaced blind and reckless confidence."[4]

President Michel of the commercial tribunal of Paris lamented in August 1838 that the legislature had adjourned without considering reform legislation. Government surveillance of all joint-stock companies, according to Michel, could protect small shareholders without hindering the development of industry. He recommended the formation of a commission to verify the balance sheets of all joint-stock companies, both *anonymes* and *commandites*.[5] A year later, Michel's successor as president, Pépin-Lehalleur, reaffirmed in his inaugural speech the need for reform. He blamed the depression of 1839 on the fraudulent promotion of *commandites par actions* during the preceeding years.[6]

The Chamber of Commerce of Paris devoted its meeting of 26 December 1839 to discussing whether restrictive legislation was needed. Some argued that, with the current depression, it was more important to encourage enterprise than to discourage it by passing a new law. Others favored restrictive legislation that would abolish bearer shares, stop committees of surveillance from engaging in management, and prevent *gérants* from liquidating their financial interests in enterprises. Because the chamber was divided, no resolution was taken. The only issue to evoke unanimity was the necessity of keeping commercial cases out of the civil courts.[7]

After the fall of the Molé government, another extraparliamentary commission, consisting of sixteen members, was appointed toward the end of 1839 to consider anew the question of reform. There were six holdovers from the 1837 commission,[8] and among the newcomers were Charles Legentil, the *rapporteur* of the Chamber's committee, which had drafted a milder alternative to the government bill; Louis Wolowski, whose articles in 1838 had greatly influenced the Chamber's committee bill; Pellegrino Rossi, one of the foremost economists of the day; and two distinguished legists, Horson and A. Frémery. At the beginning of the commission's deliberation, one member suggested that legislation was unnecessary as the boom had died and the question had not been raised during the 1839 session of the Chamber.[9] This view was supported by several members. Others thought a new law was necessary to rescue the *commandite par actions* from the complete discredit into which it had fallen since the collapse of the boom. Still another group expressed the opinion that the lull was temporary and that a new law was necessary before the next boom got underway.[10]

First the commission examined the main provisions of the bill produced by the Chamber's committee, after which Legentil prepared a draft text based upon the committee's bill to serve as the basis for discussion. Not surprisingly, the draft finally produced by the new commission resembled the Chamber's bill. However, neither this proposal nor any other was submitted to the legislature during the July Monarchy.

The *commandite par actions*, in any event, revived. The boom of the forties, spearheaded by the railroad mania, saw a rise in the formation of *commandites*, though not comparable to the boom of 1836–38 (table 5.1).

The belief that restrictive legislation was necessary did not disappear. Claude Alphonse Delangle, in his two-volume *Des sociétés commerciales*, after presenting the usual lurid account of the boom of the mid-1830s, expressed the view that *commandites par actions* should be subjected, like *sociétés anonymes*, to government authorization.[11] Horace Say, reviewing Delangle's work in the *Journal des économistes*, while not subscribing to Delangle's extreme view, called for legislation which would outlaw bearer shares.[12] One discordant voice, that of Charles Coquelin in the *Revue des deux mondes*, although agreeing with the general view that the *commandite par actions* had been diverted from its original purpose and distorted, argued that the remedy was to liberalize the formation of *anonymes*. The *anonyme* was "the veritable form of business organization of our time, required by the present needs of industry, and the form to which the future belongs."[13] According to Coquelin, if the *anonyme* were freed from

TABLE 5.1 Registration of *Sociétés en Commandite par Actions*, 1839–1849

Year	France	Paris
1839	121	—
1840	176	80
1841	89	15
1842	123	—
1843	151	—
1844	114 (104)[a]	54
1845	229 (151)[a]	65
1846	276	—
1847	239	—
1848	147	—
1849	182	—

Source: Based upon Bresson, *Annuaire de 1840*, p. i; *Compte général de l'administration de la justice*, volumes for 1840–45; *Annuaire de l'économie politique et de la statistique*, 1861, p. 537.

[a]The figures for 1844 and 1845 in the annual *Compte général de l'administration de la justice* are not the same as those reported in the *Annuaire de l'économie politique et de la statistique*. Those in parentheses come from the *Annuaire*.

the necessity of government authorization, the *commandite* would no longer be forced to serve needs for which it was ill fitted.

The government continued to show some interest in *commandites*. At the end of 1845, one of the matters on which Minister of Commerce L. Cunin-Gridaine solicited the advice of the Conseils Généraux de l'Agriculture, des Manufactures, et du Commerce concerned the reform of legislation governing joint-stock companies. These three councils, which normally were convened for a month every three years to advise the minister on matters he submitted to them, were composed of prominent individuals in their respective fields of agriculture, industry, and commerce. The three councils were asked their opinions on a series of questions concerning *commandites par actions.* Although there were some differences in the recommendations of the individual councils, they all agreed that: (1) the *commandites par actions* should be retained, (2) their formation should not require government authorization, (3) shares of high denomination (5000 francs minimum) should be required, (4) bearer shares should be eliminated, and (5) safeguards were needed to prevent the *gérant* from overvaluing his contribution.[14] The government took no action on these recommendations.

After the depression and the Revolution of 1848, the coup d'état of 2 December 1851 set the stage for another boom. Political stability, the advent of joint-stock investment banks, and a favorable world economic climate, buoyed by a great expansion in gold production, underlay the boom of the 1850s. State, department, and municipal investment in public works reached new highs in the early 1850s. Large sums were channeled not only into railroads but into a host of derivative and unrelated enterprises, many of which employed the joint-stock form of business organization.

The formation of *sociétés en commandite par actions* increased from an annual average of 173 for the decade of the 1840s to an annual average of 348 for the five-year period 1852 to 1856. Although figures for the 1840s are lacking, the increase in the nominal capital of these enterprises was probably even greater. Figures for the Paris area, where the boom got underway after mid-1852, show a spectacular rise (table 5.2). The capital figures were greatly inflated, but if only one-fifth of the nominal capital was realized, the amount would equal the huge sums being invested in the securities of *sociétés anonymes*.

It may be inferred from the Paris figures that the increase in the average size of enterprises was marked, the *commandite* becoming more and more the vehicle of large enterprise, such as Jules Mirès's Caisse Général des Chemins de Fer (1856), capitalized at 50 million francs, an enterprise that had been refused authorization as a *société anonyme*.

Of 253 enterprises registered in 1855 at the commercial tribunal of Paris (including 8 registered elsewhere but designating Paris the seat of the enterprise), 14 were capitalized (nominally) at 20 million francs or more, 32 at 10 million or more, and 48 at 5 million or more. These enterprises encompassed a wide range of activities, with banking, transport, and mining and metallurgical enterprises accounting for about one-third of the number and almost two-thirds of the nominal capital (table 5.3). Some of these companies were stillborn, and others lasted no more than a few years. Many commenced operations after raising only a portion of their capital. Although the boom had its unhealthy aspects, some successful enterprises, which would have been unable to raise their capital in quieter times, were founded by imaginative promoters. The number and range of enterprises attests to the vitality of Parisian entrepreneurial talent.

A large number of the promoters sported noble names, but many of these "de's" were self-bestowed. Investors were presumed to be more

TABLE 5.2 Nominal Capitalization of *Commandités par Actions*, Paris Area, 1851–1857

Year (1 July–30 June)	Initial Nominal Capitalization (Francs)
1851–52	98,315,000
1852–53	1,013,109,000
1853–54	650,049,150
1854–55	967,822,944
1855–56	1,928,671,000
1856–57	580,779,000

Source: Charles Lescoeur, *Essai historique et critique sur la législation des sociétés commerciales en France et à l'étanger*, p. 66.

willing to entrust their savings to noble *gérants* than to commoners. But if the nobility of many *gérants* was spurious, those who served on councils of surveillance were generally the real article. Most *gérants* made an effort to recruit men of prominence or title to dress up their councils. With the distribution of free shares, most of which could be disposed of at once, the recruitment of these councils was not difficult. Though the Compagnie Française de Navigation à Vapeur, de Roulage, et de Messageries was founded in 1856, its councils of surveillance afford a typical example. To the members of the first two councils of surveillance, the *gérant*, one D. Galland (his real name was Guillier), distributed 830 shares, worth nominally 415,000 francs. Among

TABLE 5.3 Registration of *Commandites par Actions*, Paris Area, 1855, by Sector

Sector	Number	Initial Nominal Capitalization (Francs)
Banking	26	440,000,000
Transport	18	216,600,000
Mining and metallurgy	33	120,690,000
Commerce and real estate development	23	110,472,000
Manufacturing	40	62,228,170
Insurance	13	42,950,000
Distilling and food processing	15	40,400,000
Publishing and publicity	23	19,898,000
Gas	8	18,582,000
Cesspool cleaning and fertilizer	9	15,200,000
Textile	10	8,880,000
Miscellaneous	35	81,519,000
Total	253	1,177,419,170

Source: Compiled from the *Gazette des tribunaux*, 1855.

the five members of the second council were two nobles, one a senator and the other a member of the Institute. A third was a deputy. According to Caignard de Saulcy, the member of the Institute, his lawyer had brought the opportunity to his attention and advised him to accept the post and the shares, on the grounds that he might make some money and that, even if the shares proved to be valueless, nothing was lost.[15]

To attract investors, some promoters vied with one another in advertising spectacular returns. M. de Ponthieux, *gérant* of the Compagnie de Vidange Atmosphérique Perfectionnée, "believed he could assure" dividends of 40 percent to his stockholders. The Société Générale de Conservation de Substances Alimentaire indicated that dividends would be more than 60 percent, in addition to 5 percent interest on shares. Stockholders of the Baleine Française were to receive 5 percent interest and were "assured on the basis of past performance" of an annual dividend of between 35 and 40 percent. The Compagnie des Mines de Charbon et Chaux Hydraulique de Montjoyer paid 5 percent interest and a dividend "of which the expected size is between 35 and 45 percent annually." More modest were the claims for the Gaz Hydrogène pour l'Eclairage et Chauffage dans la Ville de Havre, which, in addition to the usual 5 percent interest, "assured" shareholders of dividends of more than 10 percent.[16]

Although shares of low denomination came in for much subsequent criticism, their prevalence was exaggerated. The shares of most Paris companies in 1855 ranged from 100 to 500 francs. Only thirty companies issued shares ranging from 5 to 50 francs, and nine issued shares of 5,000 francs or more. Some companies issued shares of varying denominations.

The same abuses to be found in the earlier boom of the 1830s accompanied that of the 1850s, but on a greater scale. Critics raised the same objections and, with slight variation, proposed the same remedies. Not only did the boom offer opportunities for new men, but the *commandite* form afforded them particular advantages, as described by Horace Say in the *Journal des économistes*:

It often occurs that a person with little or no funds conceives the idea of creating a large, joint-stock enterprise, and if he possesses energy and *savoir faire*, he can succeed in having considerable funds placed at his disposal. In order to attract public attention, he gives the enterprise a pompous title, taking care to list the legal name [of the enterprise] in a subordinate position. For some years our newspapers have carried a large number of prospectuses for companies having all the appearances of *sociétés anonymes*, with no mention of the name of the *gérant*. In companies of this sort the *gérant* goes to a notary and alone stipulates all the conditions to which the investors are subsequently considered to have adhered by their subscription of shares. The *gérant* is thus the veritable dictator of the enterprise. The investors who subscribe can exercise only an imperfect surveillance over his administration. They are restrained by the fear of losing their status of *commanditaires* and becoming indefinitely liable by having participated in policy making. The liability of the *gérant* in these companies is illusory, for, when the company goes bankrupt, he usually disappears.[17]

Some promoters lent credence to their claims of high dividends by paying them from the enterprise's capital, giving the firm a temporary aura of prosperity that assisted it in disposing of unsubscribed shares. It has been estimated that at least one-third of all *commandites* were floated by dishonest promoters whose sole purpose was to fleece unwary shareholders.[18]

The flood of shares of both *commandites* and *anonymes* inundated the capital market. The shares of railroads floated in 1852 and after were still draining the capital market in 1855. Because the costs of railroad construction were spread over a number of years, most railroad shares were subscribed at a quarter down and the other three quarters payable at a quarter a year. The Bank of France, after noting a decline in its reserves, took a first step toward choking off the boom in the fall of 1855. The bank's reserves had fallen from 451 million francs on 29 March, to 310 million on 11 July, to 246 million on 4 October. Some of these losses were attributable to increased food imports owing to the poor harvest of 1855, some to the effects of the Crimean War, and some to growing demand for payment in bullion in the provinces. In addition, advances of the bank on *rentes* and railroad stocks and bonds had risen, fueling the speculative boom, which the Council of Regents attempted to halt. The bank raised the discount rate from 4 to 5 percent on 4 October and to 6 percent on 18 October, on the latter date reducing the maximum term from ninety to seventy-five days.[19]

Alarmed by the flood of new *commandites*, the prefect of police of Paris, Joachim Pietri, advised the minister of commerce in September

1855 that legislation was needed to correct abuses. His remedy for this "disastrous state of affairs" was to subject *commandites* to government authorization.[20] The government's concern over the speculative mania was expressed publicly early in 1856. Pierre Magne, the minister of finance, warned of the dangers of speculation and announced the adjournment of new public works projects in a report to the emperor that appeared in the *Moniteur* in January.[21] Concern for the speculative mania spilled over into the theater. The craze for shares was ridiculed in François Ponsard's popular comedy *La Bourse*, which opened at the Théatre Française in Paris on 6 May 1856, with the emperor in attendance.[22] On 9 March 1856, as we have seen earlier, the emperor announced that no new *société anonymes* giving rise to new capital issues would be authorized for the rest of the year. This edict did not apply to *commandites par actions*, as the government had no direct control over their formation. In order to curb the *commandites*, the government decided again, after an eighteen-year interval, that restrictive legislation had to be enacted.

In the last days of May 1856, the government introduced a bill, prepared by the Conseil d'Etat, ostensibly to repress fraudulent practices in the formation of *commandites*. The *exposé des motifs* preceding the bill complained in a manner reminiscent of 1838:

> Unhappily, investors have allowed themselves to be seduced by the maddest hopes, and have fallen for the most extravagant exaggerations. Persons of bad faith have known how to take advantage of this speculative frenzy: They have given rise to hopes of impossible dividends by lying in their prospectuses; they have appeared to offer guarantees of credit and morality by placing their enterprise under the nominal patronage of honorable persons; they have, in exaggerating the value of the assets they have contributed to the enterprise, absorbed for their own gain a large portion of the capital furnished by the shareholders; they have found in the mechanism of the *commandite par actions* the means to realize illicit advantages, entirely independent of the success of the enterprise.[23]

The correction of these faults was the stated purpose of the bill, but with the government's concern over the state of the capital market, repression of fraud was not the only motive.

If the rhetoric was reminiscent of 1838, so were the solutions. The provisions of the government's bill were similar to the provisions of the Chamber's committee bill in 1838. Within the Corps Législatif, a committee of seven presided over by the industrialist Eugène Schneider examined the bill.[24] The committee considered a large number of amendments proposed by members of the Corps Législatif. When the bill emerged, it was even more restrictive than the government's bill.[25] In his report to the legislature, the *rapporteur* of the committee, J. Langlois, impressively stated what the bill would accomplish: "What will the new law do? It prevents fraud; it stops the most usual types of fraud; it obliges the founders of enterprises to be wise and honest; it asks shareholders to investigate and be prudent; it protects small investors; it diminishes and represses speculation; it ends the illicit dividends; it forms a barrier to the creation of fraudulent enterprises; it institutes an effective surveillance; it attempts, insofar as possible, to replace deceit and lies with truth and fairness."[26]

The bill, which passed without change, mandated shares of at least 100 francs for enterprises with capital of under 200,000 francs; for enterprises with capital of over 200,000 francs, the shares could be no less than 500 francs. All shares had to be subscribed and at least a quarter of the capital had to be paid in on each share before the company could be definitively constituted. Shares were to be *nominatives*—that is, registered in the name of their owner—until entirely paid up, and the original subscriber was ultimately liable for all calls in the event subsequent shareholders defaulted. Although the shares could be negotiated after two-fifths of their capital had been paid in, the responsibility of the original subscribers for all calls rendered this provision illusory. In contrast to the committee bill of 1838, bearer shares were permitted if the shares were fully paid up.

Before the company could be definitively constituted, a special stockholders' meeting had to be held to review the evaluation of the assets contributed by the *gérant* and any advantages stipulated on his behalf in the by-laws. This provision aimed at preventing the *gérant* from overvaluing his contribution and providing exorbitant privileges for himself. In adopting this provision, the committee rejected several proposals that the assets furnished by the *gérant* be subjected to the appraisal of experts.[27]

In order to prevent the *gérant* from misrepresenting the financial situation of the company, the establishment of councils of surveillance was made mandatory, even for existing *commandites*. These councils were to be elected at the first stockholders' meeting (in the past, the members had often been selected by the *gérant*). The duties of these councils, heretofore, vague, were spelled out in detail and given statutory force. Council members were responsible for seeing that the prescriptions of the law had been observed in the formation of the company. They were further responsible for verifying financial statements of the *gérant* and preventing the payment of dividends not covered by net earnings. To fulfill their task, they were to have access to all the necessary records. Members of these councils were subject to both civil and criminal suits for failure to perform their duties.

Although passage of the bill through the docile legislature of the Second Empire was never in doubt, and amendment was impossible, several provisions of the bill were attacked during the short debate. Two members opposed the provision requiring shares of 500 francs for enterprises with a capital superior to 200,000 francs, on the grounds that it would banish the small capitalist from the market: "The figure of 500 francs is already an aristocratic figure, and small savers cannot aspire to shares of 500 francs."[28] Three speakers criticized the provisions rendering the members of the councils liable,[29] foreseeing an avalanche of irresponsible litigation. They argued that few conscientious and honorable men would be willing to serve on such councils, for even baseless suits would damage their reputations. Maxmilian Koenigswarter, a deputy and banker, claimed that the law would render the formation of large *commandites* impossible, thus attenuating competition and giving the masters of *sociétés anonymes* virtual monopolies.[30] Finally, he predicted prophetically that "in the not distant future, the government will be obliged itself to request the modification of the law."[31] The critics of the bill were to see their views justified shortly, but the legislature ignored their observations. The bill passed on 1 July 1856 by a vote of 221 to 12. The Senate also approved, and the emperor promulgated the new law on 17 July.

The bill also had its critics outside the legislative chambers. The liberal-oriented Société d'Economie Politique discussed the bill at a meeting on 5 July 1856, where majority sentiment opposed at least parts of the impending law. Joseph Garnier declared that the law would not prevent the abuses it was designed to repress. He attacked the restrictions placed on the *commandites* and predicted that the whole question would have to be taken up again soon.[32] Another speaker, Hippolyte Peut, claimed that the result of the new law would be "the expatriation of domestic capital, the repulsion of foreign capital, and the impoverishment of the country for these two reasons.''[33] Others, in attacking the restrictions of the law, pointed out the need for a more liberal approach to the whole question of business organization. Yet, even here, the new law was not without its defenders, including the financial columnist Alphonse Courtois.

Criticism of the bill appeared in the pages of the influential *Journal de chemins de fer* from the pen of its editor, Jules Mirès, who objected to the obstacles that would impede the formation of *commandites* and also to the provisions that would subject the *gérants*, of which he was one, to suits from individual shareholders. He foresaw the bringing of many nuisance suits, which would embarrass *gérants*. For Mirès, the solution was not to restrict the *commandite* but to lower the barriers to the formation of *sociétés anonymes*, as had been done in Belgium.[34] His advice was not disinterested, for his Caisse Générale des Chemins de Fer had only recently been refused authorization by the Conseil d'Etat.

The law had the effect desired by the government. The number and nominal capitalizations of *commandites par actions* declined sharply during the year following the passage of the law, falling precipitously after mid-1857. By that time *gérants* and members of councils of surveillance had been subjected to numerous suits under the provisions of the law, and the boom of the mid-fifties had collapsed. Certainly,

TABLE 5.4 Nominal Capitalization of *Commandites par Actions*, Paris Area, 1855–1860

Year (1 July–30 June)	Initial Nominal Capitalization (Francs)
1855–56	1,928,671,000
1856–57	580,779,000
1857–58	74,238,000
1858–59	61,767,000
1859–60	29,874,000

Source: Lescoeur, *Essai historique et critique sur la législation des sociétés*, pp. 66, 120–21.

the depression of the late fifties contributed to reducing the number of new *commandites*, but the continued eclipse of the *commandite* form after recovery can be attributed to the law. The nominal capitalization of new *commandites par actions* for the Paris area dropped steadily (table 5.4), although outside Paris, the boom and subsequent decline of *commandites* was less pronounced (table 5.5).

Even with the economic recovery of the 1860s, the formation of *commandites* remained at a low level. The giant *commandite* virtually disappeared. In the five years between 1858 and 1862, only two *commandites* capitalized at 20 million francs or more were formed.[35] Hostile reaction to the law was prompt, and numerous suggestions for reform were forthcoming. Some critics even blamed the law for the collapse of the boom. As time passed, there was general agreement that the law had vitually eliminated the *commandite par actions* as a vehicle for investment. Some argued that the law was responsible for diverting French capital into foreign investment.[36] Illustrative of this view was the judgment on the law given by T. N. Bénard to the Société d'Economie Politique on 5 March 1863: "It is precisely the law of 1856 that has killed the *commandite* by deforming the position and character of the *gérant*, and by eliminating honorable and prudent

TABLE 5.5 Registration of *Commandites par Actions*, France and Selected Commercial Tribunals, 1851–1867

Locale	1851	1852	1853	1854	1855	1856	1857	1858
All France	166	200	384	305	387	463	217	126
Paris	75	120	230	174	243	273	68	32
Lyon	12	8	24	26	36	47	48	21
Aix	16	19	40	14	16	24	7	18
Bordeaux	8	6	5	10	13	12	8	9
Douai	13	3	13	6	12	15	18	12
Rouen	0	5	13	12	8	16	12	4

Source: *Compte général de l'administration de la justice civile et commerciale*, annual volumes, 1851–67. The most active commercial tribunals were selected. The jurisdiction of these tribunals encompass the following departments: Paris: Seine, Aube, Eure et Loire, Marne, Seine et Marne, Seine et Oise, and Yonne; Lyon: Ain, Loire, and Rhône; Aix: Basse Alpes, Bouches du Rhône, and Var; Bordeaux: Charente, Dordogne, and Gironde; Douai: Nord and Pas de Calais; Rouen: Eure and Seine Inférieure.

men from their functions as members of councils of surveillance. The best proof that the depression has not affected for long the accumulation of savings is the large amount of French capital that has gone abroad for investments that it can no longer find in France. Is it not regrettable that the imperfections of our laws have not permitted capital to be easily placed in French investments that are sure and advantageous?''[37]

Even without the 1856 law, the downturn of the business cycle in the late fifties would have reduced the number of *commandites par actions*. This had been the case in the 1830s when the legislature had failed to pass restrictive legislation. Even in the absence of the law, investors certainly would have become wiser and more discriminating. Even those who are incapable of learning from past mistakes soon find themselves in a position of being unable to repeat them. The law of 1856 was the last triumph of the lawyers and bureaucrats. Time and events were putting them on the defensive. Their victory in 1856 was Pyrrhic, because it helped to intensify the pressures for more far-reaching reform that resulted in the triumph of free incorporation.

The law of 1856 ended the golden age of the *commandite par actions*. The form continued to exist, but its role was modest. Before

1859	1860	1861	1862	1863	1864	1865	1866	1867
141	111	96	116	111	106	152	131	101
66	46	34	41	50	40	89	61	17
25	16	12	10	13	15	8	10	27
3	6	3	4	3	6	4	0	4
3	10	5	5	1	1	2	5	2
6	4	8	3	7	6	8	10	2
3	5	5	11	8	6	6	1	7

its decline, however, it played a vital role in facilitating French economic growth over five decades. It offered entrepreneurs a viable alternative to the *société anonyme*. In particular, it afforded opportunities to "new men" who could not expect to meet the social and economic qualifications generally required for government authorization. The contribution of *commandites* in the banking sector was of special importance, because the government bureaucracy was hostile to authorizing banks as *anonymes*. Although many of the *commandite* banks were spectacular or ignominious failures, hundreds of banks specializing in discount were formed from the 1830s on. Some of the better known *caisses* operated in Paris, such as those of Laffitte, Béchet-Dethomas, and Lehideux; the greater number operated in large and small provincial centers from Lille to Lons-le-Saunier. The partial list, in Auguste Vitu's *Guide financier*, consisting of forty-eight provincial *commandite* banks existing in 1864, capitalized from 200,000 to 12 million francs, gives an indication of their geographical diffusion and importance.[38] For large metallurgical enterprises, the *commandite* form provided a convenient way station on the road to *anonyme* status, and for some, such as Fourchambault and Creusot, it was more than a temporary expedient. The use of the *commandite* form in the manufacturing and service sectors was even more extensive than in banking or metallurgy. In spite of the many ill-conceived, ill-managed, and fraudulent *commandites*, their contribution far outweighed their faults and was probably equal in importance to that of *sociétés anonymes* for French economic development.

6 The End of an Era

A mon avis, il y aurait avantage a dégager le gouvernement de la grave responsabilité qui resulte de son droit de contrôle et de surveillance.

Minister of Finance Achille Fould
to the minister of commerce, 9 May 1863

The Last Years of Government Authorization, 1860–1867

Even with the disfavor into which the *commandite par actions* had fallen, there was no increase in the formation of *sociétés anonymes*. The average annual number of *sociétés anonymes* authorized in the seven and a half years between 1860 and mid-1867 was 12.7, about the same as for the preceding period, 1847–59. The number might have been larger except for the appearance in 1863 of an alternative form of business organization, the *société à responsabilité limitée*.[1] The founders of the Crédit Lyonnais, for example, chose to utilize this new form rather than run the authorization gauntlet.[2] But, as with most substitutes, it was not as good as the real thing. There was a drop in the average nominal capitalization of *sociétés anonymes* from approximately 18 million francs per enterprise to 10 million, reflecting the absence of large railroad companies (table 6.1). Whereas railroads accounted for the lion's share of nominal capitalization of *anonymes* for 1847–59, that preeminence was taken over by financial institutions for 1860–67 (table 6.2).

Among financial institutions, the nominal capitalization of eleven banks accounted for 376 million francs and that of thirty-three insurance companies for 83,700,000 francs. More banks were authorized than ever before, but the reluctance of the administration still kept the number relatively small (table 6.3). Most of these banks were spawned by other banks to provide for more specialized services or for geographical coverage. The Société de Dépôts et de Comptes Courants,

the Société Lyonnaise, the Société Marseillaise, and the Crédit du
Nord were offspring of the Crédit Industriel et Commercial.[3] These
banks, modeled on their parent, were to specialize in deposit and
discount. The Crédit Agricole and the Comptoir de l'Agriculture, both
specializing in credit for agriculture, were founded under the patronage of the Crédit Foncier, whose office they shared. L'Approvisionne-
ment, Société de Crédit des Halles et Marchés, another specialized
credit institution, was an offspring of the Crédit Agricole. The Crédit
Colonial, primarily a mortgage bank designed to operate in the French
colonies, was an offshoot of the Comptoir d'Escompte. The Crédit
Colonial was rebaptized the Crédit Foncier Colonial in 1863, and its
capital was at that time increased to 12 million francs.

The Société Générale pour Favoriser le Développement du Commerce et de l'Industrie en France was an investment bank resembling
the Crédit Mobilier, or, in the view of Bertrand Gille, more truly
modeled on its Belgian namesake.[4] The Société Générale was the
descendant of the ill-fated Comptoir Impérial des Travaux Publics, du
Commerce, et de l'Industrie, which failed to receive authorization in
1856; it included many of the same founders, with the notable exception of James de Rothschild. In the absence of Rothschild, Paulin

TABLE 6.1 Formation of *Sociétés Anonymes*, 1860–1867

Year	Number	Initial Nominal Capitalization (Francs)
1860	12	11,200,000 (for 7)
1861	9	33,500,000 (for 7)
1862	11	13,200,000 (for 5)
1863	25	278,500,000 (for 19)
1864	11	150,550,000 (for 8)
1865	12	57,000,000 (for 8)
1866	8	125,400,000 (for 6)
1867	7	10,000,000 (for 6)
Total	95	679,350,000 (for 66)

Source: Compiled from company charters in the *Bulletin des lois*.

Talabot took the leading role. Two years later, Talabot was the prime mover in creating an analogous bank for Algeria, the Société Générale Algerienne.

Most of these banks called only a fraction of their capital. Although the Crédit Agricole called only 100 francs on its shares, securities worth 150 francs had to be deposited as a guarantee for each share. The minister of finance was reluctant to allow less than 40 percent to be paid in, although a precedent existed, for only one-quarter had been paid on the shares of the Crédit Industriel et Commercial (1859). Achille Fould thought this precedent ill advised and recommended that the realized capital of the Société de Dépôts et de Comptes Courants be raised, from the one-fifth desired by the promoters, to two-fifths.[5] Fould was skeptical of the argument much used by promoters that the uncalled capital was a "guarantee capital." In time of financial crisis, Fould asserted, calls on shares would not be honored.[6] His advice was not followed in this case; only 25 percent was paid in on the shares of the Société de Dépôts and, in the following years, 25 percent was the usual amount for other banks and was the amount for the Société Générale.

In some instances, only part of the total number of shares were issued, the rest being reserved for future issue. The Société Générale Algerienne issued only one-quarter of its shares, an exception to the

TABLE 6.2 *Sociétés Anonymes,* 1860–1867, by Sector

Sector	Number	Initial Nominal Capitalization (Francs)
Banking and insurance	44	459,700,000
Transport	16	71,300,000 (for 11)
Mining and metallurgy	8	unknown
Warehouses, shops, apartments	8	84,500,000 (for 2)
Other	19	63,850,000 (for 9)
Total	95	679,350,000 (for 66)

Source: Compiled from company charters in the *Bulletin des lois.*

long-enforced rule that all the capital of the enterprise had to be subscribed. The stockholders of the Caisse des Associations Coopéra-tives were empowered to raise the capital of the enterprise from 1 million francs up to a maximum of 4 million. The motives for the founding of this organization were partly philanthropic, as it "aimed at the improvement and progress of the working classes" by lending to co-ops.[7] Napoleon III was among the founders, and his support facilitated the authorization process.

TABLE 6.3 Banks Authorized, 1860–1867

Bank	Year	Initial Nominal Capitalization (Francs)
Crédit Colonial	1860	3,000,000
Crédit Agricole	1861	20,000,000
Comptoir de l'Agriculture	1863	6,000,000
l'Approvisionnement, Crédit des Halles et Marchés	1863	6,000,000
Société de Dépôts et de Comptes Courants	1863	60,000,000
Société Générale pour favoriser le Developpement du Commerce et de l'Industrie en France	1864	120,000,000
Société Lyonnaise de Dépôts et de Comptes Courants et de Crédit Industriel (Lyon)	1865	20,000,000
Société Marseillaise de Crédit Industriel et Commercial et de Dépôts (Marseille)	1865	20,000,000
Crédit Industriel et de Dépôts du Nord (Lille)	1866	20,000,000
Société Générale Algerienne	1866	100,000,000
Caisse des Associations Coopératives	1866	1,000,000

Most of the approximately fifty unsuccessful authorization requests for banks to be found in the files of the National Archives for this period were not serious attempts to found enterprises. All of them, including those with solid backing, appear to have been interred by the ministries without having been submitted to the Conseil d'Etat.[8]

Of the thirty-three insurance companies, twenty-four were for maritime insurance, and half of these were Parisian companies. Six were for fire insurance and two for life insurance. The first *anonyme* for accident insurance, La Securité Sociale, was capitalized at 2,500,000 francs.[9]

In the transport sector, there were eleven railroads, all for feeder or suburban lines; three steamship companies; the Compagnie Générale de Omnibus de Bordeaux; and the Compagnie Générale de Voitures à Paris. The largest was the Compagnie Générale des Voitures, organized originally as a *commandite par actions* in 1855 and capitalized at 40 million francs. Uniting a number of smaller companies into a giant one, which possessed for a time an exclusive privilege for *voitures à place* in Paris, it obtained authorization in 1866 after eleven years of effort.[10]

Among the mining and metallurgical companies, the Forges de Chatillon et Commentry, after unsuccessfully attempting to gain authorization in 1846–47 and again in 1857, finally succeeded on its third try. The company had been denied authorization in 1857 because its liabilities amounted to more than 20 million francs. It was informed by the ministry that a requirement for authorization was that all assets be free and clear of debts and mortgages. If anything, the company was in even worse shape in 1861. It had not fared too well in the intervening four years, and its liabilities stood at 24 million francs. This time, however, Minister of Commerce Rouher decided to allow the request to be processed. Precedents existed for authorizing enterprises whose assets were not free and clear. The four successor companies of the old Compagnie des Mines de la Loire (1854), the Mines de la Grand'Combe (1855), and, more recenlty, the Houillères de Carmaux (1860) were cases in point. Thus, while affirming the general principle that all assets be free and clear of all debts and mortgages, the ministry decided to treat Chatillon-Commentry as an "exceptional case."[11]

All the mining engineers and prefects of the five departments where the company had operations favored authorization, except for the prefect of the Allier and the mining engineers of the Allier and Côte d'Or. They advised either for adjournment or for rejection of the request. The prefect and mining engineer of the Allier objected mainly to the company's huge debt. The mining engineer of the Côte d'Or raised this and other objections. According to him, many of the company's operations were in a precarious state because of their great distance from coal mines and because of the inferiority of the company's products. He advised that the company be forced to sell these marginal properties, which had been idle for some time anyway, and apply the proceeds to its debt. He also observed that the company needed more working capital.[12] The prefect of the Côte d'Or saw the situation differently. If many of the company's factories were idle, it was only a temporary situation because of the general depression, which periodically affected the whole metallurgical industry. New railroad construction would bring better times. Although the debt was large, it was more than covered by the firm's assets, affording ample protection to third parties.[13] Two of the company's creditors were not so certain. They registered their opposition with the ministry, alleging that the *commandite* afforded greater protection to creditors because of the personal liability of the *gérants*, than would an *anonyme*.[14]

A more liberal attitude toward authorizing an enterprise with substantial liabilities is apparent in the success of Chatillon-Commentry's 1861 application. Why accord authorization then, after the company had operated for seventeen years as a *commandite par actions*? How many "exceptional cases" can be allowed before a policy is relegated to the dustbin? Obviously, some motives of the chief actors from Rouher on down may escape us.[15] It cannot be entirely ruled out that they, their relatives, or their friends may have had a pecuniary interest in authorization. Some weight was given to the plight of the stockholders, who alleged that the enterprise could not be properly administered as a *commandite par actions* because of its vast size and numerous *gérants*, each placed at the head of a group of factories and each going his own way. "Thus, there is no unity in the direction of the business, nor any control possible by the stockholders, who, if they intervene in the administration of the enterprise, assume the risks of unlimited liability."[16] In any case, without the *anonyme* form, the enterprise certainly would have experienced great difficulty in raising the additional working capital it needed.

Of the warehouses and shops authorized, two were in Paris and one each in Bordeaux, Tours, Lyon, Amiens, and Nevers. On a grander scale, the Compagnie Immobilière, authorized in 1863 and capitalized at 80,000,000 francs, undertook the construction and exploitation of shops, apartments, hotels, and streets in Paris and Marseille. The company was formed by the fusion of two previously authorized *anonymes*, the Compagnie Immobilière de Paris, a Pereire enterprise (the former Compagnie de l'Hotel et des Immeubles de la Rue de Rivoli authorized in 1854), and the Société des Ports de Marseille (1859), the creation of Jules Mirès during better days. Also included was the unincorporated but ongoing development of the rue Impériale in Marseille, controlled by the Pereires, who had also wanted to include in the new combination—yet another of their creations—the Compagnie des Entrepôts et Magasins Généraux de Paris, authorized in 1860—but this latter idea was vetoed by the Conseil d'Etat.[17]

The basis of the fusion agreed to by the stockholders of the Paris Immobilière and the Ports de Marseille in October 1862 had been determined primarily by the market value of the shares. The shareholders in the old Immobilière were to exchange eleven shares (par value 100 francs each) for four shares in the new company (par value 500 francs each), and shares of the Ports de Marseille were to be exchanged one for one. This plan amounted to evaluating the Immobilière at more than 43 million francs and the Ports de Marseille at 15 million. Rouher, the minister of commerce, interfered with this arrangement, ordering an appraisal of the assets of the companies, which was to be the basis for the division of shares.

When a few dissident shareholders of the Ports de Marseille brought suit against the merger, Rouher informed Emile Pereire on 9 February 1863 that, until the suit was settled, the processing of the request for authorization would be suspended.[18] Normally, the ministry was insensitive to the inconveniences caused by interminable delays, but on this occasion, after a warning from the prefect of Bouches du Rhône, a high official in the ministry expressed some qualms over the possible political consequences:

> There will be in this manner of proceeding a serious objection: If we wait until the courts have decided, and the processing of the affair has not even begun, a delay of several weeks will take place before the authorizing decree can be issued. However, the basis of the fusion among the companies, having been decided last October, the Paris and Marseille companies cannot under-

take new operations; they can only continue those that were already underway. Any new operation will change the relative financial status of the Companies and affect the basis of the fusion.

In this situation, thousands of workers, in both Paris and Marseille, will find themselves temporarily unemployed, as the works in progress are coming to an end.

If the authorization of the combination is delayed until April, the new company will not be able to begin new works in time for the coming electoral campaign, and a large number of workers will be idle at the time of elections.

If authorization comes during March, two months will be sufficient for the company for preparation, and the great operations it will undertake in Paris and Marseille will be well underway at the time of the elections.

Therefore it is urgent that the Conseil d'Etat immediately begin processing the matter without waiting for the decision of the courts.

It would also be useful, in view of the importance of this question, if the Court of First Instance was called upon to make its decision quickly.[19]

However, Rouher was not to be stampeded by pressure from the promoters. He wrote to the prefect at Marseille that normal procedures would be followed: "In addition, I cannot admit for a single instant that the matter of authorization can be linked to the question of continuing operations. All the companies and M. Em. Pereire personally have contracted individually certain obligations. These obligations must be fulfilled within the time set whatever the outcome of the authorization process."[20]

The dossier was sent to the Conseil d'Etat but was held up there awaiting the report of the appraisers. Meanwhile, the dissident stockholders withdrew their suit.[21] The Conseil rendered its opinion on 20 May, just ten days before the 1863 legislative elections. In addition to excluding the Compagnie des Entrepôts et Magasins Généraux de Paris from the merger, the Conseil wanted to change the stock apportionment in the new enterprise in accordance with the appraisals, which showed the assets of the Compagnie Immobilière to be overvalued by more than 4.5 million francs and those of the Ports de Marseille to be undervalued by 3 million francs. A meeting of Pereire with Rouher resolved these and other difficulties. The demand of the Conseil d'Etat in regard to stock reapportionment, which Rouher had originally favored, was dropped. The company was finally authorized on 13 June. The appraisals ordered by Rouher were to become an issue later in a stockholders' suit to dissolve the company. Although this suit was brought in 1869, after government authorization had been ended, even by 1863 some government officials were beginning to see the advantages of free incorporation.

Authorization Policy in the Railroad Age

By the 1830s an established set of principles governed authorization. Most of these continued to be enforced without change until government authorization came to an end in 1867. Others were strengthened or weakened as circumstances required, and some new policies evolved. Although it sometimes did not get its own way, the Conseil d'Etat continued to dominate the formulation of authorization policy.

The Conscil d'Etat underwent important changes in organization, powers, and personnel after 1814. Wholesale turnovers in personnel occurred in 1830, 1848, and 1852, but after each upheaval a core of experienced personnel remained to provide continuity. The gradual creation of the Conseil's administrative jurisprudence regarding the authorization of *sociétés anonymes* was virtually unaffected by revolutions, coups d'état, and personnel purges. The outlook, background, and education of the Conseil's personnel did undergo some change but with no perceptible effect on the Conseil's unsympathetic view of the business world. Here legitimists and republicans saw eye to eye. The social and psychological gulf between members of the Conseil and the new breed of company promoters remained unbridgeable.

The Conseil conceived its role as that of the guardian of business probity. Though protesting frequently that authorization was not an official guarantee, it acted as if the opposite were true. Even the language of its *avis* often belied the disclaimers. Members of the Conseil, particularly members of the section of agriculture, public works, and commerce, were likely to know if, and when, authorization would occur. Under certain circumstances this was valuable information. It is impossible to know to what extent members, directly or indirectly, engaged in speculation or passed along information to friends and relatives. It appears that their conservative outlook extended to their investments, which were overwhelmingly in government *rentes* and landed property.[22]

The other important molders of authorization policy were the ministers and the bureaucrats within the ministries, particularly those of commerce, public works, and finance. Ministers came and went, but changes were less frequent than during the Third Republic. The professional cadres within the ministries, usually willing to serve any regime, changed less frequently, though political upheaval, death, and retirement took their inevitable tolls. Insofar as their collective outlook was concerned, these professionals were a little less conservative on authorization policy than the Conseil d'Etat, the difference arising from a slightly greater political and economic awareness. Although the Conseil and the ministries were generally in accord, conflicts between them over authorization policy did occur.

As in the earlier period, the Conseil d'Etat continued its attempt to limit the *anonyme* form to large enterprises of public utility. In 1836, the Conseil refused to authorize the Manufacture de St. Clément, an old firm engaged in the manufacture of faience, principally on the grounds that there was "no motive of Public interest," as there were only ten stockholders, all members of four families. The Conseil also objected to provisions mandating unlimited calls on shares to maintain their value at 700 francs and restrictions on the right to sell shares to outsiders.[23]

In the same year the Conseil also refused to authorize the Berlines Mantaises Accélerées because of the small size of its capital (20,000 francs).[24] The minister of commerce ordered that the request be returned to the Conseil for reconsideration. The ministry argued that precedents existed, a number of *anonymes* with small capital, varying from 15,000 to 66,000 francs, having been authorized previously.[25] The ministry also invoked the opinion issued by the Conseil Générale du Commerce in 1825 when the Conseil d'Etat had refused to authorize the Verrerie de Thuison for similar reasons.[26] Not to authorize small enterprises, the ministry argued, "would be to create a restriction that the law has not established."[27] The request was resubmitted to the Conseil in April 1837, and it is not clear why the enterprise was not authorized.

That the ministry was partly successful, however, is evident from the subsequent authorization of a small sugar refinery. The authorization of the Sucrerie de Bergerac, capitalized at 100,000 francs divided into twenty shares of 5,000 francs each, with only ten shareholders, was refused by the Conseil d'Etat in June 1837 on the grounds of its small capital and few shareholders. The Conseil observed that the enterprise could be formed easily as a partnership.[28] The minister immediately ordered the request to be returned to the Conseil for reconsideration. The ministry noted that the Berlines de Chateau Thierry, a smaller company (capital 60,000), had been authorized in February and that the Berlines Mantaises Accélerées had been resubmitted in April.[29] The Conseil reversed itself and authorized the Sucrerie de Bergerac in November.

In September 1837, the Conseil d'Etat approved the authorization of the Forges et Fonderies d'Axat (Aude), capitalized at 420,000 francs, reversing the decision of its own committee. Three members of the committee voted against authorization in December 1836 because of "serious objections," the most serious of which was that the company had only three stockholders; and two members voted for authorization on the grounds that "a sufficient reason to refuse authorization does not exist."[30] The delay between the action of the committee and final authorization suggests that the minister may have intervened in the case: if the General Assembly had immediately overruled the committee, authorization should have occurred earlier. Probably the ministry's insistence at this time that small enterprises and enterprises with a small number of shareholders should be permitted to employ the *anonyme* form was not unrelated to the effort to secure legislative restrictions on the formation of *sociétés en commandite par actions*.

During the 1840s, some small enterprises continued to be authorized. In 1842, l'Union, Messageries d'Alençon à Caen, capitalized at 50,000 francs, and the Salle de Spectacle à Saint Amand (Cher), capitalized at 38,000 francs, were authorized. The shares of both these enterprises represented derogations from the standard minimum share of 500 francs. The shares of the Messageries were 100 francs, and the 500-franc shares of the Salle de Spectacle were subdivided into four coupons of 125 francs each.[31] Most shares under 500 francs were those of small provincial enterprises, though the Conseil was overruled in the case of a few large enterprises, such as the rue de Rivoli company of the Pereire brothers, which issued 100-franc shares.[32] In a few instances the Conseil did permit large companies to issue shares of 250 francs.[33] Railroads popularized the 500-franc share, though many companies continued to issue shares of a higher denomination. The shares for the Filature de Danlot (1841) were for 20,000 francs.

Sentiment for limiting the *anonyme* form to large enterprises always remained, reasserting itself when the climate was favorable. In 1843, l'Union, Bateaux à Vapeur entre Rouen et la Bouille, capitalized at 240,000 francs with twelve shareholders, was authorized. In 1859, upon the expiration of its term, the Conseil d'Etat denied reauthorization. Its capital had been reduced to 160,000 francs divided among nine shareholders; "moreover, this enterprise, in spite of its undoubted utility, is not among those whose size satisfies the criteria that, from the beginning, the administration has required for the *anonyme* form."[34] Restriction was again in the ascendancy.

The attitude of the Conseil Générale des Mines was even more restrictive than that of the Conseil d'Etat. The Conseil Générale des Mines recommended rejection of the request for authorization of a company to mine pozzolana (used to manufacture cement) in the Hérault department: "An enterprise that requires only 300,000 francs of working capital is not among those for which the *anonyme* form has been introduced in our commercial legislation. This form is designed . . . for huge speculations that would otherwise not be formed."[35] In transmitting the dossier to the minister of commerce, the minister of public works concurred in the recommendation, because (1) the enterprise was risky, as the deposits were uncertain, and (2) the *commandite* form could be used.[36]

The hostility to small enterprise with few stockholders was replaced, at the other extreme, by fear of gigantic enterprise with thousands of stockholders. Ministry officials and the Conseil d'Etat often reduced the projected capital of large enterprises, particularly if only part of the shares were to be issued immediately. The projected capital of the Compagnie Générale des Eaux, authorized in 1853, was reduced from 100 million francs to 25 million by the ministry and from 25 to 20 million by the Conseil d'Etat.[37]

Certain types of enterprise were denied authorization. The ministry of commerce refused to process the request for authorization of a retail trade enterprise.[38] Questions concerning the interpretation of Article 30 of the *Code de Commerce*, which forbade *anonymes* from engaging in "multiple operations of a diverse nature," continued to arise. Almost from the beginning, insurance companies were limited to a single type of risk. The Messageries Nationales was denied the right to extend its operations to the high seas; a separate company was necessitated. Although it came to be accepted that the union of coal mines and metallurgical enterprises was legitimate, a conflict arose between the ministry and the Conseil d'Etat over whether the Decize Coal Mines should be permitted to acquire a small glass works.[39] Some banks were denied authorization in the 1850s on the grounds that they combined too many "diverse operations." What separated legitimate "diverse operations" from those coming under the ban of Article 30 was a matter of arbitrary judgment.

The government scrutinized enterprises carefully for adequate working capital. Instances of enterprises forced to raise their capitalization to provide what government officials regarded as adequate working capital were numerous. The projected capital of the Forges et Fonderies de Bourges was set by the promoters at 600,000 francs. The government mining engineer recommended that it be raised to 1 million, and the Conseil Général des Mines decided upon 1,050,000 francs.[40] The Conseil d'Etat declared that the projected capital of 400,000 francs of the Société de Culture de la Dombe, an agricultural enterprise authorized in 1843, was too small; it was raised to 830,000 francs.[41] Promoters often balked at providing the detailed accounting on which the judgments were based.

One recurrent problem in verifying a firm's capital involved evaluation of the nonliquid assets — factories, equipment, and inventories — of the enterprise. Normally, government officials made an independent appraisal, but sometimes an appraisal by outside experts was sought. Discrepancies between the company's evaluation and the administration's appraisal, when the latter was lower, as was usually the case, gave rise to controversies. But the promoters had little choice; they had to accept the administration's figure if they wanted authorization.

The administration also had qualms about including sunk costs in the firm's capitalization figure. The timbering of a mine shaft would be worthless in case of liquidation. To include the cost of timbering as part of a company's capitalization figure misled third parties, at least in the official view. To avoid this problem, the administration adopted the policy of not listing a capitalization figure in the charter. Instead there was a simple listing of a firm's assets, with no value assigned to the physical assets. Shares were assigned no par value but simply designated as representing a fraction of ownership. This method, which became general practice in 1840, was employed primarily to protect third parties and incidentally to protect the administration from criticism by third parties. At first, some thought it might relieve the administration from the burden of detailed appraisals.[42] But appraisals continued to be made, in order to protect shareholders, actual or future, from having promoters unload on them, a greatly overvalued asset, a type of fraud commonly practiced in *commandites*.

The government required that an enterprise seeking authorization be free of all debts, obligations, and mortgages. Any exceptions allowed were permitted, Minister of Commerce Curin-Gridaine noted in 1847, when the debt or mortgage was relatively small.[43] In the 1850s a more liberal policy was followed for the four successor companies to the Loire Mining Company, authorized in 1854; for the Grand'Combe Mining Company (1855); for the Mines of Mayenne and Sarthe (1855); and for other cases. Though in 1857 the ministry refused to process the renewed request of Chatillon-Commentry on the grounds that it was encumbered by a debt of 21 million francs, the company was authorized five years later when its debt was even larger.

The principle of prohibiting the payment of interest on shares continued to be invoked, but the Conseil d'Etat, usually as the result of pressures from above, made important exceptions. Some railroad companies were permitted to pay interest on shares from capital during construction. The Compagnie Général des Eaux (1853) was permitted to pay interest of 4 percent on its shares for its first five years. The rue Impériale of Lyon (1854) paid interest of 5 percent on its shares until the end of 1858, and the shares of the rue de Rivoli company (1854) also paid 5 percent interest without any time limitation.

Although earlier the Conseil d'Etat had allowed some latitude to promoters concerning provisions on voting in stockholders' meetings, in the 1830s this discretion was confined within relatively narrow limits. The number of shares required to attend and vote varied with the value and number of shares issued by the company. Rarely were the holders of single shares allowed a vote, and then only in the smallest companies. Forty shares were required for one vote in the Société Générale Algerienne—a figure raised by the Conseil d'Etat from the twenty stipulated in the company's draft charter.[44] The Conseil lowered the number of shares required for a single vote from forty to twenty in the draft charter of the Société Lyonnaise de Dépôts et de Comptes Courants et de Crédit Industriel, which had only 40,000 shares, against the 200,000 for the Société Générale Algerienne.[45] Provisions to limit the meetings to a fixed number of the largest stockholders, as in the case of the Bank of France, had been permitted for departmental banks but were refused by the Conseil for all other enterprises.[46]

If shareholder democracy was rejected at one extreme, control by a single or small group of large shareholders was rendered theoretically impossible at the other. Strict limitations were placed on the total number of votes a shareholder might cast. Few companies, regardless of size, permitted a single shareholder more than five votes. When the Paquebots à Vapeur entre Le Havre et Londres (1837), with 600 shares, proposed to give each shareholder a vote to a maximum of ten votes, the Conseil proposed instead two or three shares for a single vote and a maximum of four or five votes. Too many shareholders attending the stockholders' meetings, the Conseil stated, "could hinder the proper administration of the company."[47] The Conseil also exhibited hostility to proxy voting, imposing limitations on the number of proxy votes in those charters that permitted it.[48]

As earlier, prefectural reports on the solvency and morality of shareholders continued with few exceptions to be pro forma. However, the authorization of the Société Marseillaise de Crédit Industriel et Commercial et de Dépôts (1865) was held up for what proved to be well-justified fears about the solvency of two of its promoters, Charles and Alfred Rostand.[49] When foreign investors were involved, the ministry of foreign affairs was pressed into service.[50] A different kind of objection was raised in 1843 about A. Lebaudy, a holder of 583 of the 1,200 shares of the Compagnie des Antilles. The par value of the shares was 5,000 francs, of which only a quarter had been called. Because Lebaudy's call obligation exceeded 2 million francs, the Conseil deferred authorization until the company's shares were more equally distributed, the final decision being left to the minister of commerce. The minister, Cunin-Gridaine, did not prove to be too demanding. When informed by Ernest André and d'Audiffret, two of the promoters, that Lebaudy's portion had been reduced to 503 shares, and that three new stockholders had been added, he approved authorization.[51]

When more than the usual apprehension about the future operations of an enterprise existed, the charter would include a provision requiring the appointment of government commissioners to exercise surveillance over its operations. In the case of some banks, the government went even further, reserving the right to appoint, or approve the appointment, of the chief executive. Actually, government commissioners did little. Their reports usually consisted of summaries of the annual stockholders' meetings, containing no more information than could be found in the financial press. The commissioners were paid by the enterprises on which they were supposed to inform. The four government commissioners of the Crédit Foncier each received 6,000 francs annually, not bad pay for what was essentially a sinecure. In 1855, the report to the committee of the Conseil d'Etat that was considering the request for authorization of the Mines de Houille de la Mayenne et de la Sarthe called government commissioners an "illusory guarantee" against abuse.[52] Fears existed about the future pricing policies of the company, which possessed fourteen of the sixteen mining concessions in the area (and five of the six mines actually being exploited).

Other safeguards were no more effective. Requiring the submission of the firm's balance sheet to the ministry, the local commercial tribunal, and the local chamber of commerce every six months was originally intended to serve as a means of official surveillance. That many firms were not complying with this requirement became evident in 1838 when concern over joint-stock enterprise was at a peak. The ministry directed the prefects to remind all *anonymes* of their obligations. Some of the balance sheets submitted testify to a woeful state of accounting practice. A few firms did not know what a balance sheet was. After being forcefully reminded of their obligations, *anonymes* submitted these reports with greater regularity, but from time to time the ministry had to mount a new campaign to remind those in default.[53] There is almost no evidence that the administration put these records, once in their possession, to any use.[54] But if the reports did not serve the regulatory purpose originally intended, their publicity function came to be recognized as essential.

Government authorization by the end of the 1850s was being subjected to increasing attack. The old catalogue of complaints continued unabated: excessively stringent conditions, long delays, and the "privilege" conferred by authorization. Further, the demise of the *commandite par actions* as a vehicle for large-scale enterprise, attributed to the restrictive law of 1856, removed a viable alternative to the *anonyme*. Liberalization of incorporation laws abroad, which affected the competitive position of French firms, contributed to the demands for reform. Finally, growing sentiment held that government involvement was both inappropriate and unnecessary. What remained to be seen was how the problem would be solved.

7 The Triumph of Free Incorporation

Une loi ne s'invente *pas, elle* se découvre.

P. J. Proudhon

The triumph of free incorporation in France was closely intertwined with events abroad. Though the French in 1856 passed legislation restricting the *commandite par actions*, in the same year the British liberalized their corporate law. Until then, French corporate law had been generally more liberal than the British. Although the British law of 1844 recognized the principle of free incorporation, it did not grant limited liability. In the early 1850s, many favored importing the *commandite par actions* into Britain to secure limited liability for shareholders.[1] But rather than imitate the French, the British created, by the Company Act of 1856, the limited liability company, a corporation with a minimum of seven persons, conferring limited liability on shareholders and requiring certain formalities of registration.

Prior to the enactment of this law, English promoters often crossed the channel to found companies that operated in Britain with wholly British capital. In 1852–53, twenty English companies were founded as *commandites par actions*, each renting office space in France and hiring a French *gérant* "who did nothing but give a power of attorney to one of the company's English directors."[2] The cost of founding and maintaining English companies in France was one of the arguments used in favor of liberalizing English law. According to the vice-president of the Board of Trade, Edward Pleydell-Bouverie, in June 1855:

So great is the demand for limited liability, that companies are frequently constituted in Paris and the United States, in order that they may obtain the security which in this respect the laws of those countries afford. When these companies are formed in Paris, they pay a heavy duty to the French government. The duty assessed upon one company of which my firm were the solicitors amounted to £750. . . . All this expense is incurred simply to get the benefit of the French law of limited liability, and it amounts generally to £400 or £500 a year. I have reason to believe that one company's expenses incurred in Paris to obtain the benefit of this law amounted to nearly £4,000. I am within the mark in saying that during the last two years at least twenty companies have been formed in France solely for the same purposes. They are, in truth, English companies, both as to capital and directors, and all this expenditure is just so much money taken from this country and paid to France as a consideration for the use of her laws.[3]

The British act and the French law of 1856 reversed the migration. English companies that had been founded in Paris recrossed the channel to become limited liability companies and escape the rigors of the French law on *commandites*. A number of purely French companies found it convenient to become limited liability companies under British law.

The migration of French companies was facilitated when the French government explicitly recognized the right of foreign corporations to operate in France. This was the result of a series of events that began when Belgian courts, during the 1840s, rendered contradictory decisions on the rights of French *sociétés anonymes* to exist as legal persons under Belgian law. This inconsistent jurisprudence was finally ended in 1849 when the Court of Cassation at Brussels decided that French *sociétés anonymes* could not exist as legal persons under Belgian law.[4] Numerous complaints from French chambers of commerce followed this decision. The Chamber of Commerce of Valenciennes pointed out to the French minister of commerce that French *sociétés anonymes* "could not operate abroad from the moment that one refused them the right to legal existence" (*d'y ester en justice*).[5] To allay this difficulty, a convention was added to the Franco-Belgian Treaty of Commerce of 27 February 1854 that obligated the Belgian government to introduce legislation guaranteeing the right of legally authorized French *sociétés anonymes* to operate in Belgium. This arrangement led to the passage of the Belgian law of 14 March 1855. Because the convention required reciprocity, the French were obliged to introduce legislation that led to the enactment of the law of 30 May 1857. Although the French Court of Cassation had consistently upheld the right of foreign companies to operate in France, they had been subjected to some harrassment by the French government.[6] The French law of 1857 permitted all Belgian companies to operate in France and provided that the government could extend this privilege to any other country by a decree in the Conseil d'Etat. After the passage of this law, French courts reversed their previous jurisprudence and refused to admit the legality of any foreign corporations except the Belgian.[7] In the following decade the French government extended full rights to the companies of almost all European states. For companies of the few countries not covered, of which Prussia was one, permission to operate in France was obtained on an individual basis. The treaty of 30 April 1862 established general reciprocity with Britain.

The liberalization of British company law with the creation of the limited liability company in 1856 and the right of British and other foreign companies to operate freely in France helped speed the liberalization of French law. Other important determinants were the harsh criticism to which the French law of 1856 on the *commandites* was subjected and the movement of the government after 1860 toward freer trade and toward political liberalization.

In 1861, two high officials of the judiciary joined the chorus favoring reform. Guillaume Denière, president of the commercial tribunal of the Seine, advocated a new law establishing the English limited liability company in France.[8] A few months later, Antoine Blanche, *avocat général* of the Court of Cassation, echoed the need for reform, noting that there were two defects in the *commandite par actions*: the omnipotence of the *gérant* and the prohibition of stockholders from participating in management.[9] He pointed out that the law of 1856 had not been successful in diminishing fraud and proposed that stockholders be given the right "to oversee the action of the *gérant*, to direct and limit it, without exposing them to the rigorous consequences [unlimited liability] of Article 28 of the *Code de Commerce*."[10] Recent decisions of the Court of Cassation, Blanche noted, already permitted the stockholders some control over the actions of the *gérant*.[11] These ideas and others were discussed by Adolphe Blaise in a series of articles in the *Journal des travaux publics*, later published as a book. Blaise, like Denière, proposed introducing the English limited liability company into France.[12] The proposals of Denière, Blanche, and Blaise were discussed in the press, and many other proposals were forthcoming, some for removing the restrictions placed on the *commandite* by the law of 1856, others for allowing the *anonyme* to be formed without government authorization.[13]

Shortly after the proposals of Denière and Blanche, the Corps Légis-latif in its reply to the emperor's speech from the throne in 1862 called attention to the need for "the reform of certain commercial laws . . . [and] the suppression of obstacles that excessive regulation opposes to the productive forces of the country."[14] The government was willing to consider reform. An appointed commission, headed by Minister of Commerce Eugene Rouher, recommended introducing the English limited liability company into France.

Although the government's bill, prepared by the Conseil d'Etat, was welcomed as a forward step, many expressed reservations over the restrictions it contained.[15] The committee of the legislature suc-ceeded in securing subsequent ameliorations from the Conseil d'Etat, some of which owed much to adverse public comment. Foremost among the critics was Adolphe Blaise, who subjected the govern-ment's bill to a minute criticism.[16] He accused government bureaucrats of betraying the emperor's desire for reform:

They think only of the traditions of the past, . . . only of preserving vested interests and prolonging the legal wardship of citizens. . . . They distrust commerce and industry, and try to preserve themselves from any contact with these inferior professions, of whose customs and needs they are ignorant. This accounts for the general attitude of the Conseil d'Etat, which, on questions of reform and commercial legislation, sees in the business world only dupes to be protected, charlatans to be restrained, and abuses to be anticipated and prevented. . . . All these preoccupations and contradictions are to be found in the bill on the *société à responsabilité limitée*, which begins with a proclama-tion of emancipation, . . . whose application the remainder of the bill para-lyzes and hinders, when it does not render it completely impossible.[17]

Blaise's criticisms helped to secure some important changes, such as the reduction of the number of associates required to found a *société à responsabilité limitée* from ten to seven and the increase of the maxi-mum capitalization from 10 to 20 million francs.[18] Michel Chevalier, liberal economist and senator, pointed out the disparity between the English law and the restrictions of the government's bill and added his weight to those pressing the legislature to liberalize the bill.[19]

The government's bill was sent to the Corps Législatif on 16 May 1862, and in June a committee was appointed to study the bill.[20] The committee's decision to obtain the advice of commercial tribunals and chambers of commerce, no doubt motivated by a desire to gain support for amendments, delayed the reporting of the bill until 1863. The character of the *société à responsabilité limitée (SARL)*, the French translation of the English "limited liability company," was described in the committee's reports as follows: "It is, in reality, a *société anonyme* without the authorization of the government and in which the inherent guarantees of authorization are replaced by a set of requirements destined to protect shareholders and third parties. . . . This new form offers all the features of security that can be found in a regular *société anonyme* and at the same time avoids the slowness and difficulties of government authorization."[21] The *SARL* also overcame one of the main problems of the *commandite par actions*: lack of stockholder control over the enterprise. In reply to criticism that the advantages of the *SARL* would lead to unfair competition with proprietorships and partnerships, the committee gave a stock nineteenth-century answer: "Businessmen whose entire credit and fortune are at stake usually will retain a superiority and advantage in the struggle against administrators having only a partial interest in the business that they run."[22] Another motive for the bill, emphasized by the committee, was the necessity of providing French businessmen with "equal arms" to compete with English companies, especially because the Cobden-Chevalier Treaty of 1860 and the Commercial Treaty of 1862 had stimulated commercial relations.[23]

The bill that emerged from the committee was less restrictive than the government's bill, for the committee was successful in persuading the Conseil d'Etat to accept some ameliorations.[24] The committee wanted to change the title to *société anonyme libre*, but this move was rejected by the Conseil. The committee did succeed, however, in reducing the minimum number of associates from ten to seven, which was the minimum number in England. The effort of the committee to remove the restriction of a maximum allowable capital failed, but the Conseil did agree to raise the maximum from 10 to 20 million francs and to eliminate a 200,000-franc minimum.

Many of the restrictions imposed on the *commandite par actions* by the law of 1856 were incorporated to prevent fraud, to assure the reality of the capital, to curb overvaluation of contributions by the promoters, and to restrain the stipulation of excessive advantages for the founders in the by-laws. Shares were to be negotiable only after at least two-fifths had been paid in, and they were *nominatives* until completely paid up. The minimum par value of shares was fixed at 500 francs for companies with capital of over 200,000 francs and 100 francs for companies with capital below 200,000 francs. All capital had to be subscribed before a company could be formed, and at least one-fourth had to be paid in. All these restrictions were taken from the 1856 law, but an important innovation required that the administrators possess at least one-twentieth of the total capital in inalienable shares, a disposition suggested by the commercial tribunal of the Seine. The bill provided for commissioners, to be chosen by the stockholders, who were to verify the accounts and watch over the actions of the administrators; they resembled the inspectors provided by the British act of 1856. Some of the commercial tribunals criticized this provision as likely to breed controversy within the enterprise.[25] The question of the dissolution of the enterprise had to be submitted to the stockholders if three-quarters of the capital were lost, a provision also taken from the English law.[26] A mandatory reserve was to be created to which 5 percent of the annual profits were to go until it equalled 10 percent of the enterprise's capitalization (10 percent and 25 percent, respectively, in the government's bill). To prevent conflicts of interest, administrators were forbidden to do business with or to have interests in firms doing business with their enterprises, a provision suggested by several commercial tribunals and added by the committee.[27]

During the debates on the bill, most of the criticism focused upon old charges that the bill was too restrictive and on the provisions concerning penalties that could be incurred by administrators.[28] The Anglomania reflected in the bill was also attacked.[29] The Vicomte de Kervéguen advocated repealing the law of 1856; for A. C. Calley de Saint-Paul, a banker and prominent company promoter, the solution was to simplify the formation of *anonymes*.[30] The Duc de Morny, president of the Corps Législatif, criticized the provision restricting the negotiability of shares until two-fifths had been paid in. This rule, he charged, failed to take into account the needs of different enterprises, in some of which the calling of one-fifth of the capital would be sufficient. According to Morny, this was true for banking and insurance companies, where the capital of the company was not the operating capital but a guarantee. The more capital called, the greater the service charges that would have to be made to provide a return on it.[31] These criticisms had no effect on the provisions of the bill. As expected, the Corps Législatif voted the bill by an imposing majority, 203 to 23.[32]

The law, even with the changes obtained by the committee, was a disappointment for the proponents of liberalization. Henri Baudrillart, the editor of the *Journal des économistes*, summarized their sentiment: "Is the law in accord with the idea of liberalization that has appeared in official quarters? We do not think so. It falls far short of the English Law."[33] If it was hoped that the law would fill the need for free incorporation, this hope was doomed to disappointment. The main advantages of the SARL were that, like the *commandite par actions*, it did not require government authorization and that, unlike the *commandite*, it was ruled not by an omnipotent *gérant* but by a board of directors chosen by and responsible (at least theoretically) to the shareholders. The main disadvantages were the requirement that the members of the board collectively had to possess at least 5 percent of the enterprise's capital in inalienable shares and the penalties that could be incurred by members of the board for violations of the law's provisions. These disadvantages made the SARL less attractive to prospective administrators than had been hoped and constituted a barrier to the formation of large enterprises.

The SARL was destined to last only four years, from mid-1863 to mid-1867, during which time 338 were founded, about equally distributed between the Paris area and the rest of France (table 7.1). Without the SARL, some of these enterprises would have been founded as *commandites par actions*, others would have elected to run the authorization gauntlet, and some would not have been founded at all. In spite of the advantages of the SARL, contemporaries were convinced, with justification, that the restrictions of the law prevented its wider use.

One of the first and most important enterprises to be founded as a SARL during the four-year life of the law was the Crédit Lyonnais, constituted two weeks after the law was promulgated. By opting for the SARL, rather than trying to obtain authorization as an *anonyme*, the promoters from Lyon were able to forgo sharing control of the enterprise with Parisian financial interests: the opposition of Parisian interests, if they had been excluded, might have been fatal to obtaining authorization as an *anonyme*. As an additional benefit, the Crédit Lyonnais escaped the restrictions that the ministries and the Conseil d'Etat normally imposed on banks. The new enterprise was capitalized at 20 million francs, the maximum allowable.[34]

The SARL proved to be a halfway house on the road toward the liberation of the *société anonyme* from government authorization. In August 1864, minister of commerce Armand Béhic announced that the government would introduce a bill extending the freedom of commercial companies.[35] The Conseil d'Etat undertook the task of preparing the draft of the government's bill in September 1864.[36] In February 1865, Napoleon III announced the impending introduction of the bill, which would "allow a greater liberty for commercial associations and disengage the responsibility, always illusory, of the government."[37] The government's bill was introduced in the Corps Législatif on 28 March 1865. It was the most comprehensive piece of legislation on business organization to be taken up since the elaboration of the *Code de Commerce*. It tempered the rigors of the law of 1856 on the *commandite par actions*, dispensed with government authorization of *anonymes*, suppressed the SARL, and introduced a new form of business organization, the *société de coopération*, designed to facilitate the growth of the cooperative movement in France.

The most important modifications in the *commandite par actions* proposed by the government allowed limiting the liability of original

TABLE 7.1 SARLs, France and Selected Commercial Tribunals, 1863–1867

Locale	1863	1864	1865	1866	1867	Total
All France	10	59	104	88	77	338
Paris	9	25	61	46	27	168
Aix	0	1	6	2	6	15
Bordeaux	0	6	0	2	1	9
Douai	0	2	2	3	3	10
Lyon	1	7	11	9	9	37
Rouen	0	4	1	2	2	9

Source: *Compte général de l'administration de la justice civile et commerciale*, annual volumes, 1863–67. The jurisdiction of each commercial tribunal encompassed two or more departments.

subscribers for uncalled amounts on their shares to half the par value of the shares, permitted the negotiation of shares after a quarter had been paid in (rather than two-fifths), and limited the responsibility and liability of members of councils of surveillance. These provisions corrected what many believed to be the chief defects of the law of 1856.

For *sociétés anonymes*, which were no longer to be authorized by the government, the *exposé des motifs* of the government's bill noted, "It has been believed for a long time . . . that the authorization and suveillance of the government afforded complete security to investors and the best guarantee that third parties could have."[38] But of late, according to the *exposé des motifs*, there had been less satisfaction with the alleged guarantees that authorization afforded than complaints about its slowness. The success of the SARL led the government to believe that authorization could be safely dispensed with.[39] This was a superficial view of the matter, however. Those who hoped for relatively unrestricted incorporation were to be disappointed. The requirements of the Conseil d'Etat for authorization were, insofar as possible, to be written into the new law, "which would define the general lines on which all company charters must be based."[40] Interested individuals were to make the same determination previously made by the Conseil d'Etat. By and large the provisions of the bill were similar to those of the 1863 law on the SARL. Life insurance companies were to remain under the regime of government authorization.

Four of the nine members of the parliamentary committee constituted to consider the government's bill had been members of the committee on the SARL in 1863.[41] The bill received long and careful study. A special government commission set up to make a comprehensive study of the proposed *sociétés de coopération* delayed the committee's report and resulted in important changes for these associations. Only in May of 1867 was the committee's report presented to the legislature. Even then some unresolved differences between the positions of the committee and the Conseil d'Etat remained.

The report represented the bill as a *juste milieu* between the opposing tendencies of freedom of contract on the one hand and the protection of public morality, third parties, stockholders, commerce, and industry on the other.[42] The bill would encourage economic growth by stimulating the "spirit of association" and by "facilitating associations of large amounts of capital.''[43] The report praised the restrictions of the law of 1856, as having been successful in preventing fraud, and ignored the inhibiting effects of the law on company formation. Attenuations in the restrictions of the law of 1856 were justified by the virtual disappearance of fraudulent practices and the increasing maturity of investors. Even with the changes, the *commandite par actions* was far from possessing the freedom it enjoyed before 1856; although lessened, the restrictions were not removed.

The committee was successful in persuading the Conseil d'Etat to remove the provision that required the directors of a *société anonyme* to possess 5 percent of the enterprise's capital in inalienable shares, to a maximum of 1.5 million francs. This provision had been borrowed from the SARL, and the committee thought it too restrictive. It was replaced by a provision allowing the charter to specify the number of inalienable shares the directors must possess as a guarantee of their administration.

The provisions of the bill were sharply criticized both inside and outside the chamber. Within a few days after the submission of the committee's report, members of the Corps Législatif offered more than fifty amendments. Except for a few minor changes in the bill, the committee systematically rejected all the amendments.[44] Two economists, J. G. Courcelle-Seneuil and Gustave de Molinari, criticized the restrictiveness of the bill in long articles that appeared in the *Journal des économistes*.[45] In the *Journal des chemins de fer*, A. Larrieu refuted the government and the committee on the allegedly beneficial effects of the law of 1856:

> Since 1856 the extraordinary prosperity of the economy has been decimated and a marvelous industrial development stopped short. The movement of capital has been diverted abroad into enterprises that have ruined stockholders and bondholders. Three billions have been lost, while the soil of France contains much unexploited wealth. . . . If the law of 1856 has prevented possible disasters by Mr. *X* or Mr. *Z*, would-be *gérants* of unformed enterprises, it is necessary to compare this with the desolation of many families beginning with the collapse of Spanish railroads and ending with those in Italy, which proves that the French *commandite* is still preferable to the foreign *anonyme*. At least the money does not leave the country.[46]

Joseph Garnier, the editor of the *Journal des économistes*, would have preferred the complete abolition of the provisions of the *Code de*

Commerce and the laws on business organization, which abolition would allow complete liberty to company promoters.[47] But he recognized that this solution had no chance of success: "Unhappily the spirit of preventive regulation has dominated the authors of the bill, the Conseil d'Etat, and the committee," he wrote; "it dominates the legislature and will result in a very imperfect law, which it will be necessary to change before long."[48]

The debates on the bill were long and, except for the intrusion of current political concerns, of a remarkably high order; altogether, thirteen meetings of the legislature were devoted to the bill. The debates afforded the opposition an opportunity to attack the empire. In a free-swinging attack on the government, Ernest Picard, a member of the republican opposition, claimed that with the aid of French commercial legislation a veritable "industrial feudalism" had been created, "whose representatives were as powerful as they were few, and who, with government authorization, possess in incalculable proportions the greatest portion of the patrimony and riches of the country."[49] Picard cited the case of an unnamed financier who, with the assistance of friends in the government to obtain authorization for *anonymes*, had become the director of twelve or fifteen companies with a total capital of 3,740,000,000 francs. The interests of individuals such as these were promoted by their control of the press: "Behind each financial institution, there is a newspaper."[50] Picard argued that they had drained into their own pockets the prosperity of the empire, a prosperity in which workers had not shared, for prices had risen faster than wages.[51]

Another opposition leader, Emile Ollivier, who had been a member of the committee, presented a complete counterproposal to the bill. Ollivier's bill, which was similar to the suggestion of Joseph Garnier, would have abrogated the laws of 1856 and 1863 and Articles 18 through 64 of the *Code de Commerce*. It contained only brief definitions of the partnership, the *commandite*, and the *anonyme*, definitions sanctioned by commercial custom, and, subject to safeguards of adequate publicity, would have allowed a rather complete liberty for promoters and investors to shape their own partnership agreements or company charters.[52] The minister of commerce, de Forcade de la Roquette, while emphasizing the liberalization provided in the government and committee bills, attacked the almost complete liberty provided by Ollivier's bill as being dangerous to public order.[53] Echoing the opinion of Napoleon I's archchancellor, Cambacérès, a member of the Conseil d'Etat who had participated in the elaboration of the *Code de Commerce*—"The public order is involved in all joint-stock companies, because in this type of enterprise public credulity is easily duped by speculators"[54]—the minister pointed out that shares of five francs were possible under Ollivier's bill. The boom of the 1850s had already seen shares selling for as little as one franc: "They were not capital shares, but simply lottery tickets."[55] Ollivier's proposal was doomed to fail, but it nevertheless rallied 44 favorable votes to 154 against.[56]

The government and the committee were successful in defeating both restrictive and liberal amendments that would have affected the bill materially. The few remaining points of difference between the government and the committee versions were settled by compromises. Article 2, allowing shareholders to limit their liability for calls on their shares to half the par value, if so stipulated in the charter, was the subject of considerable debate. An amendment to delete this article, proposed by Jules Simon and others, was narrowly defeated.[57] Simon criticized the article for allowing the capital of the company to be misrepresented. The government's version of the article limited the liability of original shareholders who had sold their shares; the committee's version applied to all shareholders alike. As finally voted, the company charter could limit the liability of all shareholders for future calls to two years from the formation of the enterprise. An amendment prohibiting directors from using the capital of the company to purchase its own shares was rejected,[58] as well as an amendment supported by many businessmen in the chamber that would have introduced a clearer statement regarding the nonliability of company directors.[59] An amendment sponsored by the Baron de Janzé, giving all shareholders a single vote in stockholders' meetings, regardless of the number of shares owned, was rejected. Janzé likened his amendment to political universal suffrage, but the author of the report, Auguste Mathieu, objected that the amendment would open the way for minority control of the company.[60]

The bill passed by an imposing majority of 223 to 7.[61] It received no serious debate in the Senate and became law on 24 July 1867. Ten years later, Charles Lescoeur, noting that the corporate law of England and Belgium was less restrictive, accurately summarized liberal objections to the law: "By attempting to regulate everything to the last details, in determining a priori the conditions by which a company must be constituted and function, without leaving anything for the unexpected, without taking into account the circumstances and varied needs which can arise, in claiming to force all efforts of large companies into two inflexible molds, more benefits are sacrificed than abuses avoided."[62] But the majority view on the law was probably expressed by the Chamber of Commerce of Paris, which in 1882 judged it favorably as "a well-made law which has given excellent results and permitted the creation of large and useful financial and industrial enterprises."[63]

The law opened the way for a large increase in the formation of *sociétés anonymes*; 191 *anonymes* were formed in 1868 and 200 in 1869.[64] In the Paris area alone, 798 *anonymes* were formed between 1868 and 1876,[65] more than for the whole of France during the entire sixty-year period of government authorization. In the single year 1881, 976 *anonymes* were founded in France.[66] With free incorporation of the *anonyme*, there existed little need for the *commandite par actions*, which ceased to be an important form of business organization. Other European countries shortly followed the lead of France and England in providing free incorporation: Spain in 1869; Germany (North German Confederation) in 1870; Belgium in 1873, and Italy in 1883.

The French law of 1867, which was to remain the fundamental charter for corporate enterprise for almost a century, marked an end as well as a beginning. During the sixty years following the promulgation of the *Code de Commerce*, the corporation, at first virtually unknown and regarded with suspicion and hostility, had emerged in large numbers and had acquired a legitimacy in the public eye. A regular external structure and a system of internal governance had been added to the bare framework of the code. Corporate securities had become an important and accepted form of wealth, and a national securities market had come into being, fueled by middle-class investors.[67] A new class of corporate promoters and managers had come into existence. And finally, the emergence of France into a new era of industrial capitalism, with all its benefits and problems, had been achieved.

Appendix:
Sociétés Anonymes, 1808–1867

This appendix is a complete list of all *sociétés anonymes* authorized between 1807 and 1867, except for three types of enterprise that took the *anonyme* form but were not, strictly speaking, *anonymes*, being instead charitable, or nonprofit, or quasi-official enterprises. The three types excluded are savings banks, mutual insurance companies, and the discount banks that were founded as a temporary expedient following the Revolution of 1848.

Each listing contains the name of the company, from which the prefix *compagnie*, *société*, or *société anonyme* usually has been omitted, followed by the official seat of the company as designated in its charter. The date of authorization is given, and then the initial nominal capitalization of the enterprise, if it is known. In some instances where the capitalization is unknown, the number of shares issued by the enterprise is given. Some changes in capitalization have been noted, as well as dissolutions and mergers, but this information is far from being complete. Finally, references to materials in the F^{12} and F^{14} series in the National Archives have been given. Some of these dossiers are fairly comprehensive; others contain only an item or two. BL (*Bulletin des lois*) references are for the companies' charters, to which are annexed, in most cases, lists of initial stockholders.

1. *Enterprise Générale des Messageries*   Paris
   2 July 1808   1,000,000F (2,000,000F, 1809)
   BL., 4th ser., 1809, 2d sem., 287–97, new charter of 1809

2. *Moulin à Scier le Bois*   Gand (Escaut), Belgium
   20 July 1808
   F^{12}6811

3. *Société Conservatrice de l'Ecole Secondaire*   Evaux (Creuse)
   3 Aug. 1808

4. *Fonderies de Romilly*   Paris
   3 Aug. 1808   1,760,000F (dissolved 1865)
   F^{14}8230

5. *Mines de Houille de Methamis*   Carpentras (Vaucluse)
   3 Aug. 1808

6. *Canal d'Aigues Mortes à Beaucaire*   Beaucaire
   27 Oct. 1808

7. *Fonderies de Vaucluse*
   27 Oct. 1808
   $F^{14}8233$

8. *Fonderies de Cuivre et Manufacture de Fer-Blanc de Dilling*   Metz
   2 Feb. 1809

9. *Théâtre de Sedan*   Sedan (Ardennes)
   2 Nov. 1810   70,000F
   $F^{12}6794$

10. *Théâtre de Niort*   Niort (Deux-Sèvres)
    25 May 1811   28,800F
    $F^{12}6794$

11. *Théâtre de Mans*   Mans (Sarthe)
    17 Jan. 1812   18,000F
    $F^{12}6794$

12. *Culture de Pastel et la Fabrication de l'Indigo*   Mulhouse
    9 Mar. 1812   40,000F
    $F^{12}6728$

13. *Fonderies et Forges de Toulouse et d'Angoumer*   Toulouse
    10 Apr. 1812
    BL, 4th ser., 1812, 1st sem., 286–93

14. *Glaces et Verres de Saint-Quirin*
    29 Sept. 1815   2,016,000F
    $F^{12}6739$

15. *Galerie Métallique des Grands Hommes Français*
    14 Aug. 1816

16. *Compagnie Royale d'Assurances Maritimes*   Paris
    11 Sept. 1816   (dissolved 1820 and reauth. as no. 41)

17. *Mines de Houille de Decize*   Paris
    4 Dec. 1816   200,000F
    $F^{14}8232$

18. *Mines de Houille de Montrelais*   Paris
    7 Mar. 1817
    $F^{14}8232$

19. *Assurances de Nantes (Maritimes)*   Nantes
    9 Apr. 1817

20. *Banque de Rouen*   Rouen
    7 May 1817

21. *Assurances Maritimes de Rouen*   Rouen
    13 Aug. 1817

22. *Théâtre Feydeau*   Paris
    27 Aug. 1817   581,000F
    $F^{12}6794$

23. *Société Lithographique de Mulhausen*   Paris and Mulhouse
    12 Nov. 1817

24. *Banque de Nantes*   Nantes
    11 Mar. 1818

25. *Forges du Bas-Rhin*
    15 Apr. 1818

26. *Pont de Bordeaux*   Bordeaux
    22 Apr. 1818   2,300,000F
    $F^{12}6748$; BL, 7th ser., 1818, 1st sem., 289–98

27. *Assurances Générales (Transport Mer et Terre)*   Paris
    22 Apr. 1818   (5,000,000F, 1832)

28. *Compagnie Commerciale d'Assurances (Maritime et Incendie)*   Paris
    22 Apr. 1818   (4,000,000F, 1820)

29. *Port du Havre*   Havre
    15 July 1818   2,000,000F
    BL, 7th ser., 1818, 2d sem., 61–67

30. *Assurances de Bordeaux (Transport Mer et Terre)*   Bordeaux
    22 July 1818   4,800,000F (dissolved 1820 to form nos. 42 and 43)
    BL, 7th ser., 1818, 2d sem., 177–99

31. *Assurances Maritimes contre les Risques de Guerre*   Paris
    19 Aug. 1818   3,000,000F (dissolved 1820)
    BL, 7th ser., 1818, 2d sem., 354–76

32. *Pont de la Dordogne*   Bordeaux
    9 Sept. 1818   2,300,000F
    $F^{12}6747$; BL, 7th ser., 1818, 2d sem., 411–23

33. *Banque de Bordeaux*   Bordeaux
    23 Nov. 1818   3,000,000F
    BL, 7th ser., 1818, 2d sem., 725–60

34. *Assurances contre l'Incendie*   Paris
    14 Feb. 1819   2,000,000F
    BL, 7th ser., 1819, 1st sem., 217–35

35. *Salines et Produits Chemique du Plan d'Aren*   Paris
    7 July 1819   1,200,000F
    F^{12}6728; BL, 7th ser., 1819, 2d sem., 113–24

36. *Compagnie Française du Phénix pour l'Assurance Générale contre l'Incendie*   Paris
    1 Sept. 1819   4,000,000F
    BL, 7th ser., 1819, 2d sem., 324–44

37. *Maison Gérante de la Caisse de Survivance et d'Accroissement*   Paris
    8 Dec. 1819   500,000F
    BL, 7th ser., 1819, 2d sem., 817–78

38. *Assurances Générales sur la Vie des Hommes*   Paris
    22 Dec. 1819   3,000,000F
    BL, 7th ser., 1820, 1st sem., 157–83

39. *Compagnie Royale d'Assurances sur la Vie*   Paris
    11 Feb. 1820   30,000,000F (15,000,000F, 1830)
    BL, 7th ser., 1820, 1st sem., 473–95

40. *Compagnie Royale d'Assurances contre l'Incendie*   Paris
    11 Feb. 1820   10,000,000F
    BL, 7th ser., 1820, 1st sem., 496–510

41. *Compagnie Royale d'Assurances Maritimes*   Paris
    11 Feb. 1820   10,000,000F
    BL, 7th ser., 1820, 1st sem., pp. 513–26

42. *Assurances Maritimes de Bordeaux*   Bordeaux
    28 Apr. 1820   2,100,000F
    BL, 7th ser., 1820, 1st sem., 740–53

43. *Assurances contre l'Incendie*   Bordeaux
    28 Apr. 1820   1,400,000F
    BL, 7th ser., 1820, 1st sem., 937–50

44. *Canal de la Sensée*   Douai (Nord)
    18 May 1820   1,750,000F
    BL, 7th ser., 1820, 1st sem., 950–58

45. *Caisse Hypothécaire*   Paris
    12 July 1820   50,000,000F
    BL, 7th ser., 1820, 2d sem., 271–94

46. *Mines de Fer de Saint-Etienne*   Saint-Etienne
    25 Oct. 1820   1,500,000F
    BL, 7th ser., 1821, 1st sem., 18–47

47. *l'Ardoisière du Moulin-Sainte-Anne*
    22 Feb. 1821   97,000F
    BL, 7th ser., 1821, 1st sem., 467–85

48. *Mines de Bouxwiller*   Bouxwiller (Bas Rhin)
    16 May 1821   1,000,000F
    $F^{14}8233$; BL, 7th ser., 1821, 1st sem., 566–78

49. *Assurances pour la Vie des Chevaux*   Paris
    16 June 1821   100,000F
    BL, 7th ser., 1821, 2d sem., 256–63

50. *Caisse d'Economie et d'Accumulation, de Garantie et d'Amortissement
    des Dettes*   Paris
    18 July 1821   600,000F
    BL, 7th ser., 1821, 2d sem., 130–44

51. *Caisse d'Economie et d'Accumulation, avec Assurance des
    Capitaux*   Paris
    18 July 1821   1,500,000F
    BL, 7th ser., 1821, 2d sem., 145–57

52. *Canal de Monsieur*   Strasbourg (Canal de Rhône au Rhin, 1832)
    19 Oct. 1821   10,000,000F
    $F^{12}6744$; BL, 7th ser., 1822, 1st sem., 67–78

53. *Société des Cinq Ponts*   Bordeaux
    16 Jan. 1822   2,900,000F
    $F^{12}6747$; BL, 7th ser., 1822, 1st sem., 258–75

54. *La Navigation de l'Isle*   Périgueux
    23 Jan. 1822   2,500,000F
    BL, 7th ser., 1822, 1st sem., 289–308

55. *Fabrique d'Aiguilles de Laigle*   Paris
    20 Feb. 1822   300,000F
    BL, 7th ser., 1822, 1st sem., 324–26

56. *l'Amélioration des Procédés de Vinification*   Paris
    27 Feb. 1822   80,000F
    $F^{12}6728$; BL, 7th ser., 1822, 2d sem., 66–71

57. *Transports Accélérés par Eau*   Paris
    27 Feb. 1822   400,000F
    $F^{12}6770$; BL, 7th ser., 1822, 2d sem., 188–99

58. *Compagnie Nantaise d'Assurances Maritimes*   Nantes
    3 Apr. 1822   600,000F
    BL, 7th ser., 1822, 1st sem., 519–28

59. *Mines de Houille de Schoenecken*   Schoenecken (Moselle)
    15 May 1822   300,000F
    $F^{14}8232$; BL, 7th ser., 1822, 1st sem., 642–54

60. *Bateau à Manège de la Dordogne*   Bordeaux
    19 June 1822   150,000F
    $F^{12}6747$; BL, 7th ser., 1822, 2d sem., 126–33

61. *Spectacle de Perpignan*   Perpignan
    3 July 1822   25,000F (dissolved 1825)
    $F^{12}6794$; BL, 7th ser., 1822, 2d sem., 83–91

62. *Compagnie d'Emprunt du Canal de Bourgogne*   Paris
    13 Nov. 1822   25,000,000F
    BL, 7th ser., 1822, 2d sem., 596–605

63. *Fonderies et Forges de la Loire et de l'Isère*   Lyon (Fonderies et Forges
    de la Loire et de l'Ardèche, 1839)
    13 Nov. 1822   1,200,000F (4,000,000F, 1823)
    $F^{14}8234$; BL, 7th ser., 1822, 2d sem., 625–44

64. *Compagnie de l'Emprunt du Canal d'Arles à Bouc*   Paris
    13 Nov. 1822   5,500,000F
    BL, 7th ser., 1822, 2d sem., 665–74

65. *Pont Neuf de Laval*   Laval (Mayenne)
    4 Dec. 1822   200,000F
    $F^{12}6747$; BL, 7th ser., 1822, 2d sem., 729–38

66. *Exploitation de l'Usine Royale d'Eclairage par le Gaz
    Hydrogène*   Paris
    18 Dec. 1822   1,200,000F (1,800,000F, 1824)
    BL, 7th ser., 1822, 2d sem., 740–52

67. *Canal des Ardennes*   Paris
    20 Feb. 1823   8,000,000F
    BL, 7th ser., 1823, I, no. 598 bis, 1–15

68. *Canal du Duc d'Angoulème*   Paris (Canal de la Somme, 1831)
    20 Feb. 1823   6,600,000F
    BL, 7th ser., 1823, I, no. 598 bis, 15–26

69. *Ponts de Montrejeau, Roche-de-Glun, Petit Vey, et Souillac*   Paris
    20 Feb. 1823   1,800,000F
    $F^{12}6747$; BL, 7th ser., 1823, I, no. 598 bis, 26–34

70. *Société pour la Manutension du Plomb*   Paris
    20 Feb. 1823   1,000,000F
    BL, 7th ser., 1823, I, no. 602 bis, 1–12

71. *Compagnie des Quatre Canaux*   Paris
    12 Mar. 1823   68,000,000F
    F¹²6744; BL, 7th ser., 1823, I, no. 602 bis, 12–61

72. *Ferme Expérimentale du Duc de Bordeaux*   Bordeaux
    30 Apr. 1823   150,000F
    F¹²6787; BL, 7th ser., 1823, I, no. 609 bis, 22–38

73. *Eaux de Saint-Maur*   Paris
    16 July 1823   6,000,000F
    BL, 7th ser., 1823, II, no. 621 bis, 1–13

74. *Pont à Aucfer*   Redon (Ille-et-Vilaine)
    30 July 1823   77,000F
    F¹²6747; BL, 7th ser., II, no. 621 bis, 14–24

75. *Compagnie des Apparaux*   Havre
    11 Feb. 1824   140,000F
    BL, 7th ser., 1824, I, no. 667 bis, 1–8

76. *Verreries et Cristalleries de Vonèche-Baccarat*   Baccarat (Meurthe)
    3 Mar. 1824   1,000,000F
    F¹²6741; BL, 7th ser., 1824, I, no. 667 bis, 28–35

77. *Coches de la Haute Seine, Yonne et Canaux*   Paris
    10 Mar. 1824   800,000F
    F¹²6758; BL, 7th ser., 1824, I, no. 661 bis, 30–48

78. *Pont Henri*   Montbrison
    16 June 1824   200,000F
    F¹²6747; BL, 7th ser., I, no. 678 bis, 2–7

79. *Eclairage de la Ville de Bordeaux par le Gaz Hydrogène*   Bordeaux
    23 June 1824   320,000F
    BL, 7th ser., 1824, I, no. 684 bis, 1–15

80. *Chemin de Fer de Saint-Etienne à la Loire*   Saint-Etienne
    21 July 1824   1,000,000F
    BL, 7th ser., 1824, II, no. 691 bis, 1–10

81. *Fonderie de Bordeaux*   Bordeaux
    4 Aug. 1824   1,000,000F
    BL, 7th ser., 1824, II, no. 691 bis, 31–40

82. *Forges d'Audincourt et Dependances*   Audincourt (Doubs)
    11 Aug. 1824   4,500,000F
    F¹⁴8230, 8233; BL, 7th ser., 1824, II, no. 697 bis, 6–16

83. *Bains Publics de Bordeaux*   Bordeaux
    24 Nov. 1824   1,000,000F
    F¹²6793; BL, 8th ser., 1824, no. 15 bis, 1–20

84. *Mines de Plomb de Chabrignac et de la Verrerie du Lardin*   Paris
    6 Jan. 1825   600,000F
    F^{14}8230; BL, 8th ser., 1825, I, no. 24 bis, 1–15

85. *Fabrique d'Acier du Bas-Rhin*   Strasbourg
    22 May 1825   300,000F
    BL, 8th ser., 1825, II, no. 62 bis, 1–14

86. *Fonderies de Vizile*   Paris
    16 Sept. 1825   800,000F
    BL, 8th ser., 1825, II, no. 62 bis, 14–24

87. *Nouveau Quartier Poissonnière*   Paris
    16 Sept. 1825   6,000,000F
    F^{12}6790; BL, 8th ser., 1825, II, no. 62 bis, 21–42

88. *Papeterie Mécanique d'Echarcon*   Paris
    28 Dec. 1825   3,000,000F
    F^{12}6737; BL, 8th ser., 1826, I, no. 73 bis, 15–29

89. *Filature du Lin par Mécanique*   Paris
    28 Dec. 1825   1,000,000F
    F^{12}6732; BL, 8th ser., 1826, I, no. 73 bis, 29–44

90. *Salines et Mines de Sel d'Est*   Paris
    2 Jan. 1826   10,000,000F
    BL, 8th ser., 1826, I, no. 73 bis, 1–14

91. *Hauts-Fourneaux et Forges de Pont Kallecq et des Mines de Houille de Quimper*   Paris
    11 Jan. 1826   1,700,000F (2,800,000F, 1830; dissolved 1830)
    F^{14}8232; BL, 8th ser., 1826, I, no. 84 bis, 1–8

92. *Bains Caroline*   Dieppe (Bains de Mer à Dieppe, 1832)
    15 Mar. 1826   500,000F
    F^{12}6793; BL, 8th ser., 1826, I, no. 84 bis, 9–16

93. *Filature et Tissage Mécanique du Bas Rhin*   Strasbourg
    11 Apr. 1826   1,800,000F (1,400,000, 1833)
    F^{12}6734; BL, 8th ser., 1826, I, no. 94 bis, 20–31

94. *Fabrique de Marcq-en-Bareuil*   Lille
    14 May 1826   4,000,000F
    F^{12}6732; BL, 8th ser., 1826, I, no. 95 bis, 28–44

95. *Verrerie de Thuison*   Thuison
    14 May 1826   400,000F (dissolved 1827)
    F^{12}6741; BL, 8th ser., 1826, I, no. 102 bis, 31–40

96. *Navigation du Rhône par la Vapeur*   Lyon
     7 June 1826   6,000,000F
     F^{12}6771; BL, 8th ser., 1826, I, no. 102 bis, 40–58

97. *Houillères et Fonderies de l'Aveyron*   Paris
     28 June 1826   1,800,000F (3,600,000F, 1829; 7,200,000F, 1832)
     F^{14}8229; BL, 8th ser., 1826, I, no. 104 bis, 1–16

98. *Ponts, Gare et Port de Grenelle*   Paris
     26 July 1826   7,000,000F
     F^{12}6792; BL, 8th ser., 1826, II, no. 109 bis, 8–21

99. *Forges de la Basse-Indre*   Nantes
     26 July 1826   500,000F
     F^{14}8232; BL, 8th ser., 1826, II, no. 109 bis, 21–26

100. *Navigation de l'Oise*   Paris
     2 Aug. 1826   3,000,000F
     BL, 8th ser., 1826, II, no. 109 bis, 26–40

101. *Filature de Poutay*   Strasbourg
     27 Sept. 1826   530,000F
     F^{12}6732; BL, 8th ser., 1826, II, no. 127 bis, 1–11

102. *Société Royale pour l'Emploi des Laines Longues et des Laines Lustrées*   Paris
     22 Nov. 1826   1,250,000F
     F^{12}6733; BL, 8th ser., 1826, II, no. 135 bis, 16 31

103. *Navigation du Drot*   Bordeaux
     21 Feb. 1827   450,000F
     BL, 8th ser., 1827, I, no. 155 bis, 1–17

104. *Chemin de Fer de Saint-Etienne à Lyon*   Paris
     7 Mar. 1827   10,000,000F
     BL, 8th ser., 1827, I, no. 155 bis, 31–56

105. *Bains Marie-Thérèse*   La Rochelle
     17 Apr. 1827   60,000F
     F^{12}6793; BL, 8th ser., 1827, I, no. 172 bis, 1–26

106. *Navigation de la Saône par la Vapeur*   Lyon
     25 Apr. 1827   1,000,000F
     F^{12}6770; BL, 8th ser., 1827, I, no. 174 bis, 1–8

107. *Assurances Maritimes de Bordeaux*   Bordeaux
     2 May 1827   2,000,000F
     BL, 8th ser., 1827, I, no. 166 bis, 1–12

108. *Institution Royale Agronomique*   Paris
     23 May 1827   600,000F
     $F^{12}6787$; BL, 8th ser., 1827, I, no. 183 bis, 1–19

109. *Construction d'une Salle de Spectacle à Laval*   Laval (Mayenne)
     29 May 1827   66,000F (dissolved 1837)
     $F^{12}6794$; BL, 8th ser., 1827, I, no. 172 bis, 26–48

110. *Bateaux à Vapeur en Fer sur la Seine*   Paris
     28 Nov. 1827   420,000F
     $F^{12}6764$; BL, 8th ser., 1827, II, no. 204 bis, 5–19

111. *L'Hotel Saint-Jean pour la Tenu des Foires*   Toulouse
     27 Jan. 1828   165,000F
     $F^{12}6790$; BL, 8th ser., 1828, I, no. 226 bis, 1–12

112. *Mines de Houille de Montrelais*   Paris
     17 Feb. 1828   1,200,000F
     $F^{14}8232$; BL, 8th ser., 1828, I, no. 226 bis, 13–30

113. *Papeteries du Marais et de Sainte-Marie*   Paris
     2 Mar. 1828   1,800,000F
     $F^{12}6735$; BL, 8th ser., 1828, I, no. 226 bis, 30–54

114. *Bulletin Universel pour la Propagation des Connaissances Scientifique et Industrielles*   Paris
     13 Mar. 1828   450,000F
     BL, 8th ser., 1828, I, no. 226 bis, 55–72

115. *Verrerie de Lamotte et Dépendances*   Châlons-sur-Saône
     11 May 1828   800,000F
     $F^{12}6741$; BL, 8th ser., 1828, I, no. 251 bis, 1–20

116. *Mines, Forges, et Fonderies du Creusot et de Charenton*   Charenton
     18 May 1828   10,400,000F (failed 1833)
     $F^{14}8233$; BL, 8th ser., 1828, I, no. 235 bis, 1–20

117. *Marbières de Montey-Notre-Dame*   Charleville
     1 June 1828   240,000F
     BL, 8th ser., 1828, I, no. 238 bis, 23–38

118. *Manufacture de Glaces et Verreries de Commentry*   Paris
     24 June 1828   5,000,000F (dissolved 1829)
     $F^{12}6738$; BL, 8th ser., 1828, II, no. 245 bis, 5–24

119. *Transports par Eau d'Elbeuf à Rouen et Retour*   Elbeuf
     24 June 1828   130,000F
     $F^{12}6771$; BL, 8th ser., 1828, II, no. 254 bis, 1–11

120. *L'Union, Assurances Contre l'Incendie*   Paris
5 Oct. 1828   10,000,000F
BL, 8th ser., 1828, II, no. 261 bis, 1–15

121. *Navigation Accélérée sur la Loire et Affluens, au Moyen de la Vapeur*   Nantes
16 Nov. 1828   600,000F
F¹²6771; BL, 8th ser., 1828, II, no. 278 bis, 5–26

122. *Pont de Thoirette*   Nantua
26 Mar. 1829   80,000F
F¹²6747; BL, 8th ser., 1829, I, no. 294 bis, 1–14

123. *Entreprise Générale des Messageries du Commerce*   Paris
5 Apr. 1829   8,000,000F
F¹²6759; BL, 8th ser., 1829, I, no. 288 bis, 1–8

124. *Chemin de Fer de la Loire*   Paris
26 Apr. 1829   10,000,000F
BL, 8th ser., 1829, I, no. 301 bis, 1–14

125. *Verreries de Saint-Louis*   Bitche (Moselle)
7 June 1829   1,200,000F
F¹²6738; F¹⁴8232; BL, 8th ser., 1829, I, no. 301 bis, 48–57

126. *L'Union, Assurances sur la Vie Humaine*   Paris
21 June 1829   10,000,000F
BL, 8th ser., 1829, I, no. 301 bis, 57–77

127. *Transports des Marchandises sur la Saône par Gondoles à Vapeur*   Lyon
19 July 1829   1,000,000F
F¹²6771; BL, 8th ser., 1829, II, no. 314 bis, 10–18

128. *Eclairage dans la Ville de Nantes, au Moyen du Gaz*   Nantes
26 July 1829   140,000F
BL, 8th ser., 1829, II, no. 316 bis, 1–16

129. *Trois Ponts sur la Seine*   Paris
2 Aug. 1829   1,700,000
F¹²6749; BL, 8th ser., 1829, II, no. 316 bis, 19–23

130. *Verrerie de Bruay*   Valenciennes
2 Aug. 1829   300,000F
F¹²6738; BL, 8th ser., 1829, II, no. 316 bis, 24–32

131. *Forges et Fonderies d'Imphy*   Paris
19 Aug. 1829   4,000,000F
F¹⁴8232; BL, 8th ser., 1829, II, no. 314 bis, 18–32

132. *Forges de la Joie*   Hennebont (Morbihan)
16 Sept. 1829   900,000F
F^{14}8232; BL, 8th ser., 1829, II, no. 320 bis, 4–14

133. *Pont de Drac*   Grenoble
31 Oct. 1829   375,000F
F^{12}6749; BL, 8th ser., 1829, II, no. 331 bis, 1–6

134. *Compagnie du Soleil*   Paris
16 Dec. 1829   6,000,000F
BL, 8th ser., 1829, II, no. 335 bis, 10–24

135. *Manufacture Royale des Glaces de Saint Gobain*   Paris
17 Feb. 1830   8,064,000F
F^{12}6740; BL, 8th ser., 1830, I, no. 349 bis, 1–16

136. *Pont de Langon*   Bordeaux
7 Apr. 1830   600,000F
F^{12}6749; BL, 8th ser., 1830, I, no. 362 bis, 1–10

137. *Bateaux à Vapeur pour la Navigation du Rhône*   Lyon
9 June 1830   1,600,000F
F^{12}6771; BL, 8th ser., 1830, I, no. 367 bis, 6–13

138. *Fabrique de Chapeaux de Paille d'Alençon*   Alençon (Orne)
16 June 1830   100,000F
F^{12}6728; BL, 8th ser., 1830, I, no. 364 bis, 1–15

139. *Exploitation des Marbres des Vosges*   Epinal
12 Aug. 1830   300,000F
BL, 9th ser., 1830, I, no. 7 bis, 1–16

140. *L'Achèvement des Travaux du Port du Havre*   Havre
26 Aug. 1830   2,800,000F
BL, 9th ser., 1830, I, no. 27 bis, 1–6

141. *Berlines de Fontainebleau*   Fontainebleau
29 Sept. 1830   60,044F
F^{12}6759; BL, 9th ser., 1830, I, no. 27 bis, 7–10

142. *Fonderies et Forges d'Alais*   Paris
20 Oct. 1830   6,000,000
F^{14}8230; BL, 9th ser., 1830, I, no. 27 bis, 11–23

143. *Banque de Secours*   Limoges
5 Jan. 1831   200,000F
BL, 9th ser., 1831, II, no. 57 bis, 1–5

144. *Caisse d'Escompte de la Ville de Reims*   Reims
22 Jan. 1831   600,000F
BL, 9th ser., 1831, II, no. 80 bis, 1–7

145. *Navigation de la Dronne*   Bordeaux
   15 Feb. 1831   315,000F
   BL, 9th ser., 1831, II, no. 57 bis, 6–15

146. *Galerie de Bordeaux*   Bordeaux
   26 Mar. 1831   2,500,000F
   F^{12}6788; BL, 9th ser., 1831, II, no. 84 bis, 1–15

147. *Navigation de la Charente*   Saintes (Charente-Inférieure)
   2 Apr. 1831   45,000F
   BL, 9th ser., 1831, II, no. 89 bis, 1–7

148. *Canal de Roanne à Digoin*   Roanne
   2 June 1831   6,500,000F
   F^{12}6745; BL, 9th ser., 1831, II, no. 80 bis, 9–20

149. *Exploitation des Papeteries Grosset*   Castres (Tarn)
   21 June 1831   375,000F
   F^{12}6736; BL, 9th ser., 1831, II, no. 89 bis, 8–16

150. *Eaux Thermales de Saint-Honoré*   Nevers (Nièvre)
   1 Aug. 1831   120,000F
   F^{12}6742; BL, 9th ser., 1831, III, 358–62

151. *Pont de l'Isle*   Bordeaux
   3 Sept. 1831   240,000F
   F^{12}6749; BL, 9th ser., 1831, III, 637–46

152. *L'Abattoir de Bordeaux*   Bordeaux
   11 Oct. 1831   970,000F
   F^{12}6788; BL, 9th ser., 1831, III, 710–21

153. *Ardoisières de Rimogne et de Saint-Louis-sur-Meuse*   Rimogne
   14 Oct. 1831   1,080,000F
   F^{14}8229; BL, 9th ser., 1831, III, 544–52

154. *Assurances Maritimes*   Havre
   14 Mar. 1832   1,086,000F
   BL, 9th ser., 1832, PS, I, 193–202

155. *Société Parisienne du Ciment Hydraulique de Pouilly*   Paris
   9 May 1832   150,000F
   F^{12}6728; BL, 9th ser., 1832, PS, I, 512–21

156. *Pont de Clairac*   Bordeaux
   11 June 1832   275,000F
   F^{12}6749; BL, 9th ser., 1832, PS, I, 675–82

157. *Ponts de l'Isle Bouchard*   l'Isle Bouchard (Indre et Loire)
   6 July 1832   250,000F
   F^{12}6756; BL, 9th ser., 1832, PS, II, 108–15

158. *Courrier de Lyon*   Lyon
    5 Aug. 1832   75,000F
    BL, 9th ser., 1832, PS, II, 233–36

159. *L'Assurances Maritimes de Nantes*   Nantes
    31 Aug. 1832   500,000F
    BL, 9th ser., 1832, PS, II, 261–67

160. *Forêt du Teich*   Bordeaux
    14 Sept. 1832   600,000F
    F^{12}6787; BL, 9th ser., 1832, PS, II, 302–14

161. *Ponts d'Asnières et d'Argenteuil*   Paris
    31 Oct. 1832   1,190,000F
    F^{12}6749; BL, 9th ser., 1832, PS, II, 486–94

162. *Canal d'Aire à la Bassée*   Paris
    13 Dec. 1832   600 shares
    F^{12}6745; BL, 9th ser., 1832, PS, II, 656–60

163. *L'Alliance, Assurances Maritimes*   Havre
    5 Apr. 1833   600,000F
    BL, 9th ser., 1833, PS, III, 320–29

164. *Paquebots à Vapeur de la Gironde*   Bordeaux
    12 June 1833   930,000F
    F^{12}6771; BL, 9th ser., 1833, PS, IV, 3–13

165. *Bazar Bordelais*   Bordeaux
    25 Sept. 1833   800,000F
    F^{12}6788; BL, 9th ser., 1833, PS, IV, 569–80

166. *Fabrique de Sucre Indigène à Beaugency*   Beaugency (Loiret)
    8 Jan. 1834   100,000F (dissolved 1835)
    F^{12}6731; BL, 9th ser., 1834, PS, V, 34–40

167. *Compagnie Française, Assurances Maritimes*   Havre
    21 Feb. 1834   500,000F
    BL, 9th ser., 1834, PS, V, 245–57

168. *Compagnie Commerciales, Assurances Maritimes*   Havre
    21 Feb. 1834   600,000F
    BL, 9th ser., 1834, PS, V, 257–68

169. *Pont de Sully-sur-Loire*   Sully-sur-Loire (Loiret)
    8 May 1834   330,000F
    F^{12}6748; BL, 9th ser., 1834, PS, V, 419–37

170. *Assurances Maritimes de Bordeaux*   Bordeaux
    13 May 1834   1,500,000F
    BL, 9th ser., 1834, PS, V, 533–42

171. *Paquebots à Vapeur entre le Havre et Hambourg*   Havre
     18 May 1834   750,000F
     F^{12}6771; BL, 9th ser., 1834, PS, V, 543–56

172. *Bateaux à Vapeur des Rives de la Garonne*   Bordeaux
     18 June 1834   350,000F
     F^{12}6771; BL, 9th ser., 1834, PS, VI, 65–77

173. *Quatre Ponts sur la Garonne*   Bordeaux
     5 July 1834   1,280,000F
     F^{12}6748; BL, 9th ser., 1834, PS, VI, 51–82

174. *Usines de Pont Saint-Ours*   Nevers
     31 July 1834   781,000F
     F^{14}8232; BL, 9th ser., 1834, PS, VI, 174–81

175. *Assurances Maritimes du Globe*   Rouen
     10 Sept. 1834   700,000F
     BL, 9th ser., 1834, PS, VI, 318–30

176. *Canal de Jonction de la Sambre à l'Oise*   Paris
     20 Oct. 1834   11,550,000F
     F^{12}6745; BL, 9th scr., 1834, PS, VI, 654–64

177. *Pont de Muret*   Toulouse
     9 Nov. 1834   155,000F
     F^{12}6748; BL, 9th ser., 1834, PS, VI, 740–50

178. *Assurances contre la Grêle pour le Dépt. du Nord*   Lille
     21 Jan. 1835   1,000,000F
     BL, 9th ser., 1835, PS, VII, 74–85

179. *Compagnie des Trois Canaux*   Paris
     3 Mar. 1835   17,600,000F (merger of nos. 67, 68, and 100)
     F^{12}6746; BL, 9th ser., 1835, PS, VII, 669–716

180. *Pont de Montpont*   Bordeaux
     19 Mar. 1835   130,000F
     F^{12}6748; BL, 9th ser., 1835, PS, VII, 638–48

181. *Pont de Saint-Jean de Blagnac*   Bordeaux
     30 May 1835   240,000F
     F^{12}6756; BL, 9th ser., 1835, PS, VII, 945–52

182. *Banque de Lyon*   Lyon
     29 June 1835   2,000,000F
     BL, 9th ser., 1835, 2d pt., XI, 63–71

183. *Pont de Villemur*   Toulouse
     30 June 1835   170,000F
     F^{12}6748; BL, 9th ser., 1835, PS, VII, 108–17

184. *Paquebots à Vapeur sur la Seine*   Havre
     15 July 1835   300,000F
     F^{12}6764; BL, 9th ser., 1835, PS, VIII, 177–205

185. *Papeterie Mécanique de Montfourat*   Bordeaux
     13 Sept. 1835   800,000F
     F^{12}6736; BL, 9th ser., 1835, PS, VIII, 454–65

186. *Pont de Condrieu*   Condrieu (Rhône)
     19 Sept. 1835   214,500F
     F^{12}6748; BL, 9th ser., 1835, PS, VIII, 498–504

187. *Banque de Marseille*   Marseille
     27 Sept. 1835   4,000,000F
     BL, 9th ser., 1835, 2d pt., XI, 316–27

188. *Chemin de Fer de Paris à Saint-Germain*   Paris
     4 Nov. 1835   6,000,000F
     BL, 9th ser., 1835, PS, VIII, 845–54

189. *Trois Ponts sur le Lot*   Bordeaux
     11 Nov. 1835   500,000F
     F^{12}6750; BL, 9th ser., 1835, PS, VIII, 861–73

190. *Pont de Cubzac sur la Dordogne*   Bordeaux
     17 Dec. 1835   2,900,000F
     F^{12}6750; BL, 9th ser., 1835, PS, VIII, 954–80

191. *La Sécurité, Assurances Maritimes*   Paris
     10 Apr. 1836   1,500,000F
     BL, 9th ser., 1836, PS, IX, 313–27

192. *L'Indemnité, Assurances Maritimes*   Paris
     27 May 1836   1,000,000F
     BL, 9th ser., 1836, PS, IX, 507–14

193. *Assurances Maritimes de la Paix*   Havre
     27 May 1836   1,000,000F
     BL, 9th ser., 1836, PS, IX, 517–31

194. *L'Union des Ports, Assurances Maritimes*   Paris
     27 May 1836   5,000,000F
     BL, 9th ser., 1836, PS, IX, 565–80

195. *Assurances Maritimes Havraise et Parisienne*   Havre
     3 June 1836   1,200,000F
     BL, 9th ser., 1836, PS, IX, 597–620

196. *Banque de Lille*   Lille
     29 June 1836   2,000,000F
     BL, 9th ser., 1836, 2d pt., XIII, 229–37

197. *Paquebots à Vapeur entre le Havre et la Hollande*   Havre
29 June 1836   400,000F
F¹²6764; BL, 9th ser., 1836, PS, IX, 810–17

198. *Pont de Valence*   Lyon
19 July 1836   569,567F
F¹²6750; BL, 9th ser., 1836, PS, X, 49–58

199. *Assurance Elbeuvienne (Incendie)*   Elbeuf
6 Aug. 1836   2,000,000F
BL, 9th ser., 1836, PS, X, 132–43

200. *Fabrication du Sucre de Betterave*   Melun
7 Aug. 1836   200,000F (dissolved 1839)
F¹²6731; BL, 9th ser., 1836, PS, X, 145–52

201. *Trois Ponts sur Charente, l'Isle, et Dordogne*   Bordeaux
25 Aug. 1836   730,000F
F¹²6750; BL, 9th ser., 1836, PS, X, 257–71

202. *Pont de Beauregard*   Messimy (Ain)
25 Aug. 1836
F¹²6750; BL, 9th ser., 1836, PS, X, 294–301

203. *Eclairage par le Gaz Hydrogène pour le Ville de Lyon*   Lyon
24 Oct. 1836   754,000F
BL, 9th ser., 1836, PS, X, 849–59

204. *Chemin de Fer de Montbrison à Montrond*   Montbrison (Loire)
31 Jan. 1837   250,000F
BL, 9th ser., 1837, PS, XI, 81–94

205. *Berlines de Château-Thierry*   Château-Thierry
8 Feb. 1837   60,000F
F¹²6759; BL, 9th ser., 1837, PS, XI, 94–106

206. *La France, Assurances contre l'Incendie*   Paris
27 Feb. 1837   10,000,000F
BL, 9th ser., 1837, PS, XI, 225–38

207. *Lloyd Français, Assurances Maritimes*   Paris
16 Mar. 1837   6,000,000F
BL, 9th ser., 1837, PS, XI, 273–83

208. *Pont de Meung*   Orléans
21 Mar. 1837   320,000F
F¹²6752; BL, 9th ser., 1837, PS, XI, 289–95

209. *L'Amélioration et l'Education des Chevaux de Luxe de Race Française*   Paris
29 Mar. 1837   400,000F
BL, 9th ser., 1837, PS, XI, 321–31

210. *L'Ocean, Assurances Maritimes*   Paris
     29 Mar. 1837   1,000,000F
     BL, 9th ser., 1837, PS, XI, 417–28

211. *Raffinerie Alsacienne*   Strasbourg
     28 Apr. 1837   300,000F
     F^{12}6731; BL, 9th ser., 1837, PS, XI, 600–607

212. *Compagnie Havraise pour Bals et Concerts*   Havre
     8 May 1837   154,000F
     F^{12}6794; BL, 9th ser., 1837, PS, XI, 593–99

213. *Pont du Carrousel*   Paris
     20 May 1837
     F^{12}6751; BL, 9th ser., 1837, PS, XI, 609–16

214. *Paquebots à Vapeur entre Havre et Londres*   Havre
     21 May 1837   600,000F
     F^{12}6764; BL, 9th ser., 1837, PS, XI, 616–26

215. *Pont de Saint-Thibault*   Saint-Thibault (Cher)
     27 May 1837   446,000F
     F^{12}6751; BL, 9th ser., 1837, PS, XI, 633–49

216. *Paquebots à Vapeur entre le Havre et le Portugal*   Havre
     9 June 1837   502,000F
     F^{12}6764; BL, 9th ser., 1837, PS, XI, 649–59

217. *Paquebots à Vapeur entre le Havre et Caen*   Havre
     25 June 1837   250,000F
     F^{12}6774; BL, 9th ser., 1837, PS, XI, 672–82

218. *Pont d'Avignon sur la Durance*   Lyon
     2 July 1837
     F^{12}6751; BL, 9th ser., 1837, PS, XII, 402–10

219. *Paquebots à Vapeur de Bordeaux au Havre*   Bordeaux
     6 July 1837   350,000F
     F^{12}6765; BL, 9th ser., 1837, PS, XII, 471–77

220. *Forges de Framont*   Framont (Vosges)
     7 July 1837   1,600,000F
     F^{14}8233; BL, 9th ser., 1837, PS, XII, 454–63

221. *Banque de Havre*   Havre
     25 Aug. 1837   4,000,000F
     BL, 9th ser., 1837, 2d pt., XV, 510–16

222. *Chemin de Fer de Paris, Meudon, Sèvres, et Versailles (Rive Gauche)*   Paris
     25 Aug. 1837   8,000,000F
     BL, 9th ser., 1837, PS, XII, 613–24

223. *Pont de Beaucaire*   Bordeaux
    31 Aug. 1837
    F¹²6751; BL, 9th ser., 1837, PS, XII, 625–40

224. *Compagnie Rouennaise pour le Remorquage des Naivres*   Rouen
    7 Sept. 1837   325,000F
    F¹²6765; BL, 9th ser., 1837, PS, XII, 661–67

225. *Chambre d'Assurances Maritimes*   Paris
    16 Sept. 1837   3,000,000F
    BL, 9th ser., 1837, PS, XII, 789–98

226. *Forges et Fonderies d'Axat*   Axat (Aude)
    19 Sept. 1837   420,000F
    F¹⁴8229; BL, 9th ser., 1837, PS, XII, 1043–49

227. *Berlines de Caen à Paris*   Caen
    13 Oct. 1837   100,000F
    F¹²6758; BL, 9th ser., 1837, PS, XII, 824–31

228. *Sucrerie de Bergerac*   Bergerac
    12 Nov. 1837   100,000F
    F¹²6731; BL, 9th ser., 1837, PS, XII, 858–62

229. *Pont de Fer de Rouen*   Rouen
    12 Nov. 1837
    F¹²6751; BL, 9th ser., 1837, PS, XII, 933–41

230. *Chemin de Fer de Paris à Saint Cloud et Versailles*   (Rive Droit)
    21 Nov. 1837   11,000,000F
    BL, 9th ser., 1837, PS, XII, 917–25

231. *Compagnie Neustrienne pour les Paquebots entre Havre et Honfleur*   Havre
    28 Nov. 1837   300,000F (400,000F, 1839)
    F¹²6765; BL, 9th ser., 1837, PS, XII, 965–73

232. *Chemin de Fer de Bordeaux à la Teste*   Bordeaux
    25 Feb. 1838   5,000,000F
    BL, 9th ser., 1838, PS, XIII, 513–23

233. *L'Urbaine, Assurances contre l'Incendie*   Paris
    4 Mar. 1838   5,000,000F
    BL, 9th ser., 1838, PS, XIII, 481–94

234. *La Sécurité, Assurances contre l'Incendie*   Paris
    15 Mar. 1838   5,000,000F
    BL, 9th ser., 1838, PS, XIII, 449–61

235. *Mélusine, Assurances Maritimes et Prêtes à la Grosse*   Paris
    15 Mar. 1838   2,000,000F
    BL, 9th ser., 1838, PS, XIII, 523–37

236. *Compagnie Elbeuvienne d'Eclairage par le Gaz*   Elbeuf
     25 Apr. 1838   225,000F (275,000F, 1840)
     BL, 9th ser., 1838, PS, XIII, 577–87

237. *Moulin à Vapeur de la Rochelle*   La Rochelle
     1 May 1838   240,000F
     F^{12}6728; BL, 9th ser., 1838, PS, XIII, 660–67

238. *Chemin de Fer de Strasbourg à Bâle*   Paris
     14 May 1838   42,000,000F
     BL, 9th ser., 1838, PS, XIII, 778–86

239. *L'Indemnité, Assurances contre l'Incendie*   Paris
     20 May 1838   3,000,000F
     BL, 9th ser., 1838, PS, XIII, 717–33

240. *Pont de Conflans-Ste-Honorine*   Paris
     7 June 1838
     F^{12}6751; BL, 9th ser., 1838, PS, XIII, 897–904

241. *Fabrication de fils et tissus de Lin et de Chanvre*   Paris (Filature de lin
     d'Amiens, 1851)
     11 June 1838   4,000,000F
     F^{12}6732; BL, 9th ser., 1838, PS, XIV, 553–75

242. *Banque de Toulouse*   Toulouse
     11 June 1838   1,200,000F
     BL, 9th ser., 1838, 2d pt., XVI, 467–79

243. *Chemin de Fer de Montpellier à Cette*   Paris
     4 July 1838   3,000,000F
     BL, 9th ser., 1838, PS, XIV, 17–26

244. *Fabrique de Sucre de Bresles*   Bresles (Oise)
     20 July.1838   150,000F
     F^{12}6731; BL, 9th ser., 1838, PS, XIV, 49–55

245. *Chemin de Fer de Paris à la Mer par Rouen, Le Havre et Dieppe*   Paris
     13 Aug. 1838   90,000,000F
     BL, 9th ser., 1838, PS, XIV, 326–37

246. *Chemin de Fer de Paris à Orleans*   Paris
     13 Aug. 1838   40,000,000F
     BL, 9th ser., 1838, PS, XIV, 338–50

247. *Canal de Givors*   Lyon
     13 Aug. 1838   6,000,000F
     F^{12}6745; BL, 9th ser., 1838, PS, XIV, 356–80

248. *Pont du Mas d'Agenais*   Bordeaux
   16 Sept. 1838   310,000F
   $F^{12}6751$; BL, 9th ser., 1838, PS, XIV, 643–54

249. *Ponts de Saint-Gervais et de la Route de Tullins*   Bordeaux
   16 Sept. 1838   475,000F
   $F^{12}6752$; BL, 9th ser., 1838, PS, XIV, 633–43

250. *Ponts de Vicq et d'Availles*   Bordeaux
   16 Sept. 1838   276,996F
   $F^{12}6752$; BL, 9th ser., 1838, PS, XIV, 665–77

251. *Pont de Fleurville*   Lyon
   16 Sept. 1838
   $F^{12}6751$; BL, 9th ser., 1838, PS, XIV, 697–702

252. *l'Avenir, Assurances Maritimes*   Paris
   16 Sept. 1838   1,000,000F
   BL, 9th ser., 1838, PS, XIV, 734–48

253. *La Providence, Assurances contre l'Incendie*   Paris
   18 Sept. 1838   5,000,000F
   BL, 9th ser., 1838, PS, XIV, 749–60

254. *La Gironde, Assurances Maritimes*   Bordeaux
   21 Sept. 1838   1,200,000F
   BL, 9th ser., 1838, PS, XIV, 761–78

255. *Paquebots à Vapeur entre Dunkerque et Hambourg*   Dunkerque
   21 Sept. 1838   550,000F (dissolved 1840)
   $F^{12}6765$; BL, 9th ser., 1838, PS, XIV, 779–89

256. *Banque de Orléans*   Orléans
   8 Nov. 1838   1,000,000F
   BL, 9th ser., 1838, 2d pt., XVII, 558–80

257. *Compagnie Riveraine d'Assurances sur la Saône et le Rhône*   Gray
   (Haute Saône)
   19 Dec. 1838   1,000,000F
   BL, 9th ser., 1838, PS, XIV, 960–78

258. *Sucrerie de Meinau*   Meinau (Bas Rhin)
   28 Apr. 1839   750,000F
   $F^{12}6731$; BL, 9th ser., 1839, PS, XV, 617 26

259. *Compagnie Lyonnaise d'Assurances contre l'Incendie*   Lyon
   16 June 1839   4,000,000F
   BL, 9th ser., 1839, PS, XV, 705–15

260. *Filature du Chanvre à Alençon*   Alençon
    4 Aug. 1839   300,000F (500,000F, 1840; dissolved 1844)
    F^{12}6733; BL, 9th ser., 1839, PS, XVI, 386–95

261. *Papeterie d'Essonne*   Paris
    4 Aug. 1839   1,600,000F (1,200,000F, 1842; 2,000,000F, 1855;
    2,400,000F, 1859; failed 1866)
    F^{12}6736; BL, 9th ser., 1839, PS, XVI, 393–401

262. *Société de Bienfaisance pour l'Emploi des Bouts de Laine et Déchets de
    Fabrique*   Elbeuf
    27 Aug. 1839   50,000F
    F^{12}6733; BL, 9th ser., 1839, PS, XVI, 436–46

263. *Diligences du Commerce de l'Ardèche et de la Drôme*   Privas
    (Ardèche)
    13 Oct. 1839   150,000F
    F^{12}6758; BL, 9th ser., 1839, PS, XVI, 577–84

264. *Constructions Mécanique de Strasbourg*   Strasbourg (Usines de
    Graffenstaden, 1846)
    7 Nov. 1839   550,000F
    F^{12}6730; BL, 9th ser., 1839, PS, XVI, 625–36

265. *Compagnie des Pyrénées, Assurances à Primes contre Mortalité des
    Bestiaux*   Tarbes (Hautes-Pyrénées)
    13 Nov. 1839   500,000F
    BL, 9th ser., 1839, PS, XVI, 673–87

266. *Le Nord, Assurances contre l'Incendie*   Lille
    24 Feb. 1840   500,000F
    BL, 9th ser., 1840, PS, XVII, 393–403

267. *Mines de Terre-Noire et des Hauts Fourneaux de Janon*   Paris
    3 May 1840   4,000,000F
    F^{14}8231; BL, 9th ser., 1840, PS, XVII, 521–34

268. *Chemin de Fer de Paris à Rouen*   Paris
    28 June 1840   36,000,000F
    BL, 9th ser., 1840, PS, XVIII, 65–75

269. *Eclairage par le Gaz des Villes de Marseille, Toulon et Nîmes*   Lyon
    5 July 1840
    BL, 9th ser., 1840, PS, XVIII, 6–14

270. *Forges et Fonderies de Montataire*   Paris
    5 July 1840   ca. 4,000,000F
    F^{14}8232; BL, 9th ser., 1840, PS, XVIII, 17–28

271. *Canalisation du Drot*   Bordeaux
   29 July 1840   1,500,000F
   BL, 9th ser., 1840, PS, XVIII, 200–12

272. *Forges de Champagney et de Ronchamp*   Champagny (Haute Saône)
   31 July 1840
   F¹⁴8233; BL, 9th ser., 1840, PS, XVIII, 225–36

273. *Papeterie de Plainfaing*   Plainfaing (Vosges)
   14 Sept. 1840   700,000F
   F¹²6736; BL, 9th ser., 1840, PS, XVIII, 291–302

274. *L'Europe, Paquebot à Vapeur entre Le Havre et la Russie*   Havre
   20 Nov. 1840   1,600,000F
   F¹²6765; BL, 9th ser., 1840, PS, XVIII, 545–56

275. *Mines de Villars*   Lyon
   29 Nov. 1840   2,500 shares
   F¹⁴8231; BL, 9th ser., 1840, PS, XVIII, 614–26

276. *Pont Suspendu sur la Charente à Tonnay*   Bordeaux
   17 Mar. 1841   575,000F
   F¹²6752; BL, 9th ser., 1841, PS, XIX, 250–59

277. *Société de Saint-Barbe (a school)*   Paris
   17 Mar. 1841   520,000F (600,000F, 1843; 1,000,000F, 1845)
   BL, 9th ser., 1841, PS, XIX, 260–83

278. *Filature de Danlot*   Poitiers
   12 Apr. 1841   340,000F
   F¹²6733; BL, 9th ser., 1841, PS, XIX, 436–48

279. *L'Amorique, Assurances Maritimes*   Paris
   28 Apr. 1841   1,000,000F
   BL, 9th ser., 1841, PS, XIX, 481–93

280. *Manufacture de Glaces et de Verres de Saint-Quirin, Cirey, et Monthermé*   Paris
   19 May 1841   10,000,000F (reauth. of no. 14)
   F¹²6739; BL, 9th ser., 1841, PS, XIX, 574–85

281. *Compagnie Reconstitué de Chemin de Fer de la Loire d'Andrezieux à Roanne*   Paris
   19 May 1841   12,000 shares (successor to no. 124)
   BL, 9th ser., 1841, PS, XIX, 621–43

282. *Pont de Peyrehorade*   Dax (Landes)
   25 May 1841   248 shares
   F¹²6752; BL, 9th ser., 1841, PS, XIX, 643–50

283. *Papeterie du Souche*   Paris
    25 May 1841   800,000F (1,100,000F, 1856)
    F¹²6737; BL, 9th ser., 1841, PS, XIX, 650–62

284. *Pont Suspendu de Bas*   Bas (Haute Loire)
    16 June 1841
    F¹²6752; BL, 9th ser., 1841, PS, XIX, 733–39

285. *Moulin de Bessières*   Bessières (Haute Garonne)
    16 June 1841   112,500F
    F¹²6728; BL, 9th ser., 1841, PS, XIX, 766–77

286. *Entrepôt Général des Sels*   Frécamp (Seine Inférieure)
    9 July 1841   80,000F
    BL, 9th ser., 1841, PS, XX, 69–78

287. *L'Equitable, Assurance contre l'Incendie*   Rouen
    25 July 1841   3,000,000F
    BL, 9th ser., 1841, PS, XX, 85–116

288. *Compagnie Agricole de Lambus*   Lambus (Pas de Calais)
    1 Aug. 1841   100,000F
    F¹²6787; BL, 9th ser., 1841, PS, XX, 368–75

289. *Papeterie d'Echarcon*   Paris
    23 Aug. 1841   800,000F (reconstitution of no. 88)
    BL, 9th ser., 1841, PS, XX, 400–16

290. *Assurances Maritimes de Bordeaux*   Bordeaux
    7 Nov. 1841   1,200,000F
    BL, 9th ser., 1841, PS, XX, 856–64

291. *Le Palladium, Assurances à Primes contre l'Incendie*   Paris
    7 Nov. 1841   2,000,000F (5,000,000F, 1847)
    BL, 9th ser., 1841, PS, XX, 892–910

292. *Pont de Champ*   Grenoble
    11 Jan. 1842   89 shares
    F¹²6752; BL, 9th ser., 1842, PS, XXI, 56–62

293. *Paquebots à Vapeur entre Dunkerque et Hambourg*   Dunkerque
    25 Jan. 1842   450,000F
    F¹²6766; BL, 9th ser., 1842, PS, XXI, 148–58

294. *L'Union, Messageries d'Alençon à Caen*   Argentan (Orne)
    13 Feb. 1842   50,000F
    F¹²6758; BL, 9th ser., 1842, PS, XXI, 221–39

295. *La Concorde, Compagnie pour la Gestion de Sociétés Mutuelles
    d'Assurances sur la Vie*   Paris

12 Mar. 1842   1,000,000F
BL, 9th ser., 1842, PS, XXI, 413–43

296. *Le Sauveur, Assurances à Primes contre l'Incendie*   Paris
25 Mar. 1842   3,000,000F
BL, 9th ser., 1842, PS, XXI, 443–56

297. *Le Dragon, Assurances à Primes contre l'Incendie*   Paris
8 May 1842   3,000,000F
BL, 9th ser., 1842, PS, XXI, 519–35

298. *Le Dragon, Assurances Maritimes*   Paris
8 May 1842   1,400,000F
BL, 9th ser., 1842, PS, XXI, 541–53

299. *Pont de Neublans*   Dôle (Jura)
14 May 1842
$F^{12}6754$; BL, 9th ser., 1842, PS, XXI, 556–62

300. *Mines de Decize*   Metz
17 May 1842   400 shares
$F^{14}8232$; BL, 9th ser., 1842, PS, XXI, 655–67

301. *Mines de Houille d'Azincourt*   Aniche (Nord)
31 July 1842   1,500 shares
$F^{14}8232$; BL, 9th ser., 1842, PS, XXII, 73–90

302. *Eclairage de la Ville de Tours par le Gaz*   Tours
31 July 1842   300,000F
BL, 9th ser., 1842, PS, XXII, 90–102

303. *Journal le* Courrier de Lyon   Lyon
6 Aug. 1842   32,000F
BL, 9th ser., 1842, PS, XXII, 121–24

304. *Eclairage par le Gaz de Saint Chamond*   Saint Chamond
20 Aug. 1842   150 shares
BL, 9th ser., 1842, PS, XXII, 245–53

305. *Théâtre à Saint Amand*   Saint Amand (Cher)
13 Oct. 1842   38,000F
$F^{12}6794$; BL, 9th ser., 1842, PS, XXII, 377–85

306. *Pont de Pouilly*   Lyon
12 Nov. 1842   320 shares
$F^{12}6753$; BL, 9th ser., 1842, PS, XXII, 413–21

307. *Moulin à Vapeur de Perrache*   Lyon
8 Dec. 1842   240 shares
$F^{12}6728$; BL, 9th ser., 1842, PS, XXII, 529–43

308. *Chemin de Fer de Rouen au Havre*   Paris
29 Jan. 1843   20,000,000F
BL, 9th ser., 1843, PS, XXIII, 161–82

309. *Société de Culture de la Dombe*   Montluel (Ain)
31 Jan. 1843   830,000F
F^{12}6787; BL, 9th ser., 1843, PS, XXIII, 193–200

310. *Compagnie Bordelaise d'Assurances Maritimes*   Bordeaux
22 Feb. 1843   1,000,000F
BL, 9th ser., 1843, PS, XXIII, 353–68

311. *La Fortune, Assurances Maritimes*   Le Havre
17 Apr. 1843   600,000F
BL, 9th ser., 1843, PS, XXIII, 645–55

312. *La France, Assurances à Primes sur la Vie*   Paris
18 May 1843   3,000,000F
BL, 9th ser., 1843, PS, XXIII, 759–79

313. *L'Aigle, Assurances contre l'Incendie*   Paris
18 May 1843   2,000,000F
BL, 9th ser., 1843, PS, XXIII, 865–75

314. *La Réparatrice, Assurances à Primes contre l'Incendie*   Paris
23 May 1843   2,500,000F
BL, 9th ser., 1843, PS, XXIII, 875–95

315. *Comptoir Parisien d'Assurances Maritimes*   Paris
15 July 1843   500,000F
BL, 9th ser., 1843, PS, XXIV, 49–58

316. *Chemin de Fer de Marseille à Avignon*   Marseille
29 Aug. 1843   20,000,000F
BL, 9th ser., 1843, PS, XXIV, 169–97

317. *L'Union, Bateaux à Vapeur entre Rouen et la Bouille*   Rouen
14 Sept. 1843   240,000F
F^{12}6766; BL, 9th ser., 1843, PS, XXIV, 388–95

318. *La Paternelle, Assurances à Primes contre l'Incendie*   Paris
2 Oct. 1843   3,000,000F (6,000,000F, 1856)
BL, 9th ser., 1843, PS, XXIV, 395–409

319. *Houillères de la Chazotte et du Treuil Réunis*   Paris
27 Oct. 1843   3,500 shares
F^{14}8231; BL, 9th ser., 1843, PS, XXIV, 543–58

320. *La Gironde, Assurances Maritimes*   Bordeaux
25 Jan. 1844   1,500,000F
BL, 9th ser., 1844, PS, XXV, 253–72

321. *L'Espérance, Assurance contre les Risques de Navigation Maritime et Intérieure*   Paris
25 Jan. 1844   500,000F
BL, 9th ser., 1844, PS, XXV, 272–82

322. *Compagnie des Antilles*   Paris
2 Feb. 1844   6,000,000F
F¹²6731; BL, 9th ser., 1844, PS, XXV, 221–32

323. *Le Neptune, Assurances Maritimes contre les Risques de Navigation Maritimes et Intérieure*   Paris
2 Feb. 1844   500,000F
BL, 9th ser., 1844, PS, XXV, 525–35

324. *Bains du Rhône*   Lyon
17 Mar. 1844   660 shares
F¹²6793; BL, 9th ser., 1844, PS, XXV, 621–27

325. *La Garonne, Assurances Maritimes*   Bordeaux
17 Mar. 1844   600,000F
BL, 9th ser., 1844, PS, XXV, 627–39

326. *Le Trident, Assurances Maritimes*   Paris
22 Apr. 1844   500,000F
BL, 9th ser., 1844, PS, XXV, 689–99

327. *Phénix, Compagnie Française d'Assurances sur la Vie Humaine*   Paris
9 June 1844   4,000,000F
BL, 9th ser., 1844, PS, XXV, 861–92

328. *Eclairage par le Gaz de la Ville d'Avignon*   Avignon
9 June 1844
BL, 9th ser., 1844, PS, XXV, 909–34

329. *L'Ille et Vilaine, Compagnie des Bateaux à Vapeur entre le Havre et Saint-Malo*   Saint-Malo
1 Aug. 1844   320,000F
F¹²6770; BL, 9th ser., 1844, PS, XXVI, 75–87

330. *Conservateur, Compagnie pour la Formation et la Gestion des Sociétés d'Assurances Mutuelles sur la Vie*   Paris
2 Aug. 1844   1,000,000F
BL, 9th ser., 1844, PS, XXVI, 110–31

331. *Lloyd Havrais, Assurances Maritimes*   Havre
26 Aug. 1844   1,000,000F
BL, 9th ser., 1844, PS, XXVI, 241–51

332. *La Boussole, Assurances Maritimes*   Havre
26 Aug. 1844   1,000,000F
BL, 9th ser., 1844, PS, XXVI, 251–61

333. *Les Deux Mondes, Assurances Maritimes*   Havre
     26 Aug. 1844   600,000F
     BL, 9th ser., 1844, PS, XXVI, 262–74

334. *Pont de Venerique*   Toulouse
     10 Sept. 1844
     F^{12}6753; BL, 9th ser., 1844, PS, XXVI, 306–14

335. *Compagnie d'Ourscamp*   Paris
     10 Sept. 1844   850,000F
     F^{12}6733; BL, 9th ser., 1844, PS, XXVI, 314–25

336. *La Confiance, Assurances à Primes contre l'Incendie*   Paris
     16 Sept. 1844   2,000,000F
     BL, 9th ser., 1844, PS, XXVI, 372–86

337. *La Providence, Assurances sur la Vie Humaine*   Paris
     6 Nov. 1844   3,000,000F
     BL, 9th ser., 1844, PS, XXVI, 529–64

338. *Pont de Vivoin*   Vivoin (Sarthe)
     8 Nov. 1844   200 shares
     F^{12}6753; BL, 9th ser., 1844, PS, XXVI, 565–72

339. *Pont d'Ivry*   Paris
     8 Dec. 1844
     F^{12}6756; BL, 9th ser., 1844, PS, XXVI, 845–57

340. *Compagnie du Rhône, Service de Bateaux à Vapeur*   Lyon
     25 Dec. 1844   540,000F (640,000F, 1846)
     F^{12}6770; BL, 9th ser., 1844, PS, XXVI, 864–72

341. *L'Urbaine, Assurances sur la Vie Humaine*   Paris
     10 Feb. 1845   5,000,000F
     BL, 9th ser., 1845, PS, XXVII, 148–66

342. *Chemin de Fer de Paris à Sceaux*   Paris
     23 Feb. 1845   3,000,000F
     BL, 9th ser., 1845, PS, XXVII, 177–94

343. *Bienfaisante, Assurances à Primes contre l'Incendie*   Paris
     17 Mar. 1845   5,000,000F
     BL, 9th ser., 1845, PS, XXVII, 560–74

344. *La Néréide, Assurances contre des Risques de la Navigation Maritime et Intérieure*   Paris
     19 Mar. 1845   600,000F
     BL, 9th ser., 1845, PS, XXVII, 574–83

345. *Mélusine, Assurances à Primes sur la Vie*   Paris
     10 Apr. 1845   1,000,000F (1,500,000F, 1846)
     BL, 9th ser., 1845, PS, XXVII, 588–607

346. *Chemin de Fer du Centre*   Paris
13 Apr. 1845   33,000,000F
BL, 9th ser., 1845, PS, XXVII, 449–91

347. *Compagnie d'Exploitation du Chemins de Fer de Montpellier à Nîmes*   Nîmes
22 Apr. 1845   2,000,000F
BL, 9th ser., 1845, PS, XXVII, 609–20

348. *Haut Fourneau de Rioupéroux*   Grenoble
8 May 1845
$F^{14}8231$; BL, 9th ser., 1845, PS, XXVII, 819–36

349. *Chemin de Fer d'Orléans à Bordeaux*   Paris
16 May 1845   65,000,000F
BL, 9th ser., 1845, PS, XXVII, 993–1004

350. *Quatre Ponts Réunis*   Bordeaux
21 May 1845
$F^{12}6756$; BL, 9th ser., 1845, PS, XXVII, 849–58

351. *La Vigie, Assurances contre les Risques de la Navigation Maritime et Intérieure*   Paris
21 May 1845   1,000,000F
BL, 9th ser., 1845, PS, XXVII, 858–68

352. *Chemin de Fer de Montereau à Troyes*   Paris
29 May 1845   20,000,000F
BL, 9th ser., 1845, PS, XXVII, 705–68

353. *Chemin de Fer d'Amiens à Boulogne*   Paris
29 May 1845   37,500,000F
BL, 9th ser., 1845, PS, XXVII, 769–815

354. *Pont Saint-Michel à Toulouse*   Bordeaux
7 June 1845
$F^{12}6755$; BL, 9th ser., 1845, PS, XXVII, 961–68

355. *Lloyd-Marseillais, Assurances contre les Risques de la Navigation Maritime et Intérieure*   Marseille
11 July 1845   1,000,000F
BL, 9th ser., 1845, PS, XXVIII, 17–27

356. *Eclairage par le Gaz de la Ville de Montpellier*   Montpellier
11 July 1845
BL, 9th ser., 1845, PS, XXVIII, 27–37

357. *Eclairage par le Gaz de la Ville de Saint-Etienne*   Saint-Etienne
11 July 1845
BL, 9th ser., 1845, PS, XXVIII, 37–47

358. *Pont d'Aiguilly*   Roanne
     29 Aug. 1845
     F¹²6755; BL, 9th ser., 1845, PS, XXVIII, 209–15

359. *L'Atlantique, Assurances contre les Risques de la Navigation Maritimes et Intérieure*   Paris
     29 Aug. 1845   500,000F
     BL, 9th ser., 1845, PS, XXVIII, 219–27

360. *Forges de Sireuil*   Bordeaux
     10 Sept. 1845   1,200 shares
     F¹⁴8230; BL, 9th ser., 1845, PS, XXVIII, 363–73

361. *Théâtre de La Rochelle*   La Rochelle
     20 Sept. 1845   120,000F
     F¹²6794, BL, 9th ser., 1845, PS, XXVIII, 394–409

362. *Pont de Belleville*   Lyon
     20 Sept. 1845   250,000F
     F¹²6755; BL, 9th ser., 1845, PS, XXVIII, 409–18

363. *Chemin de Fer du Nord*   Paris
     20 Sept. 1845   200,000,000F
     BL, 9th ser., 1845, PS, XXVIII, 289–302

364. *Chemins de Fer de Fampoux à Hazebrouck*   Paris
     22 Sept. 1845   16,000,000F
     BL, 9th ser., 1845, PS, XXVIII, 302–23

365. *Chemins de Fer de Dieppe et de Fécamp*   Paris
     14 Oct. 1845   18,000,000F
     BL, 9th ser., 1845, PS, XXVIII, 457–503

366. *Gaz Portatif Non-Comprimé*   Paris
     17 Oct. 1845   388,000F
     BL, 9th ser., 1845, PS, XXVIII, 514–24

367. *Chemin de Fer de Paris à Strasbourg (Chemin de Fer de l'Est, 1866)*   Paris
     17 Dec. 1845   125,000,000F (250,000,000F, 1854)
     BL, 9th ser., 1845, PS, XXVIII, 761–76

368. *Chemin de Fer de Tours à Nantes*   Paris
     17 Dec. 1845   40,000,000F
     BL, 9th ser., 1845, PS, XXVIII, 776–88

369. *Eclairage par le Gaz de la Ville de Metz*   Lyon
     25 Jan. 1846
     BL, 9th ser., 1845, PS, XXIX, 117–26

370. *L'Aigle, Compagnie pour la Formation et la Gestion de Sociétés d'Assurances Mutuelles sur la Vie*   Paris
    25 Jan. 1846   1,000,000F
    BL, 9th ser., 1846, PS, XXIX, 165–89

371. *Compagnie du Soleil pour la Formation et la Gestion de Sociétés d'Assurances Mutuelles sur la Vie*   Paris
    25 Jan. 1846   1,000,000F
    BL, 9th ser., 1846, PS, XXIX, 209–34

372. *L'Exploitation de l'Entrepôt Réel de la Ville de Mulhausen*   Mulhouse
    27 Jan. 1846   45,000F
    BL, 9th ser., 1846, PS, XXIX, 135–42

373. *Chemin de Fer de Paris à Lyon*   Paris
    1 Mar. 1846   200,000,000F
    BL, 9th ser., 1846, PS, XXIX, 349–65

374. *Eclairage par le Gaz de la Guillotière, Vaise et Lyon*   Guillotière (Rhône)
    10 Mar. 1846   2,400 shares
    BL, 9th ser., 1846, PS, XXIX, 630–38

375. *L'Océanie, Assurances contre les Risques de la Navigation Maritime et Intérieure*   Paris
    10 Mar. 1846   500,000F
    BL, 9th ser., 1846, PS, XXIX, 666–77

376. *Pont d'Abzac*   Libourne (Gironde)
    31 Mar. 1846   100,000F
    F^{12}6758; BL, 9th ser., 1846, PS, XXIX, 763–70

377. *Chemin de Fer de Creuil à Saint-Quentin*   Paris
    24 Apr. 1846   30,000,000F (merged wtih no. 363, 1847)
    BL, 9th ser., 1846, PS, XXIX, 812–24

378. *La Sauvegarde, Assurances Nautiques*   Paris
    4 May 1846   1,000,000F
    BL, 9th ser., 1846, PS, XXIX, 863–74

379. *Société Générale des Remorqueurs Parisiens*   Paris
    26 May 1846   500,000F
    F^{12}6770; BL, 9th ser., 1846, PS, XXIX, 1004–12

380. *La Sphere, Assurances Maritimes*   Havre
    8 Sept. 1846   500,000F (600,000F, 1852; 2,000,000F, 1857)
    BL, 9th ser., 1846, PS, XXX, 397–409

381. *Dock Flottant du Havre*   Havre
     8 Sept. 1846   335,000F
     BL, 9th ser., 1846, PS, XXX, 431–40

382. *Chemin de Fer de Bordeaux à Cette*   Paris
     24 Sept. 1846   140,000,000F
     BL, 9th ser., 1846, PS, XXX, 233–362

383. *L'Alliance; Exploitation d'un Service de Voitures de Place*   Paris
     4 Oct. 1846   800,000F
     F^{12}6758; BL, 9th ser., 1846, PS, XXX, 482–89

384. *Pont de Couthares*   Bordeaux
     4 Oct. 1846   205,000F
     F^{12}6754; BL, 9th ser., 1846, PS, XXX, 493–501

385. *La Garonne, Assurances Maritimes*   Bordeaux
     21 Nov. 1846   1,200,000F (2,500,000F in 1854)
     BL, 9th ser., 1846, PS, XXX, 641–54

386. *Pont de Pertuiset*   Pertuiset (Loire)
     26 Dec. 1846
     F^{12}6754; BL, 9th ser., 1846, PS, XXX, 881–88

387. *Chemin de Fer de Lyon à Avignon*   Lyon
     2 Jan. 1847   150,000,000F
     BL, 9th ser., 1847, PS, XXXI, 161–77

388. *L'Universelle, Formation et l'Administration de Sociétés d'Assurances Mutuelles sur la Vie*   Paris
     2 Jan. 1847   2,000,000F
     BL, 9th ser., 1847, PS, XXXI, 178–201

389. *L'Avenir des Familles, Formation et la Gestion de Sociétés d'Assurances Mutuelles sur la Vie*   Mans
     19 Jan. 1847   1,000,000F
     BL, 9th ser., 1847, PS, XXXI, 209–33

390. *L'Aquitaine, Assurances Maritimes*   Bordeaux
     21 Feb. 1847   500,000F
     BL, 9th ser., 1847, PS, XXXI, 573–85

391. *Fonderie de Niort*   Niort (Deux-Sèvres)
     9 June 1847   160,000F
     F^{14}8233; BL, 9th ser., 1847, PS, XXXI, 955–65

392. *Houillères de Layon et Loire*   Paris
     9 June 1847   1,850 shares
     F^{14}8232; BL, 9th ser., 1847, PS, XXXI, 975–89

393. *Fonderies et Forges de l'Horme*   Lyon
2 July 1847   5,000,000F
F¹⁴8234; BL, 9th ser., 1847, PS, XXXII, 114–24

394. *Pont de Quincy-sur-Cher*   Mehun-sur-Yèvre (Cher)
22 July 1847   200 shares
F¹²6754; BL, 9th ser., 1847, PS, XXXII, 126–34

395. *Verrerie de Penchot*   Penchot-sur-Lot (Aveyron)
13 Nov. 1847   327,000F (440,000F, 1856; dissolved 1866)
F¹²6738; F¹⁴8229; BL, 9th ser., 1847, PS, XXXII, 497–505

396. *Pont de Couzon*   Couzon (Rhône)
3 Jan. 1848
BL, 9th ser., 1848, PS, XXXIII, 281–90

397. *Mines de Plomb Argentifère de Pontgibaud*   Paris
20 Feb. 1848
F¹⁴8232; BL, 9th ser., 1848, PS, XXXIII, 329 43

398. *Canal de Pierrelatte*   Pierrelatte (Drôme)
16 Mar. 1848
BL, 10th ser., 1848, PS, I, 231–42

399. *La Providence des Enfants, Gestion des Associations Mutuelles sur la
Vie*   Paris
19 Mar. 1848   1,000,000F
BL, 10th ser., 1848, PS, I, 4–21

400. *L'Expansion, Constructions de Machines et de Mécaniques*   Mulhouse
7 Apr. 1848   1,050,000F
F¹²6728; BL, 10th ser., 1848, PS, I, 210–19

401. *Union des Interêts Municipaux et Industriel pour Fournir du Travail aux
Etablissements du Filature, de Tissage et d'Impression de
Rouen*   Rouen
10 May 1848   2,000,000F
F¹²6733; BL, 10th scr., 1848, PS, I, 320–24

402. *Bateaux à Vapeur de Cette*   Montpellier
3 Aug. 1848   800,000F
F¹²6770; BL, 10th ser., 1848, PS, II, 310–19

403. *Transports sur la Saône et sur le Rhône*   Lyon
8 Aug. 1848   3,000,000F
F¹²6770; BL, 10th ser., 1848, PS, II, 328–38

404. *Société d'Avances sur Dépot de Soie Ecrue*   Lyon
21 Oct. 1848   100,000F
BL, 10th ser., 1848, PS, II, 652–58

405. *Manufacture de la Trivalle (wool yarn)*   Carcassonne
     15 Jan. 1849   300,000F
     F^{12}6733; BL, 10th ser., 1849, PS, III, 125–33

406. *Hauts Fourneaux et Forges de Denain et d'Anzin*   Paris
     6 Apr. 1849   10,000,000F
     F^{14}8232; BL, 10th ser., 1849, PS, III, 685–97

407. *La Fertilisante, Fabrication et la Vente des Engrais*   Caen
     19 Apr. 1849   40,000F
     BL, 10th ser., 1849, PS, III, 697–708

408. *La Progressive, Formation et la Gestion des Sociétés d'Assurances
     Mutuelles sur la Vie*   Paris
     9 May 1849   1,000,000F
     BL, 10th ser., 1849, PS, III, 714–38

409. *Eclairage par le gaz de la Ville du Mans*   Mans
     21 June 1849
     BL, 10th ser., 1849, PS, IV, 41–50

410. *Hauts Fourneaux de Montluçon*   Montluçon (Allier)
     27 July 1849   3,000,000F
     F^{14}8229; BL, 10th ser., 1849, PS, IV, 169–78

411. *Le Commerce, Assurances Maritimes*   Havre
     9 Aug. 1849   600,000F
     BL, 10th ser., 1849, PS, IV, 309–19

412. *Assureurs Orléanais (Assurances Maritimes)*   Orléans
     12 Sept. 1849   400,000F
     BL, 10th ser., 1849, PS, IV, 345–54

413. *Entreprise Général des Coches de la Haute Seine, de l'Yonne et des
     Canaux*   Paris
     19 Oct. 1849   970,000F
     F^{12}6758; BL, 10th ser., 1849, PS, IV, 575–86

414. *Hauts Fourneaux de Maubeuge*   Valenciennes
     26 Oct. 1849   6,000,000F
     BL, 10th ser., 1849, PS, IV, 586–98

415. *Caisse Paternelle*   Paris
     19 Mar. 1850   4,000,000F
     BL, 10th ser., 1850, PS, V, 453–78

416. *L'Union de Grasse, Navigation à Vapeur entre Cannes et Cette*   Grasse
     (Var)
     15 Apr. 1850   200,000F
     F^{12}6770; BL, 10th ser., 1850, PS, V, 520–28

Appendix: *Sociétés Anonymes*, 1808–1867   [179]

417. *Pont de Fourchambault*   Nevers
 2 July 1850   412 shares
 F¹²6754; BL, 10th ser., 1850, PS, V, 98–105

418. *Houillères et du Chemin de Fer d'Epine*   Paris
 2 July 1850   2,400 shares
 F¹⁴8233; BL, 10th ser., 1850, PS, VI, 81–96

419. *Messageries du Midi et de l'Auvergne*   Montpellier
 1 Oct. 1850   120 shares (dissolved 1875)
 F¹²6758; BL, 10th ser., 1850, PS, VI, 481–88

420. *Assurances Maritimes*   Havre
 26 Nov. 1850   2,000,000F
 BL, 10th ser., 1851, PS, VII, 122–43

421. *Compagnie Commerciale d'Assurances Maritimes*   Havre
 26 Nov. 1850   1,200,000F
 BL, 10th ser., 1851, PS, VII, 145–57

422. *Sambre Française Canalisée*   Paris
 20 Dec. 1850   6,000 shares
 BL, 10th ser., 1851, PS, VII, 158–70

423. *Théâtre de Lons-le-Saunier*   Lons-le-Saunier (Jura)
 7 Jan. 1851   520 shares
 F¹²6794; BL, 10th ser., 1851, PS, VII, 190–201

424. *Société Lyonnaise des Déchets*   Lyon
 28 Jan. 1851   300 shares
 F¹²6733; BL, 10th ser., 1851, PS, VII, 361–73

425. *Filature de Poutai*   Strasbourg
 10 May 1851   520,000F
 F¹²6733; BL, 10th ser., 1851, PS, VII, 878–86

426. *Services Maritimes des Messageries Nationales, Messageries Maritimes*
 Paris (*Messageries Maritimes Impériales, 1853*)
 22 Jan. 1852   24,000,000F (60,000,000F, 1861)
 F¹²6767; BL, 10th ser., 1852, PS, IX, 161–71

427. *Chemin de Fer de l'Ouest*   Paris
 27 Jan. 1852   50,000,000F (70,000,000F, 1853)
 BL, 10th ser., 1852, PS, IX, 171–284

428. *Chemin de Fer de Paris à Lyon*   Lyon
 20 Mar. 1852   120,000,000F (132,000,000F, 1854)
 BL, 10th ser., 1852, PS, IX, 321–36

429. *Chemin de Fer de Lyon à Avignon* (*Chemin de Fer de Lyon à la Mediterranée, 1852*)   Paris
 27 Mar. 1852   35,000,000F (45,000,000F, Nov. 1852)
 BL, 10th ser., 1852, PS, IX, 289–303

430. *Eclairage par le Gaz de la Ville de Montélimar*   Lyon
     7 Apr. 1852   700 shares
     BL, 10th ser., 1852, PS, IX, 373–83

431. *Chemin de Fer de Blesme et Saint Dizier à Gray*   Paris
     4 June 1852   16,000,000F
     BL, 10th ser., 1852, PS, IX, 712–29

432. *Le Pilote; Assurances contre les Risques de Navigation Maritime et Intérieure*   Paris
     23 June 1852   1,000,000F
     BL, 10th ser., 1852, PS, X, 2–12

433. *Les Antilles, Assurances Maritimes*   Havre
     23 June 1852   600,000F
     BL, 10th ser., 1852, PS, X, 12–23

434. *Terrains et Entrepôts du Bassin Vauban, au Havre*   Paris
     29 July 1852   128,850F
     BL, 10th ser., 1852, PS, X, 140–52

435. *Chemin de Fer de Mulhouse à Thann*   Paris
     30 July 1852   2,600,000F
     BL, 10th ser., 1852, PS, X, 152–59

436. *Banque Foncière de Paris*   Paris (*Crédit Foncier de France, 1853*)
     30 July 1852   25,000,000F (60,000,000F, 1853)
     F¹²6775; BL, 10th ser., 1852, PS, X, 169–201

437. *Chemin de Fer de Paris à Caen et à Cherbourg*   Paris
     11 Sept. 1852   30,000,000F
     BL, 10th ser., 1852, PS, X, 335–66

438. *Chemin de Fer de Dijon à Besançon*   Paris
     11 Sept. 1852   16,600,000F
     BL, 10th ser., 1852, PS, X, 399–415

439. *Banque Foncière de Marseille, Société de Crédit Foncier*   Marseille
     12 Sept. 1852   3,000,000F (merged with no. 436, 1856)
     F¹²6775; BL, 10th ser., 1852, PS, X, 464–84

440. *Palais de l'Industrie*   Paris
     20 Oct. 1852   13,000,000F
     BL, 10th ser., 1852, PS, X, 622–33

441. *Crédit Foncier de Nevers*   Nevers
     20 Oct. 1852   2,000,000F (merged with no. 436, 1856)
     F¹²6775; BL, 10th ser., 1852, PS, X, 701–22

442. *Chemins de Fer du Midi et du Canal Latéral à la Garonne*   Paris
     6 Nov. 1852   67,000,000F (125,000,000F, 1856)
     BL, 10th ser., 1852, PS, X, 685–99

443. *Société Générale de Crédit Mobilier*   Paris
    18 Nov. 1852   60,000,000F (120,000,000F, 1866)
    F¹²6791; BL, 10th ser., 1852, PS, X, 781–96

444. *Forges et Chantiers de la Méditerranée*   Marseille
    29 Jan. 1853   5,000,000F (9,000,000F, 1857)
    BL, 11th ser., 1853, PS, I, 146–54

445. *Chemin de Fer de Graisseac à Béziers*   Paris
    26 Feb. 1853   18,000,000F
    BL, 11th ser., 1853, PS, I, 289–310

446. *Mines de Plomb Argentifère et Fonderies de Pontgibaud*   Paris
    8 Apr. 1853   10,000 shares
    F¹⁴8232; BL, 11th ser., 1853, PS, I, 689–702

447. *Eclairage par le Gaz de la Ville de Carpentras*   Carpentras
    15 Apr. 1853   150 shares
    BL, 11th ser., 1853, PS, I, 703–12

448. *Eclairage de la Ville de Libourne par le Gaz Hydrogène*   Libourne
    9 June 1853   160 shares
    BL, 11th ser., 1853, PS, I, 945–61

449. *Lloyd Bordelais, Assurances Maritimes*   Bordeaux
    14 June 1853   1,000,000F
    BL, 11th ser., 1853, PS, I, 899–909

450. *Compagnie Française de Prêts à la Grosse*   Paris
    16 July 1853   1,000,000F
    BL, 11th ser., 1853, PS, II, 2–10

451. *Chemin de Fer Grand Central de France*   Paris
    30 July 1853   90,000,000F (merged with no. 457, 1854)
    BL, 11th ser., 1853, PS, II, 11–28

452. *L'Equité, Assurances Maritimes*   Havre
    30 July 1853   600,000F
    BL, 11th ser., 1853, PS, II, 353–63

453. *Chemin de Fer de Lyon à Genève*   Paris
    6 Aug. 1853   40,000,000F
    BL, 11th ser., 1853, PS, II, 389–421

454. *L'Univers, Assurances Maritimes*   Havre
    17 Aug. 1853   600,000F
    BL, 11th ser., 1853, PS, II, 421–31

455. *Ardoisières de Chattemove*   Chattemove (Mayenne)
    8 Sept. 1853   2,160 shares
    F¹⁴8232; BL, 11th ser., 1853, PS, II, 609–19

456. *Hauts Fourneaux de l'Alélik*   Paris
8 Sept. 1853   1,200,000F
BL, 11th ser., 1853, PS, II, 621–34

457. *Chemins de Fer de Jonction du Rhône à la Loire*   Paris
30 Sept. 1853   30,000,000F (merged with no. 451, 1854)
BL, 11th ser., 1853, PS, II, 813–31

458. *Raffinerie et Huilerie Bordelaises*   Paris
12 Oct. 1853   2,500,000F (dissolved 1855)
F^{12}6731; BL, 11th ser., 1853, PS, II, 877–86

459. *Chemin de Fer de Provins aux Ormes*   Provins
12 Oct. 1853   1,650,000F
BL, 11th ser., 1853, PS, II, 890–907

460. *L'Aigle, Navigation du Rhône et de la Saône*   Lyon
22 Oct. 1853   1,800 shares
F^{12}6769; BL, 11th ser., 1853, PS, II, 831–38

461. *Houillères de Saint-Chamond*   Paris
29 Oct. 1853   3,275 shares
F^{14}8231; BL, 11th ser., 1853, PS, II, 859–69

462. *Houillères de Stiring*   Paris
5 Nov. 1853   12,000 shares
F^{14}8232; BL, 11th ser., 1853, PS, II, 909–19

463. *L'Espérance, Assurances Maritimes*   Havre
5 Dec. 1853   600,000F
BL, 11th ser., 1854, PS, III, 82–95

464. *Phare Maritime, Assurances Maritimes*   Paris
5 Dec. 1853   1,000,000F
BL, 11th ser., 1854, PS, III, 96–105

465. *Compagnie Générale des Eaux*   Paris
14 Dec. 1853   20,000,000F
F^{12}6785, 6742; BL, 11th ser., 1854, PS, III, 55–77

466. *Eclairage par le Gaz de la Ville de Bourges*   Lyon
13 Feb. 1854
BL, 11th ser., 1854, PS, III, 609–21

467. *Chemin de Fer de Saint-Rambert à Grenoble*   Paris (*Chemin de Fer du Dauphiné, 1857*)
18 Feb. 1854   25,000,000F
BL, 11th ser., 1854, PS, III, 683–707

468. *Compagnie Linière de Pont-Remy*   Paris
25 Feb. 1854   2,250,000F
F^{12}6734; BL, 11th ser., 1854, PS, III, 801–15

469. *L'Alliance Maritime, Assurances Maritimes*   Bordeaux
3 Mar. 1854   500,000F
BL, 11th ser., 1854, PS, III, 929–38

470. *La Provence, Assurances Maritimes*   Grasse (Var)
22 Mar. 1854   500,000F
BL, 11th ser., 1854, PS, III, 723–31

471. *La Maritime, Prêts et d'Armements Maritimes*   Paris
25 Mar. 1854   1,000,000F (dissolved 1857)
F^{12}6770; BL, 11th ser., 1854, PS, III, 753–65

472. *Paquebots de Paris*   Paris
29 Mar. 1854   450,000F (dissolved 1857)
F^{12}6766; BL, 11th ser., 1854, PS, III, 833–44

473. *L'Impériale, Assurances sur la Vie Humaine*   Paris
29 Mar. 1854   5,000,000F
BL, 11th ser., 1854, PS, III, 961–93

474. *Pont de Mallemort*   Marseille
6 Apr. 1854   280,000F
F^{12}6754; BL, 11th ser., 1854, PS, III, 1020–28

475. *La Globe, Assurances et de Réassurances contre l'Incendie et l'Explosion du Gaz*   Paris
6 May 1854   2,000,000F
BL, 11th ser., 1854, PS, III, 1071–87

476. *Rue Impériale de Lyon*   Lyon
3 July 1854   7,000,000F (10,750,000F, 1856)
F^{12}6789; BL, 11th ser., 1854, PS, IV, 104–120

477. *Clouteries Mécaniques de Charleville*   Charleville
3 July 1854   500,000F
F^{12}6730; F^{14}8229; BL, 11th ser., 1854, PS, IV, 122–28

478. *Assurances Maritimes du Finistère*   Brest
3 July 1854   300,000F (1,300,000F, 1856)
BL, 11th ser., 1854, PS, IV, 193–204

479. *Paquebots à Vapeur entre le Havre et Honfleur*   Havre
17 July 1854   535 shares (merged with no. 217 to form no. 572)
F^{12}6774; BL, 11th ser., 1854, PS, IV, 229–39

480. *Comptoir d'Escompte de Paris*   Paris
25 July 1854   20,000,000F (40,000,000F, 1860; 80,000,000F, 1866)
BL, 11th ser., 1854, PS, IV, 178–89

481. *Usines de Gouille*   Gouille (Doubs)
3 Oct. 1854   700 shares
F^{14}8230; BL, 11th ser., 1854, PS, IV, 830–42

482. *Le Midi, Assurances à Primes contre l'Incendie*   Marseille
12 Oct. 1854   2,000,000F
BL, 11th ser., 1854, PS, IV, 877–88

483. *Houillères de Saint-Etienne*   Lyon
17 Oct. 1854   80,000 shares
F^{12}6729; F^{14}8231; BL, 11th ser., 1854, PS, IV, 1037–50; BL, 11th ser., 1855, PS, V, 186–250

484. *Houillères de Rive-de-Gier*   Lyon
17 Oct. 1854   80,000 shares
F^{12}6729; F^{14}8231; BL, 11th ser., 1854, PS, IV, 1050–63; BL, 11th ser., 1855, PS, V, 186–250

485. *Houillères de Montrambert et de la Béraudière*   Lyon
17 Oct. 1854   80,000 shares
F^{12}6729; F^{14}8231; BL, 11th ser., 1854, PS, IV, 1064–77; BL, 11th ser., 1855, PS, V, 186–250

486. *Compagnie des Mines de la Loire*
17 Oct. 1854   80,000 shares
F^{12}6729; F^{14}8231; BL, 11 ser., 1854, PS, IV, 1077–90; BL, 11th ser., 1855, PS, V, 186–250

487. *Assurances Générales à Primes Fixes contre la Grêle*   Paris
25 Oct. 1854   10,000,000F
BL, 11th ser., 1854, PS, IV, 888–99

488. *Mines de Kef-Oum-Théboul*   Marseille
15 Nov. 1854   8,000 shares
BL, 11 ser., 1854, PS, IV, 992–99

489. *Compagnie Centrale d'Assurances Maritimes*   Paris
23 Nov. 1854   5,000,000F
BL, 11th ser., 1854, PS, IV, 1117–29

490. *Hotel et des Immeubles de la Rue de Rivoli (Cie. Immobilière de Paris, 1858; merged into no. 588, 1863)*   Paris
9 Dec. 1854   24,000,000F
F^{12}6780, 6781; BL, 11th ser., 1854, PS, IV, 1149–61

491. *Entreprise Générale des Omnibus*   Paris
   22 Feb. 1855   24,000 shares
   F¹²6760, 6761; BL, 11th ser., 1855, PS, V, 349–61

492. *Mines de Sel et Salines de Rosières et Verangéville*   Nancy
   15 Mar. 1855   800 shares
   F¹⁴8232; BL, 11th ser., 1855, PS, V, 713–25

493. *Compagnie Générale Maritime (Compagnie Générale Transatlantique, 1861)*   Paris
   2 May 1855   30,000,000F
   F¹²6772, 6773; BL, 11th ser., 1855, PS, V, 879–93

494. *Le Réunion, Assuranes Maritimes*   Paris
   6 June 1855   6,000,000F
   BL, 11th ser., 1855, PS, VI, 33–44

495. *Chemins de Fer de l'Ouest*   Paris
   16 June 1855   150,000,000F (merger of nos. 188, 222, 230, 268, 308, 365, 427, and 437)
   BL, 11th ser., 1855, PS, V, 1121–34

496. *Eclairage par le Gaz de la Ville d'Alais*   Lyon
   22 June 1855   840 shares
   BL, 11th ser., 1855, PS, VI, 44–53

497. *Chemin de Fer de Montluçon à Moulins*   Paris
   23 June 1855   22,000,000F
   BL, 11th ser., 1855, PS, VI, 81–94

498. *L'Abattoir de Beauvais*   Beauvais
   27 June 1855   130,000F (dissolved 1867)
   F¹²6788; BL, 11th ser., 1855, PS, VI, 164–73

499. *Mines de Charbon Minéral de la Mayenne et de la Sarthe*   Laval
   4 July 1855   13,200 shares
   F¹⁴8234; BL, 11th ser., 1855, PS, VI, 193–208

500. *Chemin de Fer des Ardennes et de l'Oise (Chemins de Fer des Ardennes, 1857)*   Paris
   11 July 1855   21,000,000F (63,000,000F, 1857; 42,000,000F, 1859)
   BL, 11th ser., 1855, PS, VI, 305–37

501. *Touage de la Basse Seine et de l'Oise*   Paris
   14 July 1855   1,500,000F
   F¹²6768; BL, 11th ser., 1855, PS, VI, 338–49

502. *Paquebots à Vapeur du Finistère*   Havre
   4 Aug. 1855   720,000F
   F¹²6768; BL, 11th ser., 1855, PS, VI, 384–94

503. *Eaux du Havre*   Havre
     4 Aug. 1855   1,500,000F
     F^{12}6785; BL, 11th ser., 1855, PS, VI, 394–407

504. *Chemin de Fer de Bessèges à Alais*   Paris
     16 Aug. 1855   4,000,000F (6,000,000F, 1857)
     BL, 11th ser., 1855, PS, VI, 517–30

505. *L'Eole, Assurances contre les Risques de Navigation Maritime et
     Intérieure*   Paris
     29 Aug. 1855   1,000,000F (2,000,000F, 1863)
     BL, 11th ser., 1855, PS, VI, 565–74

506. *Tattersale Française, Compagnie pour le Vente des Chevaux et
     Voitures*   Paris
     19 Sept. 1855   1,400 shares
     BL, 11th ser., 1855, PS, VI, 625–33

507. *Mines de la Grand'Combe*   Paris
     3 Oct. 1855   24,000 shares
     F^{14}8230; BL, 11th ser., 1855, PS, VI, 662–72

508. *Compagnie Parisienne d'Eclairage et de Chauffrage par le Gaz*   Paris
     22 Dec. 1855   110,000 shares
     BL, 11th ser., 1855, PS, VI, 1166–1201

509. *Eclairage par le Gaz de la Ville de Saint-Quentin*   Saint-Quentin
     13 Feb. 1856   1,000 shares
     BL, 11th ser., 1856, PS, VII, 193–203

510. *L'Indemnité, Assurances contre les Risques de Navigation Maritime et
     Intérieure*   Paris
     7 May 1856   2,000,000F
     BL, 11th ser., 1856, PS, VII, 792–802

511. *Verreries de Plaine-de-Valsch et de Vallerysthal*   Vallerysthal (Meurthe)
     7 May 1856   1,000,000F
     F^{12}6738; BL, 11th ser., 1856, PS, VII, 818–30

512. *Dorgogne, Assurances contre les Risques de Navigation Maritime et
     Intérieure*   Bordeaux
     7 May 1856   1,200,000F
     BL, 11th ser., 1856, PS, VII, 864–76

513. *Verreries d'Epinac*   Lyon
     14 May 1856   400,000F (500,000F, 1858)
     F^{12}6741; BL, 11th ser., 1856, PS, VII, 886–98

514. *L'Abeille Bourguignonne, Assurances à Primes contre la Grêle*   Dijon
     25 June 1856   1,000,000F (3,000,000F, 1857; 6,000,000F, 1858)
     BL, 11th ser., 1856, PS, VIII, 49–61

515. *Chemin de Fer et Docks de Saint-Ouen*   Paris
11 July 1856   20,000 shares
BL, 11th ser., 1856, PS, VIII, 209–20

516. *Compagnie Marseillaise, Assurances Maritimes*   Marseille
2 Aug. 1856   500,000F
BL, 11th ser., 1856, PS, VIII, 321–31

517. *Pont de la Haute-Chaîne à Angers*   Paris
16 Oct. 1856   480 shares
F^{12}6754; BL, 11th ser., 1856, PS, VIII, 1016–24

518. *La Seine, Assurances contre les Risques de Navigation Maritime et Intérieure*   Paris
19 Nov. 1856   1,000,000F
BL, 11th ser., 1856, PS, VIII, 1260–69

519. *Du Triton, Assurances contre les Risques de Navigation Maritime et Intérieure*   Paris
24 Dec. 1856   1,000,000F (1,500,000F, 1861)
BL, 11th ser., 1856, PS, VIII, 1396–1406

520. *L'Universelle, Assurances contre les Risques de Navigation Maritime et Intérieure*   Paris
24 Dec. 1856   1,500,000F
BL, 11th ser., 1856, PS, VIII, 1406–17

521. *Comptoir Maritime, Assurances contre les Risques de Navigation Maritime et Intérieure*   Paris
31 Jan. 1857   2,000,000F
BL, 11th ser., 1857, PS, IX, 217–27

522. *L'Abeille Bourguignonne, Assurances à Primes contre l'Incendie*   Dijon
27 May 1857   2,000,000F (5,000,000F, 1859; 8,000,000F, 1860; 10,000,000F, 1861)
BL, 11th ser., 1857, PS, IX, 1149–60

523. *Chemins de Fer de Paris à Lyon et à la Mediterraneé*   Paris
3 July 1857   588,000,000F (merger of nos. 428 and 429)
BL, 11th ser., 1857, PS, X, 113–27

524. *Exploitation des Sources et Etablissements Thermaux de Plombières*   Plombières
24 July 1857   900,000F
BL, 11th ser., 1857, PS, X, 466–86

525. *Nus Proprietaires, Compagnie d'Operations sur les Nus Proprietaires et Usufruits*   Paris

12 Oct. 1857   6,000,000F (merged with no. 619, 1866)
BL, 11th ser., 1857, PS, X, 950–64

526. *Canal de Séclin*   Séclin (Nord)
16 Dec. 1857   250,000F
BL, 11th ser., 1857, PS, X, 1370–79

527. *La Minerve, Assurances Maritimes*   Paris
27 Jan. 1858   1,000,000F
BL, 11th ser., 1858, PS, XI, 173–82

528. *L'Abattoir de Châteaudun*   Châteaudun
22 May 1858   60,000F
$F^{12}6788$; BL, 11th ser., 1858, PS, XI, 921–31

529. *Compagnie de l'Approuague*   Cayenne
28 May 1858   2,000,000F (4,000,000F, 1863)
BL, 11th ser., 1858, PS, XI, 1105–16

530. *Manufactures de Glaces et Produits Chemiques de Saint-Gobain, Chauny et Cirey*   Paris
11 June 1858   3,600 shares (merger of nos. 135 and 280)
BL, 11th ser., 1858, PS, XI, 1145–59

531. *La Transatlantique, Assurances contre les Risques de Navigation Maritime et Intérieure*   Paris
13 Aug. 1858   1,500,000F
BL, 11th ser., 1858, PS, XII, 477–87

532. *Compagnie de Navigation Mixte*   Lyon
23 Aug. 1858   5,000,000F
$F^{12}6766$; BL, 11th ser., 1858, PS, XII, 424–33

533. *Compagnie Générale de Navigation*   Lyon
15 Sept. 1858   17,600 shares
$F^{12}6769$; BL, 11th ser., 1858, PS, XII, 628–42

534. *Caisse Générale des Familles, Assurances sur la Vie*   Paris
1 Oct. 1858   3,000,000F
BL, 11th ser., 1858, PS, XII, 675–94

535. *Entrepôt Général de la Villette*   Paris
13 Oct. 1858   8,400 shares
BL, 11th ser., 1858, PS, XII, 764–74

536. *L'Etoile de la Mer, Assurances Maritimes*   Paris
11 Dec. 1858   2,000,000F
BL, 11th ser., 1858, PS, XII, 1187–98

537. *Caisse Générale des Assurances Agricole*   Paris
   30 Dec. 1858   1,000,000F (12,000,000F, 1864)
   BL, 11th ser., 1858, PS, XII, 1265–86

238. *Docks et Entrepôts de Marseille*   Paris
   23 Feb. 1859   20,000,000F (40,000,000F, 1863)
   BL, 11th ser., 1859, PS, XIII, 457–79

539. *La Marine, Assurances Maritimes*   Paris
   26 Mar. 1859   1,000,000F
   BL, 11th ser., 1859, PS, XIII, 644–53

540. *Compagnie du Jardin Zoologique d'Acclimation*   Paris
   2 Apr. 1859   1,000,000F
   F¹²6784; BL, 11th ser., 1859, PS, XIII, 754–66

541. *Société Générale de Crédit Industriel et Commercial*   Paris
   7 May 1859   60,000,000F
   F¹²6778; BL, 11th ser., 1859, PS, XIII, 968–83

542. *Ports de Marseille*   Paris
   16 Aug. 1859   15,000,000F (merged with no. 490 to form no. 588)
   F¹²6781; BL, 11th ser., 1859, PS, XIV, 382–92

543. *Assurances Maritimes de Bordeaux*   Bordeaux
   16 Aug. 1859   1,000,000F
   BL, 11th ser., 1859, PS, XIV, 392–404

544. *Le Neptune, Assurances Maritimes*   Paris
   19 Sept. 1859   2,000,000F
   BL, 11th ser., 1859, PS, XIV, 590–601

545. *Magasin Général des Soies de Lyon*   Lyon (*Société Lyonnaise de Magasins des Soies, 1863*)
   29 Oct. 1859   1,850,000F
   BL, 11th ser., 1859, PS, XIV, 882–96

546. *Compagnie Havraise de Magasins Publics et de Magasins Généraux*   Havre
   13 Nov. 1859   1,500,000F (3,000,000F, 1861; 4,500,000F, 1863)
   BL, 11th ser., 1859, PS, XIV, 1073–84

547. *Compagnie des Eaux de Maisons-sur-Seine*   Paris
   5 Dec. 1859   250,000F
   F¹²6789; BL, 11th ser., 1859, PS, XIV, 1182–96

548. *Compagnie Générale de Omnibus de Bordeaux*   Bordeaux
   7 Jan. 1860   1,306 shares
   F¹²6759; BL, 11th ser., 1860, PS, XV, 69–77

549. *Ponts de Bougival et de Croissy*   Bougival
15 Feb. 1860   600 shares
F^{12}6754; BL, 11th ser., 1860, PS, XV, 253–64

550. *Houillères et Chemins de Fer de Carmaux*   Paris
21 Apr. 1860
F^{14}8233; BL, 11th ser., 1860, PS, XV, 794–803

551. *Le Circle Commercial, Assurances Maritimes*   Paris
25 June 1860   2,000,000F
BL, 11th ser., 1860, PS, XV, 1136–44

552. *Chemin de Fer de Lyon à la Croix-Rousse*   Paris
4 Aug. 1860   2,000,000F
BL, 11th ser., 1860, PS, XVI, 218–31

553. *L'Equateur, Assurances Maritimes*   Havre
4 Aug. 1860   1,000,000F
BL, 11th ser., 1860, PS, XVI, 233–41

554. *Eclairage au Gaz et des Hauts Fourneaux et Fonderies de Marseille et des Mines de Portes et Sénéchas*   Paris
16 Aug. 1860   21,600,000F
F^{14}8230; BL, 11th ser., 1860, PS, XVI, 326–35

555. *Compagnie de Remorquage sur la Barre de Sénégal*   Bordeaux
16 Aug. 1860   200,000F (dissolved 1871)
F^{12}6774; BL, 11th ser., 1860, PS, XVI, 277–85

556. *La Garantie Maritime, Assurances Maritimes*   Paris
18 Aug. 1860   1,000,000F (1,200,000F, 1861; 1,500,000F, 1863)
BL, 11th ser., 1860, PS, XVI, 337–44

557. *Entrepôts et Magasins Généraux de Paris*   Paris
22 Aug. 1860   40,000,000F
F^{12}6781; BL, 11th ser., 1860, PS, XVI, 345–55

558. *Crédit Colonial*   Paris (*Crédit Foncier Colonial, 1863*)
24 Oct. 1860   3,000,000F (12,000,000F, 1863)
BL, 11th ser., 1860, PS, XVI, 713–23

559. *L'Abeille, Assurances Maritimes*   Dijon
26 Dec. 1860   2,000,000F
BL, 11th ser., 1860, PS, XVI, 980–88

560. *Crédit Agricole*   Paris
16 Feb. 1861   20,000,000F (40,000,000F, 1865)
F^{12}6784; BL, 11th ser., 1861, PS, XVII, 281–311

561. *L'Amphitrite, Assurances Maritimes*   Paris
15 Apr. 1861   1,000,000F
BL, 11th ser., 1861, PS, XVII, 702–10

562. *La Gironde, Assurances Maritimes*   Bordeaux
25 May 1861   2,000,000F
BL, 11th ser., 1861, PS, XVII, 835–45

563. *Bains et Lavoirs Publics de Caen*   Caen
15 June 1861   580,000F
F^{12}6742; BL, 11th ser., 1861, PS, XVII, 1003–11

564. *Polders de l'Ouest*   Paris
27 July 1861   4,000,000F
F^{12}6795; BL, 11th ser., 1861, PS, XVIII, 331–41

565. *Chemin de Fer de Lyon, Croix-Rousse au Camp de Sathonay*   Paris
5 Aug. 1861   2,500,000F
BL, 11th ser., 1861, PS, XVIII, 377–96

566. *Compagnie Française de Réassurances contre l'Incendie*   Paris
10 Aug. 1861   6,000,000F
BL, 11th ser., 1861, PS, XVIII, 437–58

567. *La Flotte, Assurances Maritimes*   Paris
1 Oct. 1861   1,000,000F
BL, 11th ser., 1861, PS, XVIII, 729–36

568. *La Persévérante, Assurances Maritimes*   Havre
30 Oct. 1861   1,000,000F
BL, 11th ser., 1861, PS, XVIII, 828–37

569. *Anciennes Salines Domaniales de l'Est*   Paris
8 Jan. 1862   7,500 shares
BL, 11th ser., 1862, PS, XIX, 125–33

570. *La Gauloise, Assurances Maritimes*   Havre
25 Jan. 1862   1,000,000F
BL, 11th ser., 1862, PS, XIX, 185–95

571. *Eclairage par le Gaz de la Ville de Tarare*   Lyon
15 Mar. 1862   640 shares
BL, 11th ser., 1862, PS, XIX, 453–59

572. *Paquebots à Vapeur entre le Havre, Caen, Honfleur et les Ports de Normandie*   Havre
2 July 1862   1,000 shares (merger of nos. 217 and 479)
F^{12}6774; BL, 11th ser., 1862, PS, XX, 18–31

573. *Forges de Châtillon et Commentry*   Paris
10 July 1862   25,000 shares
F^{14}8229; BL, 11th ser., 1862, PS, XX, 145–54

574. *La Manche, Assurances Maritimes*   Havre
28 Aug. 1862   1,000,000F
BL, 11th ser., 1862, PS, XX, 389–98

575. *Compagnie Française d'Assurances Maritimes*   Paris
22 Sept. 1862   5,000,000F
BL, 11th ser., 1862, PS, XX, 496–509

576. *La Réassurance, Incendie*   Paris
29 Sept. 1862   5,000,000F
BL, 11th ser., 1862, PS, XX, 522–34

577. *Compagnie Nouvelle d'Assurances Maritimes du Havre*   Havre
6 Oct. 1862   1,200,000F
BL, 11th ser., 1862, PS, XX, 566–75

578. *Bateaux Express de la Seine*   Paris (*Bateaux Porteurs Express de la Seine, 1865*)
1 Nov. 1862   1,000 shares (2,000 shares, 1865; dissolved 1868)
F^{12}6774; BL, 11th ser., 1862, PS, XX, 783–95

579. *Compagnie Fermière de l'Etablissement Thermal de Vichy*   Paris
27 Dec. 1862
F^{12}6743; BL, 11th ser., 1863, PS, XXI, 52–59

580. *Le Sémaphore, Assurances Maritimes*   Paris
21 Feb. 1863   3,000,000F
BL, 11th ser., 1863, PS, XXI, 389–98

581. *La Globe, Assurances Maritimes*   Havre
28 Feb. 1863   1,000,000F
BL, 11th ser., 1863, PS, XXI, 462–72

582. *L'Industrie Française, Assurances Maritimes*   Marseille
1 Apr. 1863   1,500,000F
BL, 11th ser., 1863, PS, XXI, 845–54

583. *Compagnie de Madagascar, Foncière, Industrielle et Commerciale*   Paris
2 May 1863   50,000,000F
F^{12}6778; BL, 11th ser., 1863, PS, XXI, 958–69

584. *Chemin de Fer de Libourne à Bergerac*   Paris
9 May 1863   10,000,000F
BL, 11th ser., 1863, PS, XXI, 1022–53

585. *Houillères d'A'hun*   Paris
   9 May 1863   8,000 shares
   F¹⁴8230; BL, 11th ser., 1863, PS, XXI, 1057–66

586. *Chemins de Fer des Charentes*   Paris
   30 May 1863   25,000,000F
   BL, 11th ser., 1863, PS, XXI, 1245–1349

587. *Magasins Généraux de Bercy*   Paris
   6 June 1863   12,000 shares
   BL, 11th ser., 1863, PS, XXI, 1364–73

588. *Compagnie Immobilière*   Paris
   13 June 1863   80,000,000F (merger of nos. 490 and 542)
   F¹²6781, 6782; BL, 11th ser., 1863, PS, XXI, 1373–81

589. *Guyenne Maritime*   Bordeaux
   22 June 1863   1,000,000F
   BL, 11th ser., 1863, PS, XXII, 50–59

590. *Comptoir de l'Agriculture*   Paris
   6 July 1863   6,000,000F (dissolved 1874)
   F¹²6784; BL, 11th ser., 1863, PS, XXII, 126–37

591. *L'Approuvisionnement, Crédit des Halles et Marchés*   Paris
   6 July 1863   6,000,000F (dissolved 1869)
   F¹²6786; BL, 11th ser., 1863, PS, XXII, 137–48

592. *Société de Dépôts et de Comptes Courants*   Paris
   6 July 1863   60,000,000F
   F¹²6779; BL, 11th ser., 1863, PS, XXII, 181–237

593. *La Centrale, Assurances contre l'Incendie*   Paris
   12 Aug. 1863   3,000,000F (5,000,000F, 1864)
   BL, 11th ser., 1863, PS, XXII, 398–409

594. *Caisse Générale d'Assurances Commerciales contre les Risques
   Maritimes*   Paris
   29 Aug. 1863   5,000,000F
   BL, 11th ser., 1863, PS, XXII, 530–58

595. *Caisse Generale de Réassurances et de Coassurances contre les Risques
   d'Incendie*   Paris
   29 Aug. 1863   5,000,000F
   BL, 11th ser., 1863, PS, XXII, 565–93

596. *Magasins Publics et Généraux à Bordeaux*   Paris
   2 Sept. 1863   4,500,000F
   BL, 11th ser., 1863, PS, XXII, 636–60

597. *Houillères et du Chemin de Fer de Saint Eloi*   Paris
   7 Sept. 1863   6,000 shares
   F¹⁴8232; BL, 11th ser., 1863, PS, XXII, 596–605

598. *La France Maritime, Assurances Maritimes*   Paris
   9 Sept. 1863   2,000,000F
   BL, 11th ser., 1863, PS, XXII, 606–17

599. *Magasins Généraux de Tours*   Tours
   24 Sept. 1863   300 shares
   BL, 11th ser., 1863, PS, XXII, 763–74

600. *Quatre Mines Réunis de Graissessac*   Montpellier
   7 Oct. 1863   20,000 shares
   F¹⁴8230; BL, 11th ser., 1863, PS, XXII, 774–81

601. *L'Egide, Assurances Maritimes*   Paris
   7 Oct. 1863   1,000,000F
   BL, 11th ser., 1863, PS, XXII, 782–90

602. *Chemins de Fer de la Vendée*   Paris
   31 Oct. 1863   12,000,000F
   BL, 11th ser., 1863, PS, XXII, 977–88

603. *Compagnie Française des Cotons et Produits Agricoles Algériens*   Paris
   14 Dec. 1863   2,500,000F
   BL, 11th ser., 1863, PS, XXII, 1184–96

604. *Chantiers et Ateliers de l'Océan*   Paris
   14 Dec. 1863   24,000 shares
   BL, 11th ser., 1863, PS, XXII, 1197–1216

605. *Chemin de Fer du Médoc*   Paris
   2 Mar. 1864   10,000,000F
   BL, 11th ser., 1864, PS, XXIII, 482–508

606. *Compagnie Lyonnaise des Magasins Généraux de la Gare de Vaise*   Lyon
   9 Apr. 1864   2,000 shares
   BL, 11th ser., 1864, PS, XXIII, 1029–37

607. *Le Monde, Assurances à Primes Fixes contre l'Incendie*   Paris
   27 Apr. 1864   5,000,000F
   BL, 11th ser., 1864, PS, XXIII, 1129–54

608. *Le Monde, Assurances à Primes Fixes sur la Vie des Hommes*   Paris
   27 Apr. 1864   5,000,000F
   BL, 11th ser., 1864, PS, XXIII, 1155–89

609. *Société Générale pour Favoriser le Développement du Commerce et de l'Industrie en France*   Paris
     4 May 1864   120,000,000F
     F¹²6776; BL, 11th ser., 1864, PS, XXIII, 1357–82

610. *La Garonne, Assurance Maritime*   Bordeaux
     28 May 1864   3,000,000F
     BL, 11th ser., 1864, PS, XXIII, 1304–14

611. *L'Internationale, Assurances Maritimes et Fluviales*   Paris
     18 June 1864   2,000,000F
     BL, 11th ser., 1864, PS, XXIII, 1462–71

612. *Parc et du Jardin d'Acclimatation de Bordeaux*   Bordeaux
     13 Aug. 1864   550,000F
     F¹²6788; BL, 11th ser., 1864, PS, XXIV, 340–50

613. *Immeubles de Deauville*   Deauville
     10 Sept. 1864   5,000 shares
     F¹²6783; BL, 11th ser., 1864, PS, XXIV, 592–605

614. *Compagnie de la Dombes*   Paris
     17 Sept. 1864   5,000,000F
     BL, 11th ser., 1864, PS, XXIV, 661–72

615. *Aciéries d'Imphy et de Saint-Seurin*   Paris
     24 Dec. 1864   12,000 shares
     F¹⁴8232; BL, 11th ser., 1864, PS, XXIV, 1096–1104

616. *Entrepôts et de Magasins Généraux*   Amiens
     25 Jan. 1865   1,000 shares
     BL, 11th ser., 1865, PS, XXV, 251–64

617. *Houillères de Rulhe*   Paris
     25 Jan. 1865   1,200 shares
     F¹⁴8229; BL, 11th ser., 1865, PS, XXV, 264–73

618. *Pont Saint-Pierre*   Toulouse
     4 Mar. 1865   300 shares
     BL, 11th ser., 1865, PS, XXV, 426–35

619. *L'Urbaine, Assurances à Primes Fixes sur la Vie Humaine*   Paris
     1 Apr. 1865   6,000,000F (merged with no. 525, 1866)
     BL, 11th ser., 1865, PS, XXV, 769–80

620. *Chemin de Fer de Lille à Béthune et à Bully-Grenay*   Paris
     22 May 1865   8,000 shares
     BL, 11th ser., 1865, PS, XXV, 1097–1115

621. *Magasins Généraux à Nevers*   Nevers
24 May 1865   600 shares
BL, 11th ser., 1865, PS, XXV, 1117–31

622. *Société Lyonnaise de Dépôts et de Comptes Courants et de Crédit Industriel*   Lyon
8 July 1865   20,000,000F
F^{12}6777; BL, 11th ser., 1865, PS, XXVI, 89–117

623. *La Sphère, Assurances Maritimes*   Paris
12 July 1865   2,000,000F
BL, 11th ser., 1865, PS, XXVI, 138–51

624. *Les Deux-Poles, Assurances Maritimes*   Havre
30 Aug. 1865   1,000,000F
BL, 11th ser., 1865, PS, XXVI, 403–12

625. *Société Marseillaise de Crédit Industriel et Commercial et de Dépôts*   Marseille
2 Oct. 1865   20,000,000F
F^{12}6777; BL, 11th ser., 1865, PS, XXVI, 676–95

626. *La Sécurité Sociale, Assurances à Primes Fixes contre les Accidents Pouvant Atteindre les Personnes*   Paris
11 Nov. 1865   2,500,000F
BL, 11th ser., 1865, PS, XXVI, 830–44

627. *La Créole, Assurances à Primes Fixes contre l'Incendie*   Saint-Denis
(Ile de la Reunion)
27 Nov. 1865   1,500,000F
BL, 11th ser., 1866, PS, XXVII, 78–92

628. *La Confiance Maritime, Assurances Maritimes et Fluviales*   Paris
14 Apr. 1866   3,000,000F
BL, 11th ser., 1866, PS, XXVII, 766–75

629. *Chemin de Fer de Vitré à Fougères*   Paris
18 Apr. 1866   1,100,000F
BL, 11th ser., 1866, PS, XXVII, 1093–1114

630. *Crédit Industriel et de Dépôts du Nord*   Lille
5 May 1866   20,000,000F
F^{12}6779; BL, 11th ser., 1866, PS, XXVII, 986–1015

631. *Caisse des Associations Coopératives*   Paris
5 Aug. 1866   1,000,000F (dissolved 1873)
F^{12}6779; BL, 11th ser., 1866, PS, XXVIII, 284–91

632. *Compagnie Générale des Voitures à Paris*   Paris
    5 Aug. 1866   85,000 shares
    F¹²6762, 6763; BL, 11th ser., 1866, PS, XXVIII, 291–99

633. *Eclairage et de Chauffage par le Gaz de la Ville de Versailles et de ses Environs*   Versailles
    11 Aug. 1866
    BL, 11th ser., 1866, PS, XXVIII, 354–63

634. *Maisons Ouvrières*   Amiens
    1 Oct. 1866   300,000F
    F¹²6783; BL, 11th ser., 1866, PS, XXVIII, 763–72

635. *Société Générale Algerienne*   Paris
    15 Oct. 1866   100,000,000F
    F¹²6777; BL, 11th ser., 1866, PS, XXVIII, 1033–96

636. *Association des Tisseurs de Lyon*   Lyon
    8 Feb. 1867   1,500,000F
    F¹²6796; BL, 11th ser., 1867, PS, XXIX, 508–22

637. *Chemin de Fer de Glos-Montfort à Pont-Audemer*   Evreux
    20 Feb. 1867   1,500,000F
    BL, 11th ser., 1867, PS, XXIX, 748–63

638. *Associations des Tullistes*   Lyon
    30 Mar. 1867   600,000F
    F¹²6796; BL, 11th ser., 1867, PS, XXIX, 834–42

639. *Chemin de Fer de Vassy à Saint-Dizier*   Vassy
    27 Apr. 1867   2,217 shares
    BL, 11th ser., 1867, PS, XXIX, 1102–21

640. *Association des Ouvriers Teinturiers des Villes de Lyon et de Saint Etienne*   Lyon
    1 June 1867   400,000F
    BL, 11th ser., 1867, PS, XXIX, 1369–77

641. *Maisons à Bon Marché*   Paris
    8 June 1867   3,000,000F
    F¹²6783; BL, 11th ser., 1867, PS, XXIX, 1460–69

642. *Chemin de Fer de Pont-de-l'Arche à Gisors*   Evreux
    10 July 1867   3,000,000F
    BL, 11th ser., 1867, PS, XXX, 861–88

Notes

ABBREVIATIONS TO THE NOTES
AD: Archives Departmentales
AN: Archives Nationales
BL: *Bulletin des lois*
CCP: Archives of the Chamber of Commerce of Paris
F^{12} and F^{14}: Materials in the Archives Nationales
MU: *Moniteur universel*

INTRODUCTION
1. Charles Lescoeur, *Essai historique et critique sur la législation des sociétés commerciales en France et à l'étranger*.
2. The benefits of liberalization were not, of course, part of the official wisdom of the time. Contemporaries believed that restrictions on the formation of corporations were a brake on speculation and a positive defense against economic disaster. One historian, Arthur Louis Dunham, leans toward this view (*The Industrial Revolution in France, 1815–1848*, pp. 407–19).

CHAPTER 1
1. It contained only 122 articles divided into twelve sections. The longest section was on bills of exchange (33 articles). The entire ordinance fills only sixteen pages in Isambert's *Recueil général des anciennes lois françaises depuis l'an 420 jusqu'à la révolution de 1789*, 19:91–107.
2. Two of Savary's sons continued the tradition by publishing a multivolume *Dictionnaire universel de commerce* (1st ed., 1723), a standard eighteenth-century reference work for businessmen and jurists alike.
3. The ordinance does not explicitly deny *commanditaires* the right to participate in the management of the enterprise, but, according to Savary, they could not (Jacques Savary, *Le Parfait Négociant*, p. 350).
4. Savary added a third type, the *société anonyme*, which was simply a temporary agreement involving a commercial transaction by businessmen acting in their own name (ibid.). In effect, it was not a form of business organization, although the courts accepted the distinction. Public registration was not required, and these agreements remained unknown to the public unless a conflict arising between the parties resulted in litigation. The *Code de Commerce* of 1807 was to give this designation to one of the types of joint-stock company.
5. Henri Lévy-Bruhl, *Histoire juridique des sociétés de commerce en France aux XVIIe et XVIIIe siècles*, p. 31. This is the standard work for the period.
6. Ibid., pp. 28 and 93; Jean Meyer, *L'Armement nantais dans la deuxième moitié du XVIIIe siècle*, pp. 96–117.
7. Lévy-Bruhl, *Histoire juridique des sociétés de commerce*, p. 33.
8. Ibid., p. 36.
9. Quoted in Pierre Boucher, *Institutions commerciales*, p. 167.
10. Lévy-Bruhl, *Histoire juridique des sociétés de commerce*, p. 88.
11. Ibid., p. 46. The earliest found by Lévy-Bruhl was formed in 1772.
12. Ibid., p. 48.

13. Henri Lévy-Bruhl, *Un projet de Code de Commerce à la veille de la révolution, le projet Miromesnil, 1778–1789.*

14. Ibid., p. 20.

15. Lévy-Bruhl, *Histoire juridique des sociétés de commerce*, pp. 244–45.

16. Ibid., pp. 50 and 247–48.

17. Ibid., p. 217.

18. Malachy Postlethwayt, *Universal Dictionary of Trade and Commerce*, 2:764. This work was based largely upon Jacques Savary des Bruslons, *Dictionnaire universel de commerce*, first published in 1723.

19. Fernand Braudel and Ernst Labrousse, eds., *Histoire économique et sociale de la France*, 2:255.

20. Savary des Bruslons, *Dictionnaire universel de commerce*, 1:27. The same distinctions appear in the first edition (1723).

21. Lévy-Bruhl, *Histoire juridique des societes de commerce*, p. 47.

22. Ibid., pp. 228–29.

23. Braudel and Labrousse, *Histoire économique et sociale*, 2:255.

24. Guy Richard, "La Noblesse de France et les sociétés par actions à la fin du XVIIIe siècle," p. 489.

25. Ibid., p. 493.

26. Ibid., p. 496. Cf. Meyer, *L'Armement nantais*, p. 114.

27. Richard, "La Noblesse," pp. 496–98.

28. Ibid., p. 503; Louis Joseph Gras, *Histoire économique générale des mines de la Loire*, 1: 65–67 and 204.

29. Jean Chevalier, *Le Creusot* (Paris, 1935), p. 52, quoted in Bertrand Gille, *Les Origines de la grande industrie métallurgique en France*, p. 129. For a detailed account of the founding of Le Creusot, see Denise Ozanam, "La Naissance du Creusot," 103–18.

30. Ozanam, "La Naissance," p. 116.

31. Robert Bigo, *La Caisse d'Escompte (1776–1793) et les origines de la Banque de France*, p. 97.

32. George V. Taylor, "The Paris Bourse on the Eve of the Revolution, 1781–1789," p. 967.

33. Ibid., pp. 953–54.

34. Albert Soboul, *Les Sans-culottes parisiens en l'an II*, p. 78.

35. *Réimpression de l'ancien Moniteur*, 17:484. A year earlier, the law of 27 August 1792 had ordered registration in the name of the owner of all shares and a registration of all transfers of shares. The flouting of this law was a subject of numerous denounciations in the Convention (Marcel Marion, *Histoire financière de la France depuis 1715*, 3:89–90).

36. Marion, *Histoire financière*, 3:89.

37. Gabriel Ramon, *Histoire de la Banque de France*, pp. 22–24.

38. Vital-Roux, *De l'influence du gouvernement sur la prospérité du commerce*, p. 443. The need for a new code was also echoed by Pierre Boucher, whose *Institutions commerciales* appeared in 1801, shortly after the commission finished its first draft of the code. Boucher, a former bookkeeper in Bordeaux, taught commercial law in Paris. In 1809 he went to Saint Petersburg as a councillor of state with responsibility over commercial affairs and there he remained.

39. The members of the commission, besides Vital-Roux, were: Gorneau, a judge on the court of appeal of Paris; Vignon, president of the tribunal of commerce of Paris; Boursier, a former judge on a commercial court; Legras, a legist; Coulomb, a former judge; and Mourgue, a hospital administrator.

40. *Projet de Code du Commerce*, présenté par la commission nomée par le Gouvernement le 13 Germinal an IX.

41. Ibid., p. vi.

42. Ibid., pp. x–xi.

43. Henri Lévy-Bruhl believes this to have been the case: *Un Projet de Code de Commerce à la veille de la révolution*, pp. 28–29.

44. Arrêt du 14 Frimaire, An X (5 December 1801). These institutions were given two months to formulate their observations.

45. *Observations des tribunaux de cassation et d'appel, des tribunaux et conseils de commerce, &c. sur le projet de Code du Commerce.*

46. The minister of the interior requested the prefects to urge joint deliberations ($F^{12}543$).

47. *Observations des tribunaux de cassation et d'appel*, 2:447.

48. *Révision du projet de Code du Commerce*, pp. 19–20.

49. Emile Levasseur, *Histoire du commerce de la France*, 2:46–47.

50. J. G. Locré, *Esprit du Code du Commerce*, 1:93–156. Only brief fragments of the discussions are reported in these volumes.

51. Ibid., 1:149–50.

52. Ibid., 1:150.

53. Ibid., 1:150–52

54. Ibid., 1:156.

55. This regulation assumes that the partnership agreement had granted them such power (the right of the *signature social*). In some partnerships, only one of the partners possessed the authority to bind the enterprise legally. Many partnership agreements set forth the division of labor among the partners in great detail.

56. *Code de Commerce*, p. 16.

57. Ibid., appendix.

58. I have identified fifteen *sociétés anonymes* from (1) authorizing decrees appearing in the *Bulletin des lois*, (2) the list of all *sociétés anonymes* founded in France from 1808 to 1837 contained in *Archives statistique du ministère des travaux publics et de l'agriculture et du commerce*, and (3) the records of the ministry of commerce in the Archives nationales. None of the three are complete, and each identifies enterprises not found in the other two, but the collective total may be regarded as fairly accurate. Of the fifteen, eight were authorized in 1808 and the rest between 1809 and 1812. The records of the ministry of commerce also contain some information on eight enterprises that were refused authorization.

59. $F^{12}6757$, min. of int. to the emperor, 4 May 1808.

60. Ibid.

61. $F^{12}6757$.

62. $F^{12}6809$.

63. Ibid. A provision empowering the corporation to borrow extensively was objected to as unwise.

64. $F^{12}6808$.

65. $F^{12}6740$, prefect of police to min. of int., 19 Apr. 1808.

66. $F^{14}8230$.

67. $F^{12}6794$.

68. $F^{12}6728$. The Culture de Pastel et la Fabrication de l'Indigo was required to furnish the ministry with an "exact and detailed" financial report every year.

69. $F^{12}6813$.

CHAPTER 2

1. Ministère de l'intérieur, *Circulaires, instructions, et autres actes*, 3:267–73 and 348–55.
2. Ibid., 3:268.
3. Ibid.
4. Ibid.
5. Ibid., 3:270.
6. Ibid.
7. Ibid., 3:271.
8. Ibid., 3:349.
9. Ibid., 3:350–53. After 1818 the charters of almost all companies were published in the *Bulletin des lois*.
10. It was reduced to 15 million francs in 1821.
11. Ministère de l'intérieur, *Circulaires, instructions, et autres actes*, 3:353. In 1818, the Compagnie d'Assurances de Bordeaux was denied the right to assure both marine and fire risks. Accordingly, the right to insure fire risks was dropped from its charter. In 1820, this company was reorganized as two separate companies, one for marine insurance, the other for fire (BL, 7th ser., 1820, 1st sem., 738–39).
12. Emile Vincens, *Exposition raisonnée de la législation commerciale*, 1:245–46.
13. Bertrand Gille, *La Banque et le crédit en France de 1815 à 1848*, pp. 89–91.
14. Ibid.
15. Ibid., pp. 129–31.
16. F^{12}6825.
17. A large advisory body attached to the ministry of commerce, the Conseil Général de Commerce was composed of prominent businessmen. Twenty of its members were appointed by the crown, and each chamber of commerce, of which there were thirty-one in 1821, named one member. In 1821 there were six vacancies in the first group and four in the second (*Almanach royal, 1821*, pp. 161–62).
18. F^{12}6825.
19. Ibid., min. of fin. to min. of int., 19 Oct. 1822.
20. BL, 7th ser., 1818, 2d sem., 278.
21. Fernand Lepelletier, *Les Caisses d'épargnes*, p. 22.
22. Robert Bigo, *Les Banques françaises au cours de XIXe siècle*, pp. 203–4.
23. Ministère de l'agriculture et du commerce, *Rapport au Président de la République sur les caisses d'épargnes, Année 1847*, pp. vii–viii.
24. F^{14}8232, Rapport du ingenieur en chef du Corp Royal des Mines (de Mattieu), 16 Dec. 1816. The implication is that an *anonyme* would be cost conscious in its mining methods and more interested in immediate profits than in a rational exploitation aimed at extracting all the coal.
25. Ibid.
26. Ibid.
27. F^{12}6739. These motives appear as an introduction to the company's draft charter.
28. Ibid.
29. Ibid., letter from Desrousseaux to Count Chaptal, 3 Apr. 1815.
30. BL, 7th ser., 1818, 1st sem., 177–99. The sixty-four bearer shares could be subdivided into *coupons* of 2,500 francs.
31. Banque de Bordeaux: BL, 7th ser., 1818, 2d sem., 725–60. The 3,000 shares of the bank were divided among 160 shareholders. The smallest holding was 5 shares, the largest 25. Pont de la Dordogne: BL, 7th ser., 1818, 2d sem., 411–25. Pont de Bordeaux: BL, 7th ser., 1818, 1st sem., 289–98.

32. BL, 7th ser., 1818, 2d sem., 354–76. Initially, each of the original shareholders subscribed for two bearer shares for every registered share. There were 135 shareholders.

33. The incomplete records of the ministries of commerce and public works contain some information on about sixty enterprises that did not receive authorization.

34. Gille, *La Banque et le crédit*, pp. 301–29.

35. Pierre J. Proudhon, *Manuel du spéculateur à la bourse*, p. 271.

36. The participation shares were eventually purchased by the government during the early years of the Second Empire.

37. F¹²6771; Félix Rivet, *La Navigation à vapeur sur la Saône et le Rhône, 1783–1863*, pp. 94–95.

38. Bertrand Gille, *Recherches sur la formation de la grande entreprise capitaliste*, p. 74.

39. Ordinances of 20 May 1829 and 15 May 1832 (BL, 8th ser., 1829, I, no. 301 bis, 26–32, and 9th ser., 1832, PS, I, 521–24).

40. BL, 8th ser., 1830, II, no. 340 bis, 7–20.

41. Gille, *Grande entreprise capitaliste*, p. 81.

42. F¹⁴8232, draft charter.

43. G. Villepreux, "Un Maître de forges sous quatre régimes," p. 217.

44. F¹⁴8233, Audincourt dossier; BL, 7th ser., 1822, 2nd sem., 625–44.

45. BL, 9th ser., 1830, I, no. 27 bis, 11–23.

46. Gille, *La Banque et le crédit*, pp. 128–29. One was the Caisse d'Economie et d'Accumulation, de Garantie et d'Amortissement des Dettes (BL, 7th ser., 1821, 2d sem., 130–44), capitalized at 600,000 francs. The other was the Caisse d'Economie et d'Accumulation, avec Assurances des Capitaux (BL, 7th ser., 1821, 2d sem., 145–57), capitalized at 1,500,000 francs. Both were founded by the same group. Each was to have had a commissioner, appointed by the government, who was to report every six months on the operation of his bank.

47. Gille, *La Banque et le crédit*, p. 321.

48. There is a list of the founders in Jacques Bresson, *Histoire financière de la France depuis l'origine de la monarchie jusqu'à l'année 1828*, 2:402–4.

49. Ibid., 2:404; Gille, *La Banque et le crédit*, pp. 109–13, gives the most complete account of the project.

50. M. A. Jullien, *Revue encyclopédique*, pp. 41–44.

51. Gille, *La Banque et le crédit*, p. 113.

52. F¹²6741, Avis du Conseil d'Etat, 2 Jan. 1823.

53. François Renaud, "Le Cartel des cristaux, 1830–1857," pp. 7–20.

54. Gille, *Grande entreprise capitaliste*, pp. 158–59.

55. Claude Fohlen, *L'Industrie textile au temps du Second Empire*, p. 99. Fohlen also stresses the deep-seated penchant for secrecy of textile entrepreneurs, which was incompatible with the joint-stock form of business organization.

56. F¹²6741.

57. Ibid., Rapport au ministre, 30 Aug. 1825.

58. F¹²6741, Conseil Général du Commerce to min., 12 Sept. 1825.

59. BL, 8th ser., 1826, I, no. 102 bis, 31–40.

60. F¹²6811, Avis du Conseil d'Etat, 18 Sept. 1828.

61. Ibid.

62. Occasionally the prefects were more zealous. The report of the prefect of Paris on the request for authorization of the Pont, Gare, et Port de Grenelle, authorized in 1826, discussed the credit worthiness of each of the company's forty-three stockholders. In the

prefect's opinion, the substance of a few small stockholders was questionable (F¹²6792).

63. CCP, Procès verbaux, 11 Feb. 1818. It is not clear if this letter from the minister was a reply to a request from the chamber of Paris that it be consulted.

64. Occasionally, one of the chambers would on its own initiative support the request of an enterprise for authorization.

65. For example, in the projected Société pour l'Exploitation du Théâtre de Brest, the ministry and the Conseil d'Etat suggested two-thirds or three-quarters (F¹²6832, Rapport au ministre, 24 Aug. 1829; Avis du Conseil d'Etat, 14 Oct. 1829).

66. F¹²6820, Rapport au ministre, 22 Oct. 1829; Avis du Conseil d'Etat, 25 Nov. 1829.

67. F¹²6820, Avis du Conseil d'Etat, 25 Nov. 1829. The Conseil suggested that a reserve of 100,000 francs was adequate.

68. The minister of the interior wrote to the Chamber of Commerce of Paris that these balance sheets were a convenient way to provide publicity on the enterprise (CCP, min. to chamber, 13 Oct. 1820). Earlier, the chamber of Paris had written to the minister of the interior, asking what obligation it had in regard to the balance sheets being deposited with it (CCP, chamber to min., 5 Oct. 1820). The minister did invite the chamber of Paris to submit any observations on the balance sheets "either relative to the guarantees that *sociétés anonymes* must afford the public, or in relation to the impact they could have on commerce in general" (CCP, min. to chamber, 13 Oct. 1820).

69. For example, the company Coches de la Haute Seine, authorized in 1824, was permitted to pay 6 percent interest on its shares (F¹²6758). The Compagnie du Pont, Gare, et Port de Grenelle, authorized in 1826, was permitted to pay 5 percent interest; in this case the government permitted interest payments from the enterprise's capital until construction of its bridge, port, and warehouse facilities was completed (F¹²6792, Avis du Conseil d'Etat, 5 July 1826).

70. For the Verreries de Lamotte, authorized in 1828, the Conseil d'Etat refused to allow the payment of interest (F¹²6741, Avis du Conseil D'Etat, 7 Sept. 1827).

71. The company Paquebots à Vapeur de la Gironde raised its capital from 900,000 to 930,000 francs to provide working capital (F¹²6771, Rapport au ministre, 3 Aug. 1832; Avis du Conseil d'Etat, 2 Nov. 1832). The Conseil d'Etat proposed that the capital of 320,000 francs of the Transports Accélérés par Eau be doubled (F¹²6770, Avis du Conseil d'Etat, 1 Aug. 1821). The Conseil eventually accepted a raise of 25 percent.

72. F¹²6771, Compagnie des Transport par Eau d'Elbeuf à Rouen, Avis du Conseil d'Etat, 23 May 1827.

73. F¹²6771.

74. F¹⁴8233, Rapport au Conseil Général des Mines, 18 June 1827.

75. BL, 8th ser., 1828, I, no. 251 bis, 1–20. The charter did provide for a reserve fund to be raised by a levy of 15 percent of annual net profits until it reached 100,000 francs.

76. F¹²6771, Rapport au ministre, 3 Aug. 1832.

77. Ibid.; F¹²6771, Avis du Conseil d'Etat, 3 Nov. 1832. After agreeing to many changes in its charter, the company was authorized.

78. F¹²6733. Of the enterprise's 1,250 shares, 250 were held by Charles X (BL, 8th ser., 1826, II, no. 135 bis, 16–31).

79. F¹²6787.

80. F¹²6740, Avis du Conseil d'Etat, 20 Nov. 1829; letter from Maison du Roi, 22 Jan. 1830.

81. Companies, including the major canal companies were also named after members of the royal family. For example, an experimental farm in the Gironde Department

was named after the Duc de Bordeaux; this was essentially a philanthropic enterprise that had been denied the designation of "Ecole Royale" ($F^{12}6787$). The Bains Caroline at Dieppe, authorized in 1826, was named after the Duchesse de Berry with her approval and also that of Charles X ($F^{12}6793$). The names of these companies were all changed after 1830.

82. The provision in the draft charter of the Compagnie de Paquebots à Vapeur de Bordeaux au Havre that the director could be removed only for just cause (*motifs légitimes*) was rejected ($F^{12}6771$).

83. $F^{12}6771$.

84. Ibid.

85. $F^{12}6790$. The charter of this enterprise, authorized in 1829, also provided that no one could own more than ten shares.

86. $F^{12}6792$, Avis du Conseil d'Etat, 5 July 1826.

87. $F^{14}8230$, Rapport au Conseil Général des Mines, 23 May 1831.

88. $F^{14}8230$, Avis du Conseil Général des Mines, 23 May 1831.

89. $F^{14}8233$, Rapport au Conseil Général des Mines, 11 Dec. 1822.

90. $F^{14}8233$, Avis du Conseil Général des Mines, 31 Dec. 1822.

91. $F^{14}8233$, Rapport au Conseil Général des Mines, 23 Apr. 1827.

92. Ibid.

93. $F^{14}8233$, Avis du Conseil Général des Mines, 30 May 1831.

94. $F^{14}8233$, Rapport au Conseil Général des Mines, 14 May 1832.

95. Ibid.

96. *Enquête sur les fers de 1828* (Paris, 1829), quoted in Bertrand Gille, *La Sidérurgie française au XIXe siècle*, p. 90. Beanuier was a divisional inspector of mines and a member of the Conseil Général des Mines.

CHAPTER 3

1. Under the code, the *société anonyme* was named according to the object of the enterprise; the name of a person could not be used.

2. Such a model appears in Malepeyre and Jourdain, *Traité des sociétés commerciales*, pp. 462–69.

3. The text of the decision is in Malepeyre and Jourdain, *Traité des sociétés commerciales*, pp. 144–45.

4. Dalloz, *Jurisprudence générale du royaume en matière civile, commerciale, criminelle et administrative, recueil périodique* (1832), 2d pt., pp. 107–11.

5. There was one.

6. AD, Seine, D31, U^3, cartons 54–57.

7. Sicard was apparently a man of some scruple, because these shares were nonnegotiable (AD, Seine, D31, U^3, actes nos. 1,033, 1,135, and 1,606).

8. AD, Seine, D31, U^3, nos. 934 and 1,275.

9. Ibid., no. 8, registered on 3 Jan. 1837.

10. Ibid., no. 1,401. Its shares were *au porteur* and were to bear interest of 4 percent.

11. Ibid., no. 1,367, 30 Oct. 1837; AD, Rhône, 8U, 30 Oct. 1837.

12. Louis Wolowski, *Des sociétés par actions*, p. 7. The same estimate appears in the first issue of the monthly *Le Capitaliste* in April 1838.

13. Jacques Bresson, *Annuaire de 1840 des sociétés par actions anonymes, civiles, et en commandite*, p. ii.

14. Maurice Lévy-Leboyer, *Les Banques européennes et l'industrialisation international dans la première moitié du XIXe siècle*, p. 618, n. 105.

15. *Gazette des tribunaux*, 30 Aug. 1837, p. 1061.

16. Emile Vincens, *Des sociétés par actions, des banques en France.*
17. Ibid., pp. 28–29.
18. Ibid., pp. 23–25.
19. Ibid., p. 22.
20. Ibid., pp. 89–90.
21. AN, BB³⁰278.
22. Ibid., session of 23 Nov. 1837.
23. Ibid., session of 17 Jan. 1838.
24. MU, session of 15 Feb. 1838, p. 313.
25. Ibid.
26. The minister quoted the fear expressed by Cambacérès in 1807 during the discussion in the Conseil d'Etat—which had since become reality—that Article 38 would "allow a veritable *société anonyme* to conceal itself behind the facade of a *société en commandite* to avoid obtaining government authorization."
27. MU, session of 15 Feb. 1838, p. 314.
28. These reports are in AN, BB³⁰278.
29. Charles Persil, "Des associations en commandite," pp. 89–101.
30. P[aillard de] V[illeneuve], "Des Sociétés en commandite, nécessité d'une réforme législatif."
31. Ibid., 27–28 Nov. 1837, p. 87.
32. Ibid., 1 Dec. 1837, p. 102.
33. Wolowski's work initially appeared as two articles in the *Revue de législation et de jurisprudence*. The committee acknowledged its indebtedness to him.
34. Wolowski, *Des sociétés par actions*, p. 79. P[aillard de] V[illeneuve]'s "Examen du projet de loi sur les sociétés par actions" expressed the same view (p. 401).
35. Wolowski, *Des sociétés par actions*, p. 11.
36. The committee bill was more restrictive than Wolowski's proposals. For example, Wolowski wanted to retain bearer shares, which the committee bill eliminated.
37. Other members of the committee were Odilon Barrot, Félix Real, Sylvain Dumon, and M. B. Guyet-Desfontaines.
38. MU, 25 Apr. 1838, p. 1010.
39. Ibid.
40. Ibid.
41. Ibid.
42. Most of the restrictions did not apply to *commandites* whose shares were in denominations of 5,000 francs or more.
43. The information given here is drawn from the account of the two trials published in the *Gazette des tribunaux* in the issues of 21, 22, 23, and 24 June; 1 July; and 17, 18, 19, 20, 23, and 24 August 1838. The parties were represented by some of the foremost luminaries of the Paris bar: Berryer and Baroche for the plaintiffs and Philippe Dupin, Delangle, Crémieux, and Teste for the defendants.
44. The company was registered at the commercial tribunal of Paris on 15 Aug. 1837 under the firm name Louis Cleemann et Cie. (AD, Seine, D31 U³, no. 982).
45. It appears that the value of the mines was then closer to 1,300,000 francs. However, as *maître* Delangle pointed out, it was no crime to sell something for more than you had paid for it.
46. See the advertisement for the company in the *Gazette des tribunaux*, 13 Aug. 1837, p. 1008.
47. Georges Ripert, *Aspects juridiques du capitalisme moderne*, p. 58.
48. André Cochut, "La Politique du libre échange," p. 332.

49. Paul Thureau-Dangin, *Histoire de la monarchie de juillet,* 3:238–41; Marcel Marion, *Histoire financière de la France depuis 1715,* 5:179–86; Emile Levasseur, *Histoire du commerce de la France,* 2:199. The defeats involved the pension for the widow of General Damrémont in February, the rejection of an important railroad bill in May, and the passage of a debt conversion bill over the government's opposition.

CHAPTER 4

1. The main elements of the 1842 law were planned by an extraparliamentary committee in late 1839 and early 1840. See Jean-Paul Adam, *Instauration de la politique des chemins de fer en France,* and Alfred Picard, *Les Chemins de fer français,* vol. 1.

2. Arthur Louis Dunham, *The Industrial Revolution in France, 1815–1848,* p. 62.

3. Ibid., pp. 76–77.

4. Bibliothèque de l'Institut de France, Papiers Carette, MS 4751, A. G. Aubé, "Souvenirs du passage de 18 mois au Conseil d'Etat," pp. 61–63.

5. Ibid., p. 64.

6. Ibid.

7. Bertrand Gille, *La Banque et le crédit en France de 1815 à 1848,* pp. 192–93.

8. *Le Centenaire de l'Union, Compagnie d'Assurances sur la Vie Humaine, 1829–1929,* p. 17.

9. On the rise and decline of tontines during the 1840s, see V. Senés, *Les Origines des compagnies d'assurances fondées en France depuis le XVIIe siècle jusqu'à nos jours,* pp. 333–35. Many members of the Conseil d'Etat were skeptical about tontines. The matter first came before the Conseil in 1838, when the Royale life company requested permission to administer tontines. Only three members of the committee of commerce voted in favor. To a majority of the committee, tontines resembled lotteries and hence were immoral. This decision was reversed by the General Assembly of the Conseil d'Etat by a majority of only one vote. Bibliothèque de l'Institut de France, Papiers Carette, MS 4751, Aubé, "Souvenirs," pp. 31–32. The growing popularity of tontines resulted in the issue of a regulatory ordinance on 12 June 1842.

10. *Le Centenaire de l'Union,* p. 18.

11. On departmental banks, see Gille, *La Banque et le crédit,* pp. 89–104; see Bertrand Gille's *La Banque en France au XIXe siècle,* pp. 18–75, for details on the founding of the banks of Havre, Lille, Lyon, and Marseille.

12. Ten persons, each taking 200 shares, subscribed the entire capital of the Bank of Lyon (BL, 9th ser. 1835, 2d pt, XI, 65). The capital of the Bank of Lille was subscribed by thirteen persons (BL, 9th ser., 1836, 2d pt, XIII, 231). The shares of the Bank of Lille were distributed among 127 shareholders by February 1838; ten years later there were 311 shareholders (Gille, *La Banque et le crédit,* p. 95).

13. Rondo Cameron et al., *Banking in the Early Stages of Industrialization,* p. 104.

14. Gabriel Ramon, *Histoire de la Banque de France,* pp. 198–99.

15. Ibid., pp. 223–31.

16. This figure is based upon the incomplete dossiers in the Archives Nationales, $F^{12}6829, 6830,$ and 6831.

17. One of these was the Caisse des Crédit Mutuels, projected by Hippolyte Ganneron and prominent bankers of Paris in 1838. The project was apparently abandoned before being submitted to the Conseil d'Etat ($F^{12}6829$).

18. P. Gaultier to min. of commerce, 13 June 1845, relative to the Banque Agricole ($F^{12}6829$).

19. Some of these projected banks are discussed in Gille, *La Banque et le crédit,* pp. 117–18 and 132–38.

20. This figure is based on the list of eleven in Bertrand Gille, *La Sidérurgie fran-çaise au XIXe siècle*, p. 166. I have counted Chatillon-Commentry as one firm, rather than two. The exceptions were Boigues frères at Fourchambault, de Wendel of Hayange and Moyeuvre, and Dietrich et fils in Alsace.

21. F^{14}8229.

22. In fact, the request failed to clear the preliminary hurdles and was not considered by either the Conseil Général des Mines or the Conseil d'Etat.

23. F^{14}8229, min. of pub. works to min. of commerce, 15 Dec. 1847. Most of the information in the minister's letter was drawn from the report of Baudin, engineer in chief (Allier), 4 Oct. 1847.

24. F^{14}8229, min. of commerce to min. of pub. works, 23 Feb. 1847.

25. Pierre Guillaume, *La Compagnie des Mines de la Loire, 1846–1854*, p. 42.

26. Ibid., pp. 15–16.

27. Ibid., pp. 18–19.

28. Ibid., pp. 75–76. The company was successful in obtaining the quotation of its shares on the Bourse in 1849.

29. Ibid., pp. 161–62.

30. The dossier of the company, F^{12}6729, contains a large amount of literature, both pro and con.

31. Guillaume, *La Compagnie des Mines de la Loire*, p. 198.

32. Ibid., p. 208.

33. Ibid., p. 209.

34. Ibid., p. 185.

35. Family control was facilitated by the provision in its original charter giving the board of directors the right to preempt the purchase of shares sold to outsiders. The company was permitted to retain this provision in 1841, even though the Conseil d'Etat had come to oppose such clauses.

36. Some excellent analytical essays on various aspects of the depression are to be found in Ernest Labrousse, ed., *Aspects de la crise et de la dépression, 1846–1851*.

37. Leland H. Jenks, *The Migration of British Capital to 1875*, p. 148.

38. Louis Girard, *La Politique des travaux publics du Second Empire*, p. 149.

39. Gille, *La Banque et le crédit*, pp. 159–60.

40. Jean Bouvier, *Les Rothschild*, pp. 143–44; Girard, *La Politique des travaux publics*, p. 47.

41. Girard, *La Politique des travaux publics*, pp. 181 and 293.

42. F^{12}6775; Pierre J. Proudhon, *Manuel du spéculateur à la bourse*, pp. 232–45; Pierre Dupont-Ferrier, *La Marché financier de Paris sous le Second Empire*, pp. 101–10.

43. Rondo Cameron, *France and the Economic Development of Europe, 1800–1914*, p. 129.

44. F^{12}6791; Cameron, *France and the Economic Development of Europe*, pp. 134–44; Gille, *La Banque en France au XIXe siècle*, pp. 125–43.

45. Cameron, *France and the Economic Development of Europe*, pp. 115–17.

46. Bertrand Gille, *Histoire de la maison Rothschild*, 2:100–103.

47. Cameron's *France and the Economic Development of Europe* contains the best account of the history of the Crédit Mobilier. Cameron rescues the Pereires from the hostile judgments of their enemies, which previous historians generally accepted.

48. Marcel Marion, *Histoire financière de la France depuis 1715*, 5:250; Jules Mirès, "La Banque de France et les comptoirs d'escompte," pp. 726–27; Proudhon, *Manuel du spéculateur*, pp. 227–32.

49. Dupont-Ferrier, *La Marché financier de Paris*, pp. 91–101.

50. Cameron, *France and the Economic Development of Europe*, pp. 126–27.

51. F¹²6778; Guy Beaujouan and Edmond Lebée, "La Fondation du Crédit Industriel et Commercial," pp. 6–40; Dupont-Ferrier, *La Marché financier de Paris*, pp. 145–52.

52. Although Beaujouan and Lebée, on p. 9 of "La Fondation du Crédit Industriel et Commercial," stress the desire of the government to head off a proposed investment bank projected by a syndicate of the *haute banque* and headed by Rothschild, fears concerning the general economic situation played a greater role.

53. F¹²6778, Avis du Conseil d'Etat, 20 Dec. 1856. This *avis* is printed in Beaujouan and Lebée, "La Fondation du Crédit Industriel et Commercial," pp. 33–34.

54. F¹²6778, Avis du Conseil d'Etat, 27 Jan. 1857. Beaujouan and Lebée, "La Fondation du Crédit Industriel et Commercial," p. 36. Part of the reason for the Conseil's refusal was its decision to permit the Comptoir d'Escompte de Paris to double its capital, which the Conseil claimed was sufficient to satisfy current needs.

55. In "La Fondation du Crédit Industriel et Commercial," Beaujouan and Lebée emphasize the role of Morny (p. 16). But if the role of Morny was decisive in November 1858, why not earlier? The Italian war was on the horizon, and Napoleon III may have regarded authorization as a contribution to soothing English sensibilities.

56. Ibid., pp. 17–21. The bank's official name was the Société Générale de Crédit Industriel et Commercial, but the first part of the title was soon dropped.

57. F¹²6778, Avis du Conseil d'Etat, 6 Aug. 1860.

58. Ibid.

59. Although the bank was capitalized at 60 million francs divided into 120,000 shares of 500 francs each, only 80,000 shares were initially issued, of which only a quarter (10 million francs) were called. The bank's deposits were therefore legally limited to 15 million francs until the decree of 16 February 1861 raised the figure to 60 million.

60. F¹²6827; Gille, *La Banque en France au XIXe siècle*, pp. 141–42.

61. F¹²6827.

62. F¹²6831. The chamber of Paris overturned the decision of its committee, which had suggested only modifications.

63. Ibid. It is not clear from the dossier why this attempt failed, but the project was still being pushed in 1864.

64. F¹²6329, founders to Count de Persigny, 28 Nov. 1852.

65. F¹²6830. It was a *société civile*, probably because the shareholders had no desire to trust their fate to a *gérant* of a *société en commandite*. The shareholders of a *société civile* were subject to unlimited liability.

66. Jean Bouvier, *Le Crédit Lyonnais de 1863 à 1882*, 1:120; Alphonse Courtois, fils, *Manuel des fonds publics*, pp. 497–98.

67. F¹²6830, prefect of Rhône to min. of commerce, 21 Dec. 1853. Thus, the chamber of Lyon continued to take a narrow view of what type of enterprise might appropriately be authorized.

68. Ibid., min. of fin. to min. of commerce, 6 Aug. 1853.

69. Cameron, *France and the Economic Development of Europe*, p. 131. Mirès's claim that his *caisse* afforded the idea and the model for the Crédit Mobilier has no basis. His allotment of 500 shares in the Crédit Mobilier may be attributed to the desire of the Pereires to have the *Journal des chemins de fer* on their side (Jules Mirès, *A mes juges, ma vie et mes affaires*, pp. 22–23).

70. F¹²6827, min. of commerce to J. Mirès, 17 July 1856.

71. F^{12}6827.
72. F^{12}6829.
73. In 1860, Calley de Saint-Paul announced the end of the bank. Using his broad powers as *gérant*, he employed the bank's capital to acquire the shares of the salt mining company Salines de l'Est: "The shareholders went to sleep one night co-participants in a bank; they awoke the next morning salt miners and merchants" (Georges Duchêne, *La Spéculation devant les tribunaux*, p. 174).
74. F^{12}6831. The founders subsequently proposed that the name of the enterprise be changed to Société Centrale de Commission et d'Echange. Although there is a certain resemblance between this proposal and the labor exchanges propounded by Robert Owen, and similar institutions advocated by other early socialists, in this instance the founders and their inspirer, Bonnard, were profit-oriented businessmen, not philanthropists.
75. F^{12}6830; F^{12}6831, Chamber of Commerce of Paris to min. of commerce, 15 Feb. 1853; Proudhon, *Manuel de spéculateur*, pp. 268–69.
76. F^{12}6831, Chamber of Commerce of Paris to min. of commerce, 15 Feb. 1853.
77. F^{12}6831, min. of fin. to min. of commerce, 16 June 1853.
78. F^{12}6813, 6814, 6820, 6827, and 6829.
79. This estimate is based variously upon the companies' own evaluations, the market value of the shares at the time of authorization, estimates of government engineers, and par value of shares assigned at the time of issue.
80. F^{14}8234, Jacques Ardaillon to the min. of pub. works, 3 Aug. 1845.
81. F^{14}8234, Rapport du ingénieur Garnier to the Conseil Général des Mines, 6 Apr. 1846.
82. F^{14}8232, mining engineer Comte to the chief mining engineer at Valenciennes, 2 Dec. 1847.
83. F^{14}8232, min. of commerce to min. of pub. works, 20 Dec. 1847.
84. F^{14}8232, min. of commerce to min. of pub. works, 9 Jan. 1848.
85. F^{14}8232, Serret, Lelièvre et Cie. to Citizen min. of commerce, 20 Mar. 1848.
86. F^{12}8229; Guy Thuillier, *Georges Dufaud et les débuts du grand capitalisme dans la métallurgie, en Nivernais, au XIXe siècle*, p. 90.
87. Ibid., p. 190.
88. Chatillon-Commentry made a second attempt to gain authorization in 1857. Another large *commandite*, formed by merger in 1854 and capitalized at 12.5 million francs, the Société Nouvelle des Mines, Forges, et Hauts-Fourneaux d'Herserange et Saint Nicolas, disappeared within a few years.
89. F^{14}8231.
90. In 1862, the Compagnie Générale Maritime changed its name to Compagnie Générale Transatlantique. See Marthe Barbance, *Histoire de la Compagnie Générale Transatlantique, un siècle d'exploitation maritime*, pp. 33–48.
91. F^{12}6767, min. of fin. to min. of commerce, 9 Oct. 1851; Proudhon, *Manuel du spéculateur*, pp. 363–67. The Conseil d'Etat had declared earlier that the Messageries Royales could not extend its operations to the sea (F^{12}6757, Avis du Conseil d'Etat, 20 Mar. 1847).
92. Proudhon, *Manuel du spéculateur*, p. 407.
93. By the Ordinance of 29 July 1858, the name of the company was changed to Compagnie Immobilière de Paris.
94. F^{12}6780, Avis du Conseil d'Etat, 15 Nov. 1854.
95. F^{12}6780, min. of fin. to min. of commerce, 16 Aug. 1856.
96. F^{12}6780, min. of fin. to min. of commerce, 21 July 1857.

97. F¹²6780, min. of fin. to min. of commerce, 19 Dec. 1857.

98. F¹²6782, undated memorandum prepared by the bureau of commerce in the dossier of the Compagnie Immobilière.

CHAPTER 5

1. Jacques Bresson, *Annuaire de 1840 des sociétés par actions anonymes, civiles, et en commandite*, p. i.

2. According to Michel, president of the commercial tribunal of Paris (*Gazette des tribunaux*, 26 Aug. 1838, p. 1073).

3. Jacques Bresson, *Annuaire de 1839 des sociétés par actions anonymes, civiles, et en commandite*, pp. xxi–xxvi.

4. Bresson, *Annuaire de 1840*, p. iii.

5. *Gazette des tribunaux*, 20 Aug. 1838, p. 1073.

6. Ibid., 25 Aug. 1839, p. 1081.

7. CCP, Procès verbaux, 26 Dec. 1839.

8. Jean Baptiste Teste, by then minister of justice; Lapagne Barris; Vivien; Vincens; Vandermarcq; and the Comte d'Argout.

9. AN, BB³⁰278, Procès verbaux de la commission, séance de 7 Nov. 1839.

10. Ibid. Unfortunately, the *procès verbaux* of the 1839 commission does not identify those expressing opinions by name.

11. Claude Alphonse Delangle, *Des sociétés commerciales*, 1:liii–lx. For Delangle, the love of military glory, which characterized the empire, had been succeeded by the worship of the golden calf: "Il est des époques fatales, où l'amour de l'argent se substitute à tout autre mobile de l'activité humaine. La restauration a commencé l'une de ces époques" (p. liii). These sentiments did not prevent Delangle from collecting substantial fees for defending in the courts *gérants* who were accused of fraud.

12. *Journal des économistes* 5 (1843):302.

13. Charles Coquelin, "Des sociétés commerciales en France et en Angleterre," p. 408.

14. The recommendations of the Conseil Général de l'Agriculture and the Conseil Général des Manufactures are in the published *Procès-verbaux des sessions des Conseils Généraux, session de 1845–1846*, 2 vols. (Paris, 1846), at the Archives National, AD XIX D 203. The volume for the Conseil Général du Commerce is missing, but its advice is in a printed *Notice sur les sociétés par actions* (1845) in CCP, carton 3.33.

15. *Gazette des tribunaux*, 11 Feb. 1859, pp. 146–47. De Saulcy was the victim of bad advice. The definitive constitution of the company occurred shortly after the law of 1836 established criminal penalties for certain acts or omissions, and De Saulcy suffered the indignity of being tried in a criminal court. Though he was acquitted, his experience and that of other members of councils of surveillance who were not so fortunate engendered great caution in accepting such posts.

16. These examples are all taken from advertisements in the *Gazette des tribunaux* during September and October 1855.

17. Horace Say, "Des sociétés commerciales en France et en Angleterre," pp. 349–50.

18. Charles Lescoeur, *Essai historique et critique sur la législation des sociétés commerciales en France et à l'étranger*, p. 68.

19. Gabriel Ramon, *Histoire de la Banque de France*, pp. 260–61.

20. F¹²6812, prefect of police to min. of commerce, 15 Sept. 1855, dossier of Société Générale de la Chaudronnnerie.

21. MU, 16 Jan. 1856, p. 61.

22. Although the hero lost his fortune on the Bourse, he got the girl in the final scene. So it goes in the theater. Alexandre Dumas fils tried to cash in on the same theme with his comedy *Question d'argent*, which opened in January 1857. More pretentious was the biting, though superficial, attack on speculation by Oscar de Vallée, a high official in the judiciary, whose *Manieurs d'argent* (1857) compared the speculators of his own day with those of John Law's time. The emperor sent de Vallée a letter of congratulation.

23. MU, 1 June 1856, p. 597.

24. Other members of the committee were J. Langlois, the *rapporteur*; J. H. Busson; the Vicomte de Kervéguen; L. H. Bertrand; Richer; and T. M. Vernier.

25. Under the constitution of the Second Empire, the committee amendments had to be accepted by the Conseil d'Etat. The most notable changes made by the committee were the stipulations that the original capital be integrally subscribed and that the original subscribers be legally liable for all future calls, even if the shares had changed hands. The government's bill had been more liberal on both these counts: a company could be founded with one-quarter of the shares subscribed, if they were fully paid up; and it was possible to limit the liability of shareholders to one-half the nominal value of the shares. The text of the government bill is in MU, 1 June 1856, p. 598.

26. MU, 30 June 1856, annexe, p. lxiv.

27. Ibid.

28. Maxmilien Koenigswarter, MU, 2 July 1856, p. 729; Theodore Morin, ibid., p. 730. Until 1860 only a resumé of debates in the Corps Législatif was published.

29. Keonigswarter, Morin, and Alexandre Gouin, ibid., p. 730.

30. Ibid., p. 729. According to Koenigswarter, masters of *sociétés anonymes* welcomed the introduction of the bill. As he was part of a combination that had been denied authorization for a bank, however, his views were not disinterested.

31. Ibid.

32. *Journal des économistes*, 2d ser. (1856):150.

33. Ibid., p. 151.

34. Jules Mirès, "Des sociétés en commandite," 555–56. This was also the opinion of Horace Say, "Des sociétés commerciales en France et en Angleterre," p. 350.

35. MU, 27 June 1863, annexe O, p. lviii.

36. Capital was diverted particularly into the bonds of foreign governments but also into foreign railroads, financial institutions, and gas companies (Lescoeur, *Essai historique et critique sur la législation des sociétés*, p. 125; Louis Girard, *La Politique des travaux publics du Second Empire*, p. 178).

37. *Journal des économistes*, 2d ser. 37 (1863): 538–39.

38. Auguste Vitu, *Guide financier, répertoire général des valeurs financières et industrielles*, pp. 972–73.

CHAPTER 6

1. See Chapter 7 on the *société à responsabilité limitée*.

2. Jean Bouvier, *Le Crédit Lyonnais de 1863 à 1882*, 1:126 and 139.

3. $F^{12}6777$ and 6779; Edmond Lebée, "Le Groupe des banques affiliées au Crédit Industriel et Commercial," pp. 5–39.

4. Bertrand Gille, "La Fondation de la Société Générale," p. 53.

5. $F^{12}6779$, min. of fin. to min. of commerce, 28 Mar. 1863.

6. Ibid.

7. $F^{12}6779$.

8. Among the most promising requests were those of A. Pinard for the Compagnie Générale d'Entreprises de Travaux Publics, capitalized at 20 million francs, in 1860

($F^{12}6831$); of Parent and Schaken for the Caisse de Travaux Publics des Entrepreneurs, capitalized at 40 million francs, in 1861 ($F^{12}6829$); and of E. Joliclerc for the Caisse Générale des Halles et Marchés, capitalized at 5 million francs in 1863 ($F^{12}6829$).

9. Several accident insurance companies had been founded in the 1850s as *sociétés en commandite par actions.*

10. $F^{12}6762$ and 6763.

11. $F^{14}8229$, Rapport au ministre, June 1861.

12. $F^{14}8229$, Rapport au ministre, 12 Apr. 1862.

13. Ibid.

14. Ibid.

15. The attitude of the minister of commerce was often important. It is worth noting that Rouher was generally insensitive to the problems that the authorization process created for businessmen. By contrast, Cunin-Gridaine, a former businessman who was minister from 1840 to 1848, was flexible and sympathetic.

16. $F^{14}8229$, Rapport au ministre, 12 Apr. 1862.

17. $F^{12}6781$, Avis du Conseil d'Etat, 20 May 1863.

18. $F^{12}6781$, min. of commerce to M. Pereire, 9 Feb. 1863.

19. $F^{12}6781$, "Note relative à la Compagnie Immobilière de Paris et aux Sociétés Immobilières de Marseille," undated but probably early March.

20. $F^{12}6781$, min. of commerce to prefect, Bouches du Rhône, 21 Feb. 1863.

21. $F^{12}6781$, Emile Pereire to min. of commerce, 26 Mar. 1863.

22. Vincent Wright, *Le Conseil d'Etat sous le Second Empire*, pp. 61–63.

23. $F^{12}6811$, Avis du Conseil d'Etat, 14 Jan. 1836.

24. $F^{12}8616$, Avis du Conseil d'Etat, 13 July 1836.

25. $F^{12}8616$, Rapport au ministre, 18 Aug. 1836. No company with a capital under 100,000 francs had been authorized since 1832.

26. See Chapter 2 above.

27. $F^{12}8616$, Rapport au ministre, 19 Aug. 1836.

28. $F^{12}6731$, Avis du Conseil d'Etat, 2 June 1837.

29. $F^{12}6731$, Rapport au ministre, 13 July 1837.

30. $F^{14}8229$, Avis du Conseil d'Etat, 15 Dec. 1836. Even an opinion in favor of authorization was phrased negatively.

31. $F^{12}6758$ and 6794.

32. $F^{12}6780$, Avis du Conseil d'Etat, 15 Nov. 1854.

33. E.g., the Compagnie Général des Eaux (1853) and the Compagnie Navigation Mixte of Lyon (1858).

34. $F^{12}6766$, Avis du Conseil d'Etat, 22 Nov. 1859.

35. $F^{14}8230$, Conseil Général des Mines, 21 Dec. 1851.

36. $F^{14}8230$, min. of pub. works to min. of commerce, 22 Aug. 1852.

37. $F^{12}6785$.

38. La Bisontine, Société pour le Commerce de la Boucherie (Besançon) ($F^{12}6820$, min. of commerce to prefect, 6 Oct. 1845). The ministry gave as grounds for its refusal the desire to avoid the appearance of granting a privilege or creating a monopoly and the existence of alternative forms of organization.

39. $F^{14}8232$, min. of commerce to min. of pub. works, 5 Dec. 1846; $F^{14}8234$, min. of commerce to min. of pub. works, 26 Jan. 1847; $F^{14}8234$, Rapport of E. Thirria to Conseil Général des Mines, 26 Apr. 1848.

40. $F^{14}8230$, Rapport, 13 Dec. 1842; Conseil Général des Mines, 7 Apr. 1843. This company was not authorized.

41. $F^{12}6787$, Avis du Conseil d'Etat, 11 Aug. 1842.

42. F¹⁴8233, dossier of the Compagnie de Mines de Houille d'Azincourt. The report of mining inspector Garnier to the Conseil Général des Mines, 18 Oct. 1841, advocated a hands-off policy. See also F¹⁴8232, min. of commerce to min. of pub. works, 9 Jan. 1848.

43. F¹²6728, dossier of l'Expansion, Société pour la Construction de Machines et de Mécaniqus, min. of commerce to E. Martin, attorney, 6 Aug. 1847.

44. F¹²6777.

45. Ibid.

46. For example, the Société de Dépots et de Comptes Courants (1863) wanted to limit shareholders' meetings to the 200 largest stockholders. The Conseil replaced this restriction by a requirement of forty shares for one vote, to a maximum of five votes (F¹²6779).

47. F¹²6764.

48. F¹²6767, dossier of the Société des Paquebots à Vapeur sur la Seine (1835), Avis du Conseil d'Etat, 31 May 1835.

49. F¹²6777.

50. See the report on all foreign investors in the projected Société Internationale de Crédit Commercial, a forerunner of the Crédit Industriel et Commercial (F¹²6778, min. of for. aff. to min. of commerce, 25 Apr. 1857).

51. F¹²6731, Avis du Conseil d'Etat, 26 Aug. 1843; F¹²6731, E. André and d'Audiffret to min. of commerce, 18 Dec. 1843.

52. F¹⁴8234, Rapport, 26 Mar. 1855. The rapporteur recommended refusal of authorization, but he was overruled and the company, with a government commissioner, was authorized in 1855.

53. E.g., min. of commerce A. Béhic to prefects, circulaire no. 24, 27 Dec. 1865, in F¹⁴8234.

54. One of the rare instances of use occurred in 1838 after the ministry had mounted its first campaign to obtain the records. The ministry requested the prefect of Mayenne to get from the Pont Neuf de Laval an explanation of a discrepancy of 404.16 francs between the 1837 and 1838 balance sheets. (F¹²6747, ministry to prefect, 2 July 1838).

CHAPTER 7

1. "As in the years immediately following 1850, most of the discussion was in terms of the *en commandite* partnership rather than of general limited liability" John Saville, "Sleeping Partnership and Limited Liability, 1850–1856," pp. 418–19.

2. Philip L. Cottrell, "Anglo-French Financial Cooperation, 1850–1880," p. 63. In the mid-fifties a number of Prussian companies were also founded in Paris.

3. Saville, "Sleeping Partnership and Limited Liability," p. 429, n. 6.

4. "Exposé des motifs d'un projet de loi tendant aba autoriser les associations anonyme, commerciales, industrielles ou financières, légalement constituées et autorisées en Belgique, à exercer leur droits en France," MU, 8 Apr. 1857, p. 390.

5. Ibid.

6. Charles Lescoeur, *Essai historique et critique sur la législation des sociétés commerciales en France et à l'étranger*, p. 105.

7. Ibid., p.107.

8. Ibid., p. 127; Adolphe Blaise, *Observations sur le discours de M. A. Blanche*, p. 17.

9. Lescoeur, *Essai historique et critique sur la législation des sociétés*, p. 128; Blaise, *Observations*, pp. 17–18.

10. Lescoeur, *Essai historique et critique sur la législation des sociétés*, p. 129.

11. Blaise, *Observations*, p. 18.

12. Ibid., p. 44. The articles appeared between 10 Nov. and 8 Dec. 1861.

13. For example: Henri Baudrillart, "Chronique économique" (Nov. 1861), pp. 315–17; Hippolyte Dussard, "Bibliographie," pp. 151–52; Henri Baudrillart, "Chronique économique" (Feb. 1862), pp. 338–39; Emile Jay, "Une Réforme urgente," pp. 448–52.

14. MU, 24 Nov. 1862, p. 439.

15. Among those who expressed reservations were: Alphonse Courtois fils, "Bulletin financier," p. 475; Joseph Lair, "Des Sociétés à responsabilité limitée," pp. 390–420; F. Grimaud, "Les Sociétés à responsabilité limitée," pp. 450–51; Sociéte d'économie politique, "Réunion du 5 mars 1863," pp. 526–39.

16. Adolphe Blaise, *Observations sur le projet de loi concernant les sociétés à responsabilité limitée*.

17. Ibid., pp. 12–13.

18. J. E. Horn, writing in *Journal des économistes*, 2d ser., 38 (1863): 326.

19. Michel Chevalier, "Introduction," *Rapports des membres de la section française du jury international sur l'ensemble de l'exposition*, 1: clxix.

20. The nine-man committee, under the presidency of Leclerc d'Osmonville, included Jean Baptiste Josseau, secretary; du Miral, reporter; Jules Aymé; and Emile Ollivier.

21. MU, 26 June 1863, annexe N, p. lvi.

22. Ibid.

23. MU, 27 June 1863, annexe O, p. lvii.

24. At this time, no changes could be made in a bill without the approval of the Conseil d'Etat.

25. MU, 27 June 1863, annexe O, p. lvii.

26. Ibid. The government's bill provided for mandatory dissolution.

27. Ibid.

28. The debates on the bill are in MU, 5–6 May 1863, pp. 708–10 and 716–18.

29. MU, 5 May 1863, p. 708.

30. Ibid., pp. 708–9.

31. Ibid., p. 709.

32. Ibid., 14 May 1863, p. 767.

33. *Journal des économistes*, 2d ser. 37 (1863): 368.

34. Jean Bouvier, *Le Crédit Lyonnais de 1863 à 1882*, 1:125–26 and 139–40.

35. *Journal des chemins de fer* 23 (1864): 627.

36. *Journal des économistes*, 2d ser. 43 (1864): 449.

37. MU, 16 Feb. 1865, p. 147.

38. "Exposé des motifs d'un projet de loi sur les sociétés," in Hippolyte Ferréol Rivière, *Commentaire de la loi du 24 juillet 1867 sur les sociétés*, p. 448.

39. Ibid., p. 449.

40. Ibid., pp. 451–52. This had already been done with the SARL in 1863.

41. Leclerc d'Osmonville, président of both committees; Jules Aymé; Du Miral, rapporteur for the 1863 law; and Emile Ollivier.

42. MU, 4 June 1867, p. 678.

43. Ibid.

44. "2e Rapport," MU, 10 July 1867, p. 914, and 11 July 1867, p. 920.

45. J. G. Courcelle-Seneuil's "Les Sociétés à responsabilité limitée et les jeux de bourse" is a thoughtful article that discusses the role and limits of joint-stock companies. Gustave de Molinari's article "De l'Association dans la sphère de l'économie politique" appeared in three installments in 1867.

46. A. Larrieu, "La Loi sur les sociétés," p. 355. See also the issues of the *Journal des chemins de fer* for 25 May 1867 (p. 339) and 8 June 1867 (p. 373).

47. Garnier's proposal was the subject of an earlier debate of the Société d'Economie Politique (4 November 1865). In favor—with the reservation that adequate information on the enterprise would have to be made available to interested parties—were Ferdinand Hérold, a lawyer before the Conseil d'Etat and the Cour de Cassation, and Paul Coq. Garnier's proposal was attacked by J. E. Horn; Nicholas Villiaume, a publicist; J. Dupuit, inspector general of bridges and highways; Louis Wolowski, an economist; Charles Lavollée; and Esquirou de Parieu, vice-president of the Conseil d'Etat. An account of the meeting is given in *Journal des économistes*, 2d ser. 48 (1865): 310–21.

48. Joseph Garnier, "Chronique économique," p. 472.

49. MU, 28 May 1867, p. 637.

50. Ibid., p. 638. The unnamed financier was Emile Pereire. Georges Duchêne, in his *La Spéculation devant les tribunaux*, published in 1867, listed nineteen companies in which Pereire was a director in 1863, with a total capital, including borrowing, of 3,704,000,000 francs. Duchêne was undoubtedly the source for Picard's slightly garbled version.

51. MU, 28 May 1867, p. 637.

52. Ibid., p. 640.

53. MU, 29 May 1867, p. 643.

54. Ibid.

55. Ibid.

56. Ibid., p. 652.

57. Ibid. The vote was 101 to 97.

58. MU, 31 May–1 June 1867, pp. 676–77.

59. MU, 5 June 1867, pp. 684–85.

60. MU, 6 June 1867, p. 691.

61. MU, 14 June 1867, p. 739.

62. Lescoeur, *Essai historique et critique sur la législation des sociétés*, p. 325.

63. CCP, chamber to min. of commerce, 23 May 1882.

64. *Compte général de l'administration de la justice civil et commerciale*, 1868 and 1869.

65. Lescoeur, *Essai historique et critique sur la législation des sociétés*, pp. 319–20.

66. Claudio Jannet, *Le Capital, la spéculation et la finance au XIXe siècle*, p. 169.

67. Charles E. Freedeman, "The Growth of the French Securities Market, 1815–1870," pp. 75–92.

Bibliography

MANUSCRIPT SOURCES

Paris

Archives Nationales

F^{12}6728 to 6796 and F^{14}8229 to 8234. The dossiers of about one-half of all *sociétés anonymes* authorized between 1807 and 1867. Although these dossiers are uneven in content, they constitute an incomparable source on the founding of *sociétés anonymes*. F^{14}8229 to 8234 also contain the dossiers of some mining and metallurgical enterprises that were not authorized.

F^{12}6808 to 6832. Dossiers of many projected *anonymes* that were not authorized.

BB^{30}278. Reports from the Cours Royal on all *sociétés en commandite par actions* founded in France, except for the Paris area, between 1826 and 1837 and the *procès verbaux* of the two commissions for the reform of the *commandite par actions* in 1837–38 and 1839.

F^{12}6797 to 6807. Transformation of *sociétés anonymes* into *sociétés anonymes libre* under the law of 1867.

F^{12}543 to 546. Elaboration of the *Code de Commerce*.

F^{12}6835^{1}. Depression of 1847–48.

F^{14}8514a and b. Financing of Railroads.

F^{20}723. Bankruptcies.

AD XIX D 203. *Procès-verbaux des sessions des Conseils Généraux, session de 1845–1846*. 2 vols. Paris, 1846.

Archives Départmentales, Seine

D31, U^{3}. *Sociétés en commandite par actions* registered at the Tribunal of Commerce of Paris for 1833, cartons 54 to 57, and 1837, cartons 70 to 74.

Archives of the Chamber of Commerce of Paris
Procès verbaux des délibérations
Carton 3.32. The *société à responsabilite limitee*.
Carton 3.33. The *société anonyme*.

Bibliothèque de l'Institut de France
Papiers Carette, MS 4751, A. G. Aube, "Souvenirs du passage de 18 mois au Conseil d'Etat." 107 pp.

Lyon

Archives Départmentales, Rhône
SU, Sociétés: Constitutions et modifications. I consulted the years 1821, 1825, 1829, 1833, 1837, 1838, 1841, 1845, 1853, 1857, and 1860.

GOVERNMENT DOCUMENTS

Almanach royal.
Archives statistique du minintère des travaux publics et de l'agriculture et du commerce. Paris, 1837.
Bulletin des lois.
Code de commerce. Paris: Edition des Archives de Droit Français, 1808.
Compte général de l'administration de la justice civile et commerciale.
Ministère de l'agriculture et du commerce. *Rapport au Président de la République sur les caisses d'épargnes, Année 1847.* Paris, 1851.
Ministère de l'intérieur. *Circulaires, instructions, et autres actes.*
Moniteur universel.
Observations des tribunaux de cassation et d'appel, des tribunaux et conseils de commerce &c. sur le projet de Code de Commerce. 3 vols. Paris, an XI.
Projet de Code du Commerce. Paris, an X.
Réimpression de l'ancien Moniteur. 32 vols. Paris, 1843–45.
Révision du projet de Code du Commerce. Paris, 1803.

BOOKS AND ARTICLES

Adam, Jean-Paul. *Instauration de la politique des chemins de fer en France.* Paris, 1972.
Adelson, Judah. "The Early Evolution of Business Organization in France." *Business History Review* 31 (1957):226–43.
Annuaire d'économie politique et de la statistique. Paris, 1844–.
Barbance, Marthe. *Histoire de la Compagnie Générale Transatlantique, un siècle d'exploitation maritime.* Paris, 1955.
Baudrillart, Henri. "Cronique économique." *Journal des économistes,* 2d ser. 32 (Nov. 1861):315–17, and 33 (Feb. 1862):338–39.
Bayard, Eugène. *La Caisse d'épargne et de prévoyance de Paris.* 2d ed. Paris, 1900.
Beaujouan, Guy, and Lebée, Edmund. "La Fondation de Crédit Industriel et Commercial." *Histoire des entreprises,* no. 6 (1960), pp. 6–40.
Bédarride, Jassuda. *Droit commercial, commentaire du Code de Commerce, Livre Ier, titre 3, des sociétés.* 2 vols. Paris, 1856.
Bères, Emile. *Manuel de l'actionnaire.* Paris 1839.
Bigo, Robert. *Les Banques françaises au cours de XIXe siècle.* Paris, 1947.
————. *La Caisse d'Escompte (1776–1793) et les origines de la Banque de France.* Paris, 1927.
Blaise, Adolphe. *Observations sur le discours de M. A. Blanche.* Paris, 1861.
————. *Observations sur le projet de loi concernant les sociétés à responsabilité limitée.* Paris, 1863.

Boucher, Pierre. *Institutions commerciales.* Paris, 1801.

Boudet, Jacques, ed. *Le Monde des affaires en France de 1830 à nos jours.* Paris, 1952.

Bouvier, Jean. *Le Crédit Lyonnais de 1863 à 1882.* 2 vols. Paris, 1961.

————. *Les Rothschild.* Paris, 1960.

Braudel, Fernand, and Labrousse, Ernest, eds. *Histoire économique et sociale de la France.* 4 vols. Paris, 1970–.

Bresson, Jacques. *Annuaire de 1839 des sociétés par actions anonymes, civiles, et en commandite.* Paris, 1839.

————. *Annuaire de 1840 des sociétés par actions anonymes, civiles, et en commandite.* Paris, 1840.

————. *Des Fonds publics en France et des opérations de la Bourse de Paris.* Paris, 1820; 6th ed. Paris, 1830; 9th ed. Paris, 1849.

————. *Histoire financière de la France depuis l'origine de la monarchie jusqu'à l'année 1828.* 2 vols. Paris, 1829.

Cameron, Rondo, et al. *Banking in the Early Stages of Industrialization.* New York, 1967.

————. "Economic Growth and Stagnation in France, 1815–1914." *Journal of Modern History* 30 (1958):1–13.

————. *France and the Economic Development of Europe, 1800–1914.* Princeton, 1961.

Capefigue, J. B. *Histoire des grandes opérations financières.* 4 vols. Paris, 1855–60.

Le Centenaire de l'Union, Compagnie d'Assurances sur la Vie Humaine, 1829–1929. Paris, 1929.

Chevalier, Michel. "Introduction." *Rapports des membres de le sections française du jury international sur l'ensemble de l'exposition.* 6 vols. Paris, 1862.

Clough, Shepard B. *France: A History of National Economics, 1789–1939.* New York, 1939.

Cochut, André. "La Politique du libre échange: III, La Régime économique de la France de 1815 à 1860." *Revue des deux mondes,* 2d ser. 36 (1861): 311–46.

Coquelin, Charles. "Des sociétés commerciales en France et en Angleterre." *Revue des deux mondes,* 3 (1843):397–437.

Cottrell, Philip L. "Anglo-French Financial Cooperation, 1850–1880." *Journal of European Economic History* 3 (1974):54–86.

Courcelle-Seneuil, J. G. "Les Sociétés à responsabilité limitée et les jeux de bourse." *Journal des économistes,* 2d ser. 46 (1865):35–51.

Courtois fils, Alphonse. "Bulletin financier." *Journal des économistes,* 2d ser. 34 (1862):475.

————. *Manuel des fonds publics*. 2d ed. Paris, 1856.

————. *Tableaux des cours des principales valeurs négociées et cotées aux bourses des effets publics de Paris, Lyon, et Marseille du 17 janvier 1797 à nos jours*. 2d ed. Paris, 1873.

Dalloz, *Jurisprudence générale du royaume en matière civile, commerciale, criminelle et administrative, recueil périodique*. 20 vols. Paris, 1825–44.

Daumard, Adeline. *La Bourgeoisie parisienne de 1815 à 1848*. Paris, 1963.

————, ed. *Les Fortunes françaises au XIXe siècle*. Paris, 1973.

Delangle, Claude Alphonse. *Des sociétés commerciales*. 2 vols. Paris, 1843.

Desmazières, André. *L'Evolution du rôle du notaire dans la constitution des sociétés par actions*. Paris, 1948.

Duchêne, Georges. *L'Empire industriel*. Paris, 1869.

————. *La Spéculation devant les tribunaux*. Paris, 1867.

Dumas fils, Alexandre. *Question d'argent*. Paris, 1857.

Dunham, Arthur Louis. *The Industrial Revolution in France, 1815–1848*. New York, 1955.

Dupont-Ferrier, Pierre. *La Marché financier de Paris sous le Second Empire*. Paris, 1925.

Dussard, Hippolyte. "Bibliographie." *Journal des économistes*, 2d ser. 33 (1862):151–52.

Evans, Jr., George Heberton. *British Corporation Finance, 1775–1850: A Study in Preference Shares*. Baltimore, 1936.

Fohlen, Claude. *L'Industrie textile au temps du Second Empire*. Paris, 1956.

————. "Sociétés anonymes et dévoloppement capitaliste sous la monarchie censitaire." *Histoire des entreprises*, no. 6 (1960), pp. 65–77.

————. "Sociétés anonymes et développement capitaliste sous le Second Empire." *Histoire des entreprises*, no. 8 (1961), pp. 65–79.

Freedeman, Charles E. "The Coming of Free Incorporation in France, 1850–1867." *Explorations in Entrepreneurial History*, 2d ser. 4 (1967): 211–31.

————. "The Growth of the French Securities Market, 1815–1870." In *From the Ancien Régime to the Popular Front*, edited by C. K. Warner, pp. 75–92. New York, 1969.

————. "Joint-Stock Business Organization in France, 1807–1867." *Business History Review* 39 (1965):184–204.

Frémery, A. *Etudes de droit commercial*. Paris, 1833.

Frère, Louis. *Etude historique des sociétés anonymes belges*. 2 vols. Brussels, 1951.

Garnier, Joseph. "Chronique économique." *Journal des économistes*, 3d ser. 6 (1867):472.

Gazette des tribunaux. Paris, 1825–.

Gille, Bertrand. *La Banque en France au XIXe siècle.* Geneva, 1970.

―――. *La Banque et le crédit en France de 1815 à 1848.* Paris, 1959.

―――. "Etat de la presse économique et financière en France." *Histoire des entreprises*, no. 4 (1959), pp. 61–65.

―――. "La Fondation de la Société Générale." *Histoire des entreprises*, no. 8 (1961), pp. 5–64.

―――. *Histoire de la maison Rothschild.* vols. 1 and 2. Geneva, 1965–67.

―――. *Les Origines de la grande industrie métallurgique en France.* Paris, 1947.

―――. "A propos de l'état de la presse économique et financière en France." *Histoire des entreprises*, no. 6 (1960), pp. 78–79.

―――. *Recherches sur la formation de la grande entreprise capitaliste.* Paris, 1959.

―――. *La Sidérurgie française au XIXe siècle.* Geneva, 1968.

Girard, Louis. *La Politique des travaux publics du Second Empire.* Paris, 1952.

Gras, Louis Joseph. *Histoire économique générale des mines de la Loire.* 2 vols. Saint-Etienne, 1923.

Grimaud, F. "Les Sociétés à responsabilité limitée." *Journal des chemins de fer* 21 (1862):450–51.

Guillaume, Pierre. *La Compagnie des Mines de la Loire, 1846–1854.* Paris, 1966.

Horn, J. E. *Das Creditwesen in Frankriech.* 2nd ed. Leipzig, 1857.

Hunt, Bishop C. *The Development of the Business Corporation in England, 1800–1867.* Cambridge, Mass., 1936.

Isambert, ed. *Recueil général des anciennes lois françaises depuis l'an 420 jusqu'à la révolution de 1789.* 28 vols. Paris, 1822–33.

Jannet, Claudio. *Le Capital, la spéculation et la finance au XIXe siècle.* Paris, 1892.

Jay, Emile. "Une Réforme urgente" *Journal des économistes*, 2nd ser. 33 (1862):448–52.

Jefferys, J. B. "The Denomination and Character of Shares, 1855–1885." *Economic History Review* 16 (1946):45–55.

Jenks, Leland H. *The Migration of British Capital to 1875.* New York, 1927.

Joinville, Pierre de. *Le Réveil économique de Bordeaux sous la restauration, l'armateur Balguerie-Stuttenberg et son oeuvre.* Paris, 1914.

Journal des chemins de fer. Paris, 1842–.

Journal des économistes. Paris, 1844–.

Jullien, M. A. *Revue encyclopédique,* 2d ser. 39 (1828):41–44.

Labrousse, Ernest, ed. *Aspects de la crise et de la dépression, 1846–1851.* La Roche sur Yon, 1956.

Lair, Joseph. "Des Sociétés à responsabilité limitée." *Journal des économistes*, 2d ser. 36 (1862):390–420.

Landes, David. "French Entrepreneurship and Industrial Growth in the Nineteenth Century." *Journal of Economic History* 9 (1949):45–61.

———. "The Structure of Enterprise in the Nineteenth Century." In Congrès International des Sciences Historiques, *Rapports*, vol. 5, pp. 107–28. Stockholm, 1960.

———. *The Unbound Prometheus: Technological Change and Industrial Development in Western Europe from 1750 to the Present.* Cambridge, 1969.

———. "Vieille banque et banque nouvelle: la révolution financière du dix-neuvième siècle." *Revue d'histoire moderne et contemporaine* 3 (1956): 204–22.

Larrieu, A. "La Loi sur les sociétés." *Journal des chemins de fer* 26 (1867):355.

Lebée, Edmund. "Le Groupe des banques affiliées au Crédit Industriel et Commercial: ses origines et son développement." *Histoire des entreprises*, no. 7 (1961), pp. 5–59.

Lepelletier, Fernand. *Les Caisses d'épargnes.* Paris, 1911.

Lescoeur, Charles. *Essai historique et critique sur la législation des sociétés commerciales en France et à l'étranger.* Paris, 1877.

Levasseur, Emile. *Histoire du commerce de la France.* 2 vols. Paris, 1911–12.

Lévy-Bruhl, Henri. *Histoire juridique des sociétés de commerce en France aux XVIIe et XVIIIe siècles.* Paris, 1938.

———. *Un Projet de Code de Commerce à la veille de la révolution, le projet Miromesnil, 1778–1789.* Paris, 1932.

Lévy-Leboyer, Maurice. *Les Banques européennes et l'industrialisation international dans le première moitié du XIXe siècle.* Paris, 1964.

Lhomme, Jean. *La Grande bourgeoisie au pouvoir, 1830–1880.* Paris, 1960.

Locré, J. G. *Esprit du Code du Commerce.* 9 vols. Paris, 1807–13.

Malepeyre and Jourdain. *Traité des sociétés commerciales.* Paris, 1833.

Marion, Marcel. *Histoire financière de la France depuis 1715.* 6 vols. Paris, 1914–31.

Mathieu, Auguste, and Bourguignat, A. *Commentaire de la loi sur les sociétés des 24–29 juillet 1867.* Paris, 1868.

Meyer, Jean. *L'Armament nantais dans le deuxième moitié du XVIIIe siècle.* Paris, 1969.

Mirès, Jules. "La Banque de France et les comptoirs d'escompte." *Journal des chemins de fer* 10 (1851):726–27.

———. *A mes juges, ma vie et mes affaires.* Paris, 1861.

_____. "Des sociétés en commandite." *Journal des chemins de fer* 15 (1856):555–56.

Molinari, Gustave de. "De l'association dans la sphère de l'économie politique." *Journal des économistes*, 3d ser. 5 (1867):6–30; 3d ser. 6 (1867):161–85; 3d ser. 7 (1867):5–21.

Ozanam, Denise. "La Naissance du Creusot." *Revue d'histoire de la sidérurgie* 4 (1963):103–18.

Paignon, Eugène. *Commentaire de la loi sur les sociétés en commandite.* Paris, 1856.

P[aillard de] V[illeneuve]. "Examen du projet de loi sur les sociétés par actions." *Gazette des tribunaux*, 19 Feb. 1838, p. 401.

_____. "Des Sociétés en commandite, nécessité d'une réforme législatif." *Gazette des tribunaux*, 27–28 Nov. 1837, pp. 87–88, and 1 Dec. 1837, pp. 101–2.

Payne, P. L. "The Emergence of the Large-Scale Company in Great Britain, 1870–1914." *Economic History Review*, 2d ser. 20 (1967):519–42.

Persil, Charles. "Des associations en commandite." *Revue française* 4 (1837):89–101.

Picard, Alfred. *Les Chemins de fer français.* 6 vols. Paris, 1884–85.

Ponsard, François. *La Bourse.* Paris, 1856.

Postlethwayt, Malachy. *Universal Dictionary of Trade and Commerce.* 2 vols. London, 1757.

Proudhon, Pierre J. *Manuel du spéculateur à la bourse.* 3d ed. Paris, 1856.

Ramon, Gabriel. *Histoire de la Banque de France.* Paris, 1929.

Renaud, François. "Le Cartel des cristaux, 1850–1857." *Histoire des entreprises*, no. 5 (1960), pp. 7–20.

Revue des deux mondes. Paris, 1829–.

Richard, Guy. *Noblesse d'affaires au XVIIIe siècle.* Paris, 1974.

_____. "La Noblesse de France et les sociétés par actions à la fin du XVIIIe siècle." *Revue d'histoire économique et sociale* 40 (1962):484–523.

Ripert, Georges. *Aspects juridiques du capitalisme moderne.* Paris, 1946.

Rivet, Félix. *La Navigation à vapeur sur la Saône et le Rhône, 1783–1863.* Paris, 1962.

Rivière, Hippolyte Ferréol. *Commentaire de la loi du 24 juillet 1867 sur les sociétés.* Paris, 1868.

_____. *Explication de la loi du 17 juillet 1856 relative aux sociétés en commandites par actions.* Paris, 1857.

Robert, Adolphe; Bourloton, Edgar; and Cougny, Gaston, eds. *Dictionnaire des parlementaires français, 1789–1889.* 5 vols. Paris, 1891.

Roy, Joseph Antoine. *Histoire de la famille Schneider et du Creusot.* Paris, 1962.

Sala, Adolphe E. *Manuel des placmens industriels*. Paris, 1836.

Savary, Jacques. *Le Parfait Négociant*. Paris, 1675.

Savary des Bruslons, Jacques. *Dictionnaire universel de commerce*. 5 vols. Copenhagen, 1759–65.

Saville, John. "Sleeping Partnership and Limited Liability, 1850–1856." *Economic History Review*, 2d ser. 8 (1956):418–33.

Say, Horace. "Des sociétés commerciales en France et en Angleterre." *Journal des économistes*, 2d ser. 2 (1854):348–59.

Senés, V. *Les Origines des compagnies d'assurances fondées en France depuis le XVIIe siècle jusqu'à nos jours*. Paris, 1900.

Shannon, H. A. "The Coming of General Limited Liability." *Economic History* 2 (1931):267–91.

Sherman, Dennis. "Governmental Policy toward Joint-Stock Business Organization in Mid-Nineteenth Century France." *Journal of European Economic History* 3 (1974):149–68.

Soboul, Albert. *Les Sans-culottes parisiens en l'an II*. Paris, 1968.

Société d'économie politique."Réunion du 5 mars 1863." *Journal des économistes*, 2d ser. 37 (1863):526–39.

———. "Réunion du 4 novembre 1865." *Journal des économistes*, 2d ser. 48 (1865):310–21.

Taylor, George V. "The Paris Bourse on the Eve of the Revolution, 1781–1789." *American Historical Review* 67 (1962):951–77.

Thuillier, Guy. *Georges Dufaud et les débuts du grand capitalisme dans la métallurgie, en Nivernais, au XIXe siècle*. Paris, 1959.

Thureau-Dangin, Paul. *Histoire de la monarchie de juillet*. 7 vols. Paris, 1884–92.

Todd, G. "Some Aspects of Joint-Stock Companies, 1844–1900." *Economic History Review* 4 (1932):46–71.

Troplong, Raymond Théodore. *Du Contrat de société civile et commerciale*. 2 vols. Paris, 1845.

Tudesq, A. J. "La Crise de 1847, vue par les milieux d'affaires parisiens." In *Aspects de la crise et de la dépression, 1846–1851*, edited by Ernest Labrousse, pp. 4–36. La Roche sur Yon, 1956.

———. *Les Grands Notables en France, 1840–1849*. 2 vols. Paris, 1964.

Vallée, Oscar de. *Manieurs d'argent*. Paris, 1857.

Villepreux, G. "Un Maître de forge sous quatre régimes: Nicolas Rambourg." *Revue d'Histoire des mines et de métallurgie* 3 (1971):149–258.

Vincens, Emile. *Exposition raisonnée de la législation commerciale*. 3 vols. Paris, 1821.

———. *Des sociétés par actions, des banques en France*. Paris, 1837.

Vital-Roux, *De l'influence du gouvernement sur la prospérité du commerce.* Paris, 1800.

Vitu, Auguste. *Guide financier, répertoire général des valeurs financières et industrielles.* Paris, 1864.

Vührer, A. *Histoire de la dette publique en France.* 2 vols. Paris, 1886.

Wolowski, Louis. *Des sociétés par actions.* Paris, 1838.

Wright, Vincent. *Le Conseil d'Etat sous le Second Empire.* Paris, 1972.

Index

The Author

Charles E. Freedeman is associate professor of history at the State University of New York, Binghamton.

The Book

Typeface: Mergenthaler V-I P Times Roman

Design and composition: The University of North Carolina Press

Paper: Sixty pound 1854 Regular by S. D. Warren Company

Binding cloth· Roxite B 53538 Linen by Holliston Mills, Incorporated

Printer and binder: Braun-Brumfield, Incorporated

Published by The University of North Carolina Press